Making Slavery History

Making Slavery History

Abolitionism and the Politics of Memory
in Massachusetts

Margot Minardi

OXFORD
UNIVERSITY PRESS

2010

UNIVERSITY PRESS

Oxford University Press, Inc., publishes works that further
Oxford University's objective of excellence
in research, scholarship, and education.

Oxford   New York
Auckland   Cape Town   Dar es Salaam   Hong Kong   Karachi
Kuala Lumpur   Madrid   Melbourne   Mexico City   Nairobi
New Delhi   Shanghai   Taipei   Toronto

With offices in
Argentina   Austria   Brazil   Chile   Czech Republic   France   Greece
Guatemala   Hungary   Italy   Japan   Poland   Portugal   Singapore
South Korea   Switzerland   Thailand   Turkey   Ukraine   Vietnam

Copyright © 2010 by Margot Minardi

Published by Oxford University Press, Inc.
198 Madison Avenue, New York, New York 10016

www.oup.com

Oxford is a registered trademark of Oxford University Press.

Library of Congress Cataloging-in-Publication Data
Minardi, Margot.
Making slavery history: abolitionism and the politics of memory in Massachusetts / Margot Minardi.
   p. cm.
Includes bibliographical references and index.
ISBN 978-0-19-537937-2
1. Antislavery movements—Massachusetts—History—19th century.
2. Slavery—Political aspects—United States—History—19th century.   3. Memory—Social
aspects—United States—History—19th century.   4. Slavery—Massachusetts—Public opinion.
5. Slavery—Massachusetts—History.   6. United States—History—Revolution, 1775-1783—Influence.
E445.M4M56 2010
974.4'02—dc22   2009052008

For my parents

Acknowledgments

This book exists thanks to the talents, expertise, patience, and good humor of many people. Foremost among them is Laurel Thatcher Ulrich. In a women's history class many years ago, Laurel first invited me to think about what it means to "make history." Since then, her creativity and curiosity have prompted me to find sources and ask questions that I never would have discovered on my own, and her compassion and wisdom have reminded me why the early American past is still worth examining. Joyce Chaplin taught me to think critically about race as an idea with a history, and her insightfulness and witty incisiveness have led me out of many confusions. Jill Lepore's cinematic vision of historical narrative helped me to see how a plot and subplots might emerge out of the disconnected frames before me. I still cannot believe my good fortune to have had a dissertation committee comprised of three such accomplished historians and devoted teachers.

At Harvard, I also benefited enormously from repeated conversations with Rick Bell, Lauren Brandt, Linzy Brekke, Vincent Brown, Sarah Carter, Brian DeLay, Yonatan Eyal, Linford Fisher, Rebecca Goetz, Mark Hanna, Alison LaCroix, Philip Mead, Marion Menzin, Sarah Milov, Michelle Morris, Beth Nichols, Katie Rieder, and Sara Schwebel. I am grateful to Heather Kopelson for sharing her home during a research trip to New York. Others who commented on my work or shared discoveries from their own include Barbara Berenson, Marty Blatt, Barbara Burg, Duane Corpis, Nina Dayton, Evelyn Brooks Higginbotham, Rhys Isaac, Stuart McConnell, Michelle McDonald, Cassandra Pybus, Chernoh Sesay, Len Travers, Susan Ware, Richard White, Kari Winter, and Conrad Wright, as well as audiences at the American Historical Association, the Boston Area Early American Seminar, the Consortium on the Revolutionary Era, the Dublin Seminar for New England Folklife, and the Wellesley-Deerfield Symposium. Joanne Pope Melish and an anonymous reader offered detailed and thoughtful comments for Oxford University Press, and editor Nancy Toff and her assistant Sonia Tycko skillfully shepherded this manuscript to publication.

I thank Agnieszka Flizik for cheerfully looking for Chloe Spear in a graveyard with me many years ago, before I had any sense of what this project would become. More recently, Judy Kertész understood what I was trying to do better than I did, and I am indebted to her for thinking through my ideas with me on many occasions. Amber Musser sharpened my understanding of underlying theoretical questions and listened to my research presentation far too many times. Peter Green and Susan Choi gave me the best birthday present a historian could ever ask for, but their friendship has meant even more. I am abundantly grateful to Lauren Erin Brown for keeping crazy hours, for sharing my sense of humor, and for telling me, on a few choice occasions, exactly what I needed to hear.

All of the dissertation that became this book was written in Mather House at Harvard University. I am grateful to the Mather community for providing uncountable distractions, nearly all of them welcome, during the years that I was most heavily invested in this project. Since moving on from Cambridge, I have received a warm welcome at Reed College, where I thank my students and colleagues for making a New England girl feel at home on the frontier. I especially appreciate the generosity of Jacqueline Dirks, Laura Leibman, Mary Ashburn Miller, David Sacks, and Tamara Venit-Shelton. Members of Reed's American Studies Colloquium (including Mark Burford, Devin McGeehan Muchmore, Pancho Savery, Marissa Schneiderman, and Lisa Steinman) also provided wise counsel. In the final stages of preparing this manuscript, Joel Batterman contributed his lively historical imagination and expert editing skills. At the very last minute, Sean O'Neill pulled the illustrations together for me. And like the rest of Reed, I'd be nowhere without Lois Hobbs.

I am indebted to the knowledge and professionalism of the staff members at the institutions where I conducted this research: the Andover Historical Society, Boston Athenaeum, Boston Public Library, Cambridge Historical Commission, Danvers Archival Center (Peabody Institute Library), Franklin Trask Library (Andover-Newton Theological School), Houghton Library, Longfellow National Historic Site, Lynn Museum, Massachusetts Archives, Massachusetts Judicial Archives, Massachusetts Historical Society, Massachusetts State Library, National Archives-Northeast Region (Waltham, Mass.), New England Historic Genealogical Society, New York Public Library, Phillips Library (Peabody Essex Museum), Reed College Library, Schomburg Library for Research in Black Culture, and, especially, Widener Library, along with many other libraries in the Harvard system. Funding for my graduate work and dissertation research came from the Mellon Fellowship for Humanistic Studies, the Harvard Graduate School of Arts and Sciences, the Charles Warren Center for Studies in American History, and the Gilder Lehrman Institute of American History. I later received grants from the Stillman Drake Fund and the Dean's Summer Scholarship Fund at Reed College. I thank Dean Peter Steinberger for supporting junior faculty scholarship through these grants and Christine Mack for ably administering them.

This is a book about memory, and the memories that are most important to me are those that come from my family, especially my late grandparents, Francis Derrick, Louise Derrick, Marcel Minardi, and Margaret Minardi; my brother, Michael Minardi; and my parents, Lee and Judy Minardi. My mother and father have always given me what I needed and made it possible for me to do what I wanted. Their love and support mean everything to me, and this book is for them, with gratitude.

Contents

Making Slavery History

Prologue

Two Bodies

Two dead bodies mark the entrance to this story. The first collapsed in a burst of gunfire, the second succumbed quietly to disease, but both eventually found their way to an afterlife that would not let them rest. However different their earthly circumstances and the motivations of those who revived them, they had made history in their own time, and they would be called forth to make history again in the name of sweeping abstractions: liberty, emancipation, the "nation," the "race." Crispus Attucks and Phillis Wheatley, the "mulatto" man and "African" woman whose deaths bracket Boston's Revolutionary history: a strange mix of tragedy and glory attaches to both their names.

Of the slaves or former slaves who participated in the Revolution, Attucks and Wheatley are the most frequently commemorated. Today it is impossible to imagine a history of the Revolutionary era that would exclude them.[1] Their fame is well-founded, not least because their biographies, however incomplete, are captivating. More is known of Wheatley, at least starting in 1761, when she first arrived in Boston Harbor on the slave ship *Phillis*. Legend has it that merchant John Wheatley and his wife Susanna picked the smallest, weakest child from all the human cargo and took her into their home. The eight-year-old girl quickly learned English and then Latin, read the Bible but also the poets, classical and contemporary. Then she started writing and publishing poetry of her own, including odes to the luminaries of her day, from George Whitefield to George Washington. She traveled to England, where she was welcomed as a celebrity by well-wishers who helped her publish a book in 1773. Shortly thereafter, she was freed, and from that point on, her life began to unravel—at least, so suggest the surviving sources. Her beloved mistress, who had treated the girl "more like her child than her Servant," died.[2] The colonies exploded into revolt, igniting a war that thwarted the young woman's publishing career by separating her from her circle of British supporters. She married a free black man whom her white friends considered unworthy of her, and she bore him three children. Her already precarious financial situation worsened; her children died. In 1784, she herself surrendered to illness, her last days marked by poverty and obscurity that were startling in contrast to the luxury and fame she had known only a decade earlier.[3]

When Phillis Wheatley's *Poems on Various Subjects, Religious and Moral* appeared in print at the height of her international acclaim, it did not include a poem mentioned in a book proposal she had circulated the previous year.[4] Scholars have yet to find a signed copy of "On the Affray in King-Street, on the Evening of the 5th of March," but even the idea that such a poem about the Boston Massacre once existed is intriguing for enthusiasts of early African Americana. For it is probable that in it Wheatley made reference to the one person who would eventually rival her as the best-known slave in the history of Massachusetts.[5]

If Wheatley's rise from abject slave to published poet in the span of less than a decade can be called meteoric, then Crispus Attucks's entry into history can only be judged a big bang. Most accounts of him focus on a single night, March 5, 1770, when a fight broke out between British regulars and Boston civilians gathered near the town hall. The details of what happened have been debated for centuries, but several contemporary witnesses and later historians claimed that a man of color, armed with a stick or club, was at the forefront of the American mob. As pressure on the British guards mounted, one soldier pulled the trigger on his musket, and his two bullets shot Attucks into death and immortality. Immediately, American propagandists (most famously, Paul Revere) leapt into action, turning the "Affray in King-Street" into the Boston Massacre and Attucks and his fellow victims into patriot martyrs. Some time in his past, Attucks had been a slave in Framingham, Massachusetts. Depending on whom you ask, he had been other things as well: a cattleman, a sailor, a man named Michael Johnson; a runaway, a rabble-rouser, a revolutionary; a Bahamian, a Nipmuck, a mulatto. Whatever Attucks had been before, on the fifth of March, in 1770, he became history.[6]

In Crispus Attucks's end is the beginning of the story I want to tell. Attucks and Wheatley stake out the space for this tale, by virtue of two rarely remarked coincidences in their biographies. First, although both were enslaved for parts of their lives, they lived and died not in the slave societies of the American South or the Caribbean but instead in Massachusetts, the "Cradle of Liberty." Second, they both died in the Revolutionary period, Attucks at the beginning, when the American nation was an indiscernible glimmer on the horizon, and Wheatley at the end, barely a year after the British recognized American independence. To the extent that either of them lived in the free republic, they did so primarily in other people's histories and reminiscences. And so this story is set where Attucks and Wheatley fell, as well as where they linger still: in the Commonwealth of Massachusetts, and in the space of memory.

Introduction

Who Makes History?

This is a story about storytelling, in all its myriad forms, from the narrative of national pride enshrined in a granite monument to the tales of a beloved ancestor whispered around a midnight fire. It is about who gets to tell stories about the past, whose stories get to be told, and who is around to listen. At its heart, it is about how people in a certain place and time thought about who makes history—whether in the sense of firing a bullet to start a revolution or in the sense of writing it all down—and how their answers to that question shaped their ideas about what sort of future to call into being. My subjects wrestled with these questions in the late eighteenth and nineteenth centuries, but the problem of who makes history has been no less important for historians in our own time. For the last two generations or so, social historians have understood their project as the recovery of the "agency" of those hitherto seen as passive, marginal, and inarticulate, including women, workers, and slaves. This work is impressive not least for the methodological creativity and painstaking research that it has demanded. Since marginalized people left little in the way of transparent first-person sources, historians have developed ways of wresting meaning from mute or misleading material. Social historians have become excavators, rescuing individual lives and collective mentalities from the sediment of history.[1]

But there is something troubling in this idea of "rescue."[2] The proposition of rescuing someone from obscurity puts that person in a subjected position, at the mercy of the historian, at the very moment when attention is supposedly being paid to the person's own self-determination. The language of rescue suggests that a historian today can somehow reach back in time and pluck a forgotten actor from the debris of generations of historical narration, as though the histories that were written and not written about her, in her own day and in all the generations since, could somehow be brushed aside from her historical significance. "Rescue" creates too radical a break between the present and a discrete past. There is only the historian's "now" and the

5

actor's "then," without the mediation and meaning-making of all the memory and forgetting that came in between.

My interpretation of history moves those mediating processes of memory and forgetting to the center of analysis. I am not seeking to peel away the layers of historical memory in order to reveal a hidden history; rather, I am interested in how those layers themselves came to contribute to historical transformation. Here the double entendre of the phrase "making history" is always at play. "History" refers both to a "sociohistorical process" ("what happened") and "our knowledge of that process or…a story about that process" ("that which is said to have happened"). Historian and anthropologist Michel-Rolph Trouillot stresses that these two meanings are not coincidental to each other, for there are two ways in which "human beings participate in history…: as actors and as narrators."[3] Action and narration sometimes reinforce each other and sometimes are at odds. Moreover, the relationship between them is not unidirectional. Historians generally accept that the exigencies of the moment and the position of the teller influence the shape of the tale. But the tales themselves can also lead to certain actions at certain moments. In other words, historical narratives serve as governing myths and schemes that tell people who they are or who they want to be, that raise stakes, set priorities, and determine when action is needed. In this respect, narratives have the power to facilitate certain historical events and hinder others.[4]

The setting I have chosen in which to trace the relationship between action and narration, between those who make history happen and those who tell its tale, is Massachusetts in the period spanning the American Revolution and the Civil War. The particular problem I examine was a major preoccupation of that era and that place: the ending of slavery. Bay Staters in this period participated as historical actors in three distinct projects to make slavery history. First, in the aftermath of the Revolution, they worked to build a new nation, drawing on the metaphor of emancipation from colonial enslavement to Britain. Second, some sought to eliminate chattel slavery from Massachusetts and, in succeeding generations, to secure the civil rights of local people of color. Finally, some participated in broader abolitionist movements, targeting the Atlantic slave trade in one generation and slavery in the American South in another. These three efforts—nation-building, local emancipation and civil rights activism, national and international abolition—were all "antislavery" in one way or another. Sometimes these projects complemented each other; sometimes they conflicted.[5] In working for or against these transformations, Bay Staters constantly sought to articulate and act upon what they believed that history demanded of them. As a result, narratives of slavery and freedom, nation and region, and exclusion and belonging permeate the wide range of sources they left behind.

The setting is significant because Massachusetts was the undisputed center of historical production in this period. The Bay State was home to many of the nation's first historical, genealogical, and antiquarian societies; to Harvard College and a thriving public school system; to an extensive population of writers, printers, collectors, and record-keepers. Not only did Bay Staters seek to commemorate and preserve their local past, but they also argued that their Commonwealth was the historical model and ideal for the nation. In the second quarter of the nineteenth century, the cultural element of this "sectional nationalism" was eminently effective, giving Massachusetts claim to historical preeminence in texts and images circulated throughout the United States. In projecting their past onto the nation at large, nineteenth-century Bay Staters touted an unbroken history of American freedom, from Pilgrims through to patriots and all the way into their own day, when Boston was a center of antislavery activism and sectional politicking.[6]

Given this proud history, it was not easy for people in early national and antebellum Massachusetts to recognize institutionalized chattel slavery as part of their not-too-distant past. It was no more comfortable for Bay Staters to acknowledge that slavery maintained an influence over the present fortunes of people in their state. But the influence was there. So long as the Union held together, New England's political and economic links to states in the South meant that Yankees could not claim to be truly free from the taint of slavery, even though no one was legally held as a slave in Massachusetts after 1790. Furthermore, even local emancipation did not necessarily herald an end to oppression within New England. In the decades after the Revolution, the idea of "race" became a pernicious force throughout the North. Race was a system of differentiating human beings based on bodily characteristics perceived to be immutable and inherited, whether as visible as skin color or as slippery as "blood." Racial ideology reinscribed the inequities of slavery along lines presumed to be natural, as opposed to legal or social. Hosea Easton, a nineteenth-century preacher of African, Wampanoag, and Narragansett descent, articulated the problem especially vividly: slavery's demise had only fed "the soul-and-body-destroying energies" of prejudice, a beast "with all the innate principles of the old dragon himself."[7]

For those who cared to notice it, the flowering of racial chauvinism after the death of slavery raised questions about the nature of emancipation, or, more precisely, what emancipation's goal was. Emancipation denotes a transformation from one state (slavery) to another. In evoking a process, it is fundamentally a historical term. Just as it is hard to say when history ends, it was not necessarily clear when the process of emancipation was completed—that is, when those who experienced it had reached the final state, if there even was a final state to reach. Many of Bay Staters' debates concerning the politics of history and commemoration stemmed from disagreements about

the finality and fixity of the state that followed slavery. Colloquial terminology, and much of Anglo-American political thought, labeled the antithesis of slavery as freedom. But if freedom were only that—not-slavery, or a
lack of constraint—then it would be an "empty category," as Joanne Pope
Melish puts it. Intellectual historian James Kloppenberg proposes that we
could better historicize early American political discourse if we were to
"think of autonomy rather than freedom as the aim of the American
Revolution." Similarly, we might think of autonomy as the end-state of emancipation from slavery. Compared to freedom, autonomy is both more specific
and more demanding a concept. The autonomous individual idealized by
America's foundational political thinkers was not a person who was free to
do whatever he liked; rather, he was someone who exercised both "personal
independence and moral responsibility." In short, the autonomous citizen
could proudly claim not only rights but also obligations. Foremost among the
latter was resistance to oppression, even—especially—when it meant sacri-
ficing life itself.[8]

François Furstenberg extends Kloppenberg's argument to examine how
early national notions of autonomy took shape in the presence of, and in
contradistinction to, American slavery. In the Revolution's wake, the creators
of American civic mythology represented the autonomous citizen as a man
who had sovereignty over himself, and who stalwartly and actively resisted
any threat to that self-sovereignty. With Revolutionary political discourse
claiming that death was the only respectable alternative to liberty, slaves'
abjection made them objects of contempt. That they had not fought to the
death against their enslavement signified that they had chosen their own
subjugation. This idea that enslavement demanded immediate and forceful
resistance helps to answer the nagging question about the "founding fathers"
in the American pantheon: why did they so bitterly detest the colonies' met-
aphorical enslavement to Britain, even as they tolerated the persistence of
actual human bondage? In order for white founders to argue that slaves had
effectively consented to their oppression, they had to overlook, or "unthink,"
the many examples of slaves' resistance and political activity. But what is
most striking is that the idea that the fully emancipated individual was not
merely free but autonomous, not merely a claimant of rights but an active
defender of them, was also central to the political thought of slaves and
former slaves. In Massachusetts, where the dismantling of slavery as a legal
institution happened relatively early, a major question facing people of color
was not just "are we free?" but "are we citizens?": do we have the autonomy
to make claims on the state, and are we positioned to defend such claims?[9]

If black and white Americans shared an idealization of individual moral
autonomy, it was not because this idea is, or ever has been, universal.
Intellectual histories such as Kloppenberg's and Furstenberg's allow us to see

how agency, that keyword of contemporary historiography, is itself a concept with a history. In an illuminating critique of the totalizing power of "agency" within recent social history, Walter Johnson observes that many studies oriented around agency take for granted the universal possibility and desirability of the personal autonomy that the term connotes. "Agency," he reminds us, is "saturated with the categories of nineteenth-century liberalism, a set of terms which were themselves worked out in self-conscious philosophical opposition to the condition of slavery." When reading how Bay Staters in this period asserted their autonomy as historical actors, we have to consider the historical specificity of their claims to agency. As heirs to the Revolution, Americans in the late eighteenth and early nineteenth centuries—and particularly those who lived in the "Cradle of Liberty"—measured their own efforts to make history against the promises and achievements of the most significant historical transformation of their recent past. Ultimately, their claims to historical agency matter not so much because the idealization of liberal agency has tremendous resonance in our own time but because it was so foundational to theirs.[10]

An emancipated person, then, was someone who could assert historical agency. To make their actions carry more than momentary significance, people needed the power not only to enact history but also to ensure that what they did was recognized, narrated, and commemorated. Such memorialization required the existence of others who shared a sense of the significance of their actions and who could perpetuate those meanings over time. Access to a collection of people with a shared understanding of the past—whether those people were considered family, community, or nation—was something that slavery sought to deny the enslaved. Indeed, scholars who study slavery cross-culturally have stressed that slavery might best be understood not in polarity with freedom but with belonging. In these terms, enslavement is fundamentally a process of alienation. Alienation, what sociologist Orlando Patterson calls "social death," severs the slave's capacity "to anchor the living present in any conscious community of memory."[11] If slavery involves the loss of social and historical rootedness, then emancipation must involve a reverse process, an incorporation into the community, including the "community of memory."[12]

If we consider this kind of incorporation to be an essential part of emancipation, then the ending of slavery in Massachusetts was prolonged indeed. The Bay State never legislated emancipation.[13] Instead, slavery ended due to a combination of factors, among them growing public sentiment against slavery during the Revolutionary era, a state constitution in 1780 declaring all men free and equal, and several well-timed lawsuits brought by slaves against their masters. Since chattel slavery died out in the state in the wake of the Revolutionary War, the endeavor to construct a regional and national culture rooted in a particular idea of what it meant to be a free republic coincided with the day-to-day struggles of former slaves to make lives for themselves as free individuals. In other words, the historical process of emancipation from slavery proceeded simultaneously with the crafting of historical memory about the significance of the Revolutionary era's various and uneven liberations.[14]

I relate these paired narratives over the course of five chapters that overlap in time, even as they move roughly chronologically from the Revolution to the Civil War. This story lingers longer over some moments than others, because it follows a set of characters, tales, and tropes that emerged, receded, and resurfaced from memory as the exigencies of successive moments demanded. Chapter 1 focuses on the earliest histories of slavery and emancipation in Massachusetts. It traces the historical significance and political utility of the argument that slavery ended by virtue of a Revolutionary-era shift in public opinion. First articulated by Federalist historian Jeremy Belknap in 1795 and reformulated by jurists, legislators, and antiquarians up to the Civil War, this argument made the absence of slavery a crucial yet uncontroversial part of the state's historical landscape. In linking emancipation with the Revolution, though, the public opinion argument had a divided legacy for incorporating people of color into the body politic. It both guarded against efforts to exclude them from the Commonwealth entirely and facilitated a refusal to recognize that they continued to lack substantive civil rights.

Moving from written history to a broader range of commemorative sources, chapter 2 shows how memorialization was wrapped up in the Revolution from its very beginning. With a focus on early representations of the Boston Massacre and the Battle of Bunker Hill, I argue that the individuals publicly honored as heroes in the three decades after the Revolution were primarily those with recognized political, social, and cultural authority: elite, white men. Early accounts of these pivotal Revolutionary events noted the presence, but not generally the political agency, of people of color. Advancing a generation ahead in time, chapter 3 returns to a crucial locus of chapter 2, Bunker Hill. In the late 1820s, 30s, and 40s, the long effort to build a monument on the site of Boston's first major military engagement of the Revolutionary War coincided with the development of an organized antislavery movement in the city. In this context, abolitionists and monument-builders vied for control over the legacy of the Revolution. As slavery and freedom became increasingly regionalized in political discourse, Bay Staters wondered what it meant when a black man—possibly a slave—appeared in a visible but servile position at the dedication of the Bunker Hill Monument in 1843. In contextualizing the controversy that this incident provoked, I show how the idea that slavery was fundamentally at odds with Massachusetts heritage helped abolitionists expand public support for their movement. Ultimately, abolitionists and their opponents were contesting not only what the future course of the country should be but also how to configure the relationship between the present and the past.

Moving into the city and outlying towns shadowed by Bunker Hill, chapter 4 examines less prominent, but no less significant, sites of commemorative culture in antebellum Massachusetts. This chapter reads texts memorializing individual people of color whom their white contemporaries and biographers deemed exemplary and "respectable." Foremost among these exemplary individuals was Phillis Wheatley, whom nineteenth-century accounts honored not only for her literary talents but also for her modest and deferential behavior toward whites. By presenting black agency only within a carefully circumscribed sphere, narratives like these perpetuated a feminized version of black history acceptable to white reformers. In the long run, however, people of color were not content with this vision of black respectability. Chapter 5 therefore examines how blacks strove to claim "manhood" and "citizenship" (two overlapping and at times interchangeable categories) by representing themselves and their ancestors as agents in history. This endeavor was especially pressing after 1850, when such assertions of civic belonging constituted direct affronts to the infamous Fugitive Slave Act that made African Americans vulnerable to slave catchers even on the professedly free ground of the North. It was in this context that Crispus Attucks, who had been largely forgotten in early national commemorations of the Revolutionary War, assumed his place as black America's finest example of patriotism and heroism. In this crucial period leading up to the Civil War, African Americans not only made history in America, but they also made American history their own.

The chapters that follow seek to relocate the fundamental question of recent social history—"who makes history?"—back to Revolutionary America and the early national United States.[15] The American Revolution inaugurated a debate about who could claim autonomy to make political decisions and have a stake in the distribution of power. Given these origins of the republic, the early national contestation over the meaning of the Revolution was a struggle not only to shake off slavery but also to reframe how different people were situated vis-à-vis such a monumental historical transformation. In Massachusetts, the nerve center of the nation's historical production, it was evident from the earliest days of the republic that the Revolution had destroyed the viability of chattel slavery. There was much less consensus regarding whether and how the liberations of the late eighteenth century had shaped the terms of historical agency: What were the ideals of the Revolution, and who had been responsible for fulfilling them? Who could claim the Revolution's legacy, and what did that inheritance demand of those

who received it? Was the American Revolution fixed and finished in the eighteenth century, or was it constantly being made and remade through the
very process of narrating it? This book traces how abolitionist Bay Staters
struggled to answer these questions in the context of their efforts to put
slavery into the past. In the process, they helped to create a narrative of
American history that resonates in our own time. The American Revolution
that we know in the twenty-first century—a Revolution in which a runaway
slave became the first martyr for liberty and a young African girl became an
international literary celebrity—owes as much to Massachusetts activists and
historians in the nineteenth century as it does to Crispus Attucks or Phillis
Wheatley themselves.

1

Facts and Opinion

The earliest published history of slavery in Massachusetts was instigated by an antislavery Southerner. In 1795, Judge St. George Tucker, professor of law at the College of William and Mary, sent Reverend Jeremy Belknap, founder of the Massachusetts Historical Society, a series of questions about the Bay State's history of slavery and emancipation. Belknap showed Tucker's queries to "such gentlemen as it was supposed would assist in answering them." Based on his informants' responses and his own documentary research, Belknap assembled a detailed legal and social history, in which he proposed an elegant and novel explanation for emancipation in Massachusetts: "Slavery hath been abolished here by *publick opinion*."[1] Tucker had written to Belknap hoping that the success of abolition in Massachusetts would guide Virginians working toward the same end. In his response, Belknap reinforced this connection between historical transformation and historical narration by intimating that Bay Staters had abolished slavery because it did not suit the narrative they were creating for themselves as forgers of freedom. Although he mentioned the involvement of a number of different individual actors, Belknap singled out no particular hero for initiating emancipation. Instead, by vesting responsibility in the people at large, his public opinion explanation accorded with a Revolutionary vision of historical agency. Emancipation, like the American Revolution itself, was a product of the people.

For twenty-five years after Belknap responded to Tucker's inquiries, no one else published a history of slavery and emancipation in Massachusetts. That changed in 1821, when a committee of the state legislature, led by Representative Theodore Lyman, issued a report on the treatment of the state's "Free Negroes and Mulattoes." What prompted this self-examination was the national debate over Missouri's constitution, which, in its original form, sought both to welcome slave owners and their human chattel and to keep free people of color out. Could Massachusetts claim to be any more of a refuge for the oppressed than Missouri? After an examination of the Commonwealth's history, the legislative committee's response was a resounding yes. To come to that conclusion, the committee both borrowed liberally from Belknap's version of the past and ironed out many of the complexities of his analysis.

In the decades after the Missouri compromise, various historians (some with a nod to Belknap) claimed that slavery had been fundamentally at odds with the will of the people of Massachusetts during the Revolution. Over time, Belknap's "publick opinion" argument mutated from a complex causal explanation of emancipation into an expression of a mythic identity for Massachusetts. By making principled opposition to slavery central to the Commonwealth's Revolutionary heritage, this historical identity proved politically powerful in nineteenth-century debates about slavery and citizenship. However, the argument that public opinion had emancipated the state's slaves had divergent implications. On one hand, the claim that Bay Staters had already accepted emancipation absolved them from charges of complicity with the slaveholding South. On the other, civil rights activists could point to the Revolutionary forefathers' apparent consensus around emancipation in order to argue that succeeding generations should uphold that antislavery legacy. Whether used to justify complacency or inspire action, the argument that public opinion in Massachusetts firmly opposed slavery became, in the increasingly regionalized political discourse of the antebellum decades, a mark of the state's distinctive place in the history of American slavery and freedom.

MASSACHUSETTS: THE EVIDENCE OF EMANCIPATION

Between 1780 and 1804, Pennsylvania, Rhode Island, Connecticut, New York, and New Jersey all passed gradual emancipation statutes. Massachusetts never did. Contemporaries who compared abolition in Massachusetts to other states emphasized its swiftness in the former. "All the Negroes in the commonwealth were…liberated in a day," New Haven pastor Jonathan Edwards announced to a Connecticut antislavery society in 1791. This claim highlighted the uniqueness of legal emancipation in Massachusetts. Connecticut eliminated slavery with a gradual emancipation law that did not actually free anyone who was enslaved when the act passed in 1784. Instead, it promised freedom at the age of twenty-five to children born to slaves after the law took effect. Not until 1809 would anyone become free as a result of this law; there were a handful of people still legally enslaved in Connecticut as late as 1848. In other states that legislated gradual emancipation, the story was similar.[2]

In 1795, the year Belknap and Tucker corresponded, a pamphleteer in New Hampshire mourned the persistence of slavery in his state and asserted that "in Massachusetts the negroes were freed long ago." "Long ago," of course, was entirely relative, and this writer didn't say how he knew that all the slaves were free. Still, the sense that slavery was defunct in Massachusetts was strong, both in and out of the state, even though there was no legislative record to back it up. When it came to answering Tucker's fifth query, which asked for "the mode by which slavery hath been abolished," Belknap had to piece together an explanation from a range of sources. A string of events from the 1760s through 1790 provided him with the evidence that public opinion in the Revolutionary era had turned against slavery.[3]

The first indicator was less a discrete event than a flurry of pamphlets and speeches. Dating the rise of antislavery sentiment to "the beginning of our controversy with Great-Britain," Belknap traced abolitionist ideas in the period's print and oral culture. In the 1760s, some of Boston's first antislavery literature appeared alongside writings by prominent abolitionist Quakers from the middle colonies. James Otis's *Rights of the British Colonies Asserted and Proved* (1764) questioned chattel slavery in the course of a larger critique of political tyranny, while Nathaniel Appleton's *Considerations on Slavery, in a Letter to a Friend* (1767) zeroed in on the evils of the slave trade. With the Revolution barely begun, past events nevertheless set a standard for future action. Referring to the Stamp Act crisis, Appleton proclaimed, "The years 1765 & 1766, will be ever memorable for the glorious stand which America has made for her Liberties; how much glory will it add to us, if at the time we are establishing Liberty for ourselves and children, we show the same regard to all mankind that come among us?" "Let us not wait for the example of any other of our sister colonies," Appleton implored his fellow Bay Staters, telling them that being the first to end the slave trade would "show all the world, that we are true sons of Liberty." In 1767, the legislature debated ending the trade, but the upper and lower house never agreed on a bill.[4]

The public discourse on slavery and the slave trade did not end with that legislative stalemate. The legitimacy of slavery was the topic at Harvard's commencement debate in 1773. That same year, black men brought the issue back to the legislature, submitting the first in a series of increasingly insistent petitions pointing to the irony of patriots holding slaves in the midst of their struggle for political freedom. These petitions offered some of the most pointed and moving political rhetoric of the Revolutionary era: "We have in common with all other men a naturel right to our freedoms without Being depriv'd of them by our fellow men as we are a freeborn Pepel and have never forfeited this Blessing by aney compact or agreement whatever."[5] In January 1774, an effort to outlaw the slave trade (perhaps inspired by the earliest of these petitions) stalled on the governor's desk; a ban on the slave trade would not actually be written into law until 1788. In the ensuing years, even as the exigencies of war absorbed the attention of political leaders, Belknap claimed that "the conversation of reflecting people" continued to focus on slavery. The controversy turned the hearts and minds even of some slave owners, who "condemned themselves, and retracted their former opinion."[6]

Of course, discussing the evils of slavery in pamphlets and newspapers or in taverns and lecture halls did not automatically set anyone free. As Belknap described it, the antislavery agitation of the 1760s and 1770s tipped the balance of public opinion in Massachusetts, such that by the time the Revolutionary War broke out, town meetings in several localities passed resolutions against slavery. These localized decisions were ratified into the first article of the Declaration of Rights in the Massachusetts constitution of 1780, which declared that "all men are born free and equal." This clause, Belknap explained, "was inserted not merely as a moral or political truth, but with a particular view to establish the liberation of the negroes on a general principle, and so it was understood by the people at large." The 1780 constitution was the second piece of evidence of emancipation.[7]

Not everyone at the time agreed that the constitution decisively ended slavery—even if they thought it should. Voters in the town of Hardwick proposed amending the first article to read, "'All men, whites and blacks, are born free and equal,'…lest it should be misconstrued hereafter, in such a manner as to exclude blacks." In other towns, voters suggested amendments to outlaw slavery or the slave trade explicitly. The assembled townsmen of Rochester "unanimously Voted that this be added to the above Form of Government—That there shall no Slaves be Born or Imported into this Common Wealth." For the few towns that suggested them, these constitutional amendments present the closest thing possible to poll results indicating antislavery public opinion. The novel manner by which the constitution was constructed lent support to the idea that it was an expression of the public mind. An elected convention in Boston drafted the document, then sent it out to the towns for ratification by all free adult men. In many localities, they voted on each article separately, and when any one received a significant number of "nays," voters detailed their objections. The vast majority of towns unanimously accepted the "free and equal" clause without comment. Did they—unlike their peers in Rochester and Hardwick—think that the clause invalidated slavery as it already stood? Or was the problem of chattel slavery simply of little concern to most voters? The surviving records don't say. What is evident is that in the decades to come, the Massachusetts constitution, as it was shaped and approved "by the people," would become one of the most touted examples of Bay Staters' embrace of freedom and equality.[8]

Even as he claimed that "the people at large" intended the constitution to abolish slavery, Belknap noted that "some doubted whether this was sufficient" to set all slaves free. By the time the state constitution was ratified, slavery had been debated in Massachusetts courtrooms for well over a decade. Though there had been scattered emancipation lawsuits earlier in the eighteenth century, there was a dramatic increase in slaves suing their masters for freedom throughout the Revolutionary period, with twenty such cases occurring between 1760 and 1779. Most of these cases challenged the plaintiff's enslavement within the framework of accepted law and custom, rather than attacking slavery on principle. Nevertheless, Belknap saw the lawsuits as indicative of antislavery public opinion: "The juries invariably gave their verdict in favour of liberty." The passage of the constitution with its "free and equal" clause made natural rights arguments against the institution of slavery all the stronger. In a case testing that clause in 1783, slavery in Massachusetts received what Belknap called its "mortal wound."[9]

The legal dispute later known as the "Quok Walker case" was in fact several cases, involving Quok Walker, a black man in Worcester County; his purported master, Nathaniel Jennison; and John and Seth Caldwell, brothers who employed Walker on their farm. The trouble began in the spring of 1781, when Walker fled to the Caldwells after Jennison reneged on a promise to manumit him (or so Walker claimed). Enraged, Jennison went to reclaim the man he saw as his property, eventually beating Walker before locking him up in a barn. Jennison then sued the Caldwells for their profits from the labor of his purported slave, while Walker sued Jennison for assaulting him. The details of the resulting legal actions are dizzyingly complicated. What is significant is that in the end, in a criminal assault case against Jennison, the arguments before the Supreme Judicial Court not only concerned the facts of the matter but also the legitimacy of slavery under the state constitution of 1780.[10]

Chief Justice William Cushing's charge to the jury in this case, decided in 1783, was a narrative of the history of slavery in Massachusetts. "It is true," he acknowledged, that chattel slavery "had been considered by some of the Province laws as actually existing among us, but nowhere do we find it expressly established." More than an institution with firm backing in law, slavery was, according to Cushing, a custom, or "usage," originating "from the practice of some of the European nations and the regulations…of the British government." Just as Belknap would argue some ten years later, Cushing contended that popular consensus firmly opposed slavery: "Whatever usages formerly prevailed or slid in upon us by the example of others, they can no longer exist. Sentiments more favorable to the natural rights of mankind, and to that innate desire for liberty which heaven, without regard to complexion or shape, has planted in the human breast—have prevailed since the glorious struggle for our rights began." The Massachusetts constitution, with its declaration that all men were free and equal, was "wholly incompatible and repugnant" to the existence of slavery. "Perpetual servitude can no longer be tolerated in our government," Cushing declared. The jury determined that Quok Walker was free.[11]

Cushing's statement seems to support Belknap's claim that the Massachusetts constitution of 1780, consistent with public opinion, intended to abolish slavery. The judge's stirring language also bolsters later historians' argument that the Quok Walker case ended slavery once and for all. However, Cushing's statement was not a judicial decision, entered into the official legal record, but instead a charge to jurors that was not published until the late nineteenth century.[12] The contemporary official documents pertaining to the Walker cases do not clearly invalidate slavery across the board. Furthermore, even if either the judge or jury intended to abolish slavery with these cases, it is unclear how slaves and slave owners throughout the state would have known of them. The cases received no press coverage. Even people close to the matter—including Walker's former owner and the court's clerk—seemed confused about the ramifications of the outcome, and judges in subsequent cases relating to slavery took little notice of the Walker cases as precedent.[13]

Like the establishment of the constitution of 1780, the conclusion of the Walker cases is a singular event sometimes credited with ending slavery in Massachusetts. Belknap did call it the "mortal wound" to slavery, but in the context of his lengthy narrative of emancipation, it seems more accurate to call it a fatal injury to an already languishing body. In the wake of the Revolution, enslaved Bay Staters had not waited for jurors or judges to interpret the "free and equal" clause. As Belknap explained, many took "advantage of the *publick opinion* and of this general assertion in the bill of rights."[14] In numbers impossible to quantify, slaves in the 1780s insisted that their masters manumit them; others simply left service. Numerous enslaved men had already abandoned their masters in the War for Independence, when military service proved an appealing, if risky, alternative to slavery. Perhaps aware of the Walker cases or similar legal actions, perhaps sensing popular opinion's turn against slavery, many slave owners didn't bother to pursue their runaways, or else agreed to manumit their slaves.[15] It helped that slave labor was not so central to local economies as it was in other parts of the new nation. Demographics helped, too. The thousands of slaves in Massachusetts on the eve of the Revolution constituted about 2 percent of the total population, though the fraction in seaport cities was considerably higher. Emancipation in Massachusetts thus seemed less economically and socially disruptive than in states with larger slave populations.[16]

In 1790, the first federal census reported that there were no slaves in Massachusetts. This result seems to prove that emancipation was complete by this point; Belknap called it "the formal evidence of the *abolition of slavery in Massachusetts.*" Yet despite the scientific impulse behind it, census-taking is a very human craft. In the form of peer pressure, the power of public opinion might well have influenced the count of slaves (or lack thereof). In 1847, this tantalizing anecdote about the 1790 Massachusetts census appeared in a biography of Jeremy Belknap, written by his granddaughter:

> When [the census taker] inquired for *slaves*, most people answered none,—if any one said that he had one, the marshal would ask him if he meant to be singular, and would tell him that no other person had given in any. The answer then was, 'If none are given in, I will not be singular;' and thus the list was completed without any number in the column for slaves.

Could this story be true? In 1790, Marshal Jonathan Jackson, the man in charge of the state census, seemed reasonably, but not entirely, certain that slavery was defunct. He instructed his deputies (the men who carried out most of the door-to-door counting) that "slaves (if any such are to be found among us) must be distinguished also from coloured persons who are free." While these instructions don't prove that Jackson or his deputies pressured census respondents to deny that they owned slaves, they do suggest that by 1790 slavery was something that Bay Staters sensed was not to be "found among us."[17]

Antislavery print and oral culture, a constitution declaring all men "free and equal," a court case that confirmed a man's freedom, and a census that counted no slaves: no one of these freed all of the Bay State's bondspeople. Taken together, however, they provide evidence that a general emancipation took place in Massachusetts over the course of the Revolutionary period. Later writers would single out one or another of these events (usually the constitution of 1780 or the Quok Walker decision) as the decisive emancipating act. But in 1795, Belknap came up with a far more nuanced explanation of emancipation, one that aggregated all the evidence into a larger phenomenon. "The principal cause," he declared, "was *publick opinion.*"[18]

At three points in his response to Tucker, each time attributing abolition to "*publick opinion*," Belknap underscored the phrase. His emphasis called attention to the relative novelty of the idea. While "public opinion" appeared only occasionally in British and Continental political philosophy before the eighteenth century, historian Mark Schmeller argues that over the course of the American Revolution and its aftermath, "opinion" gradually came to replace "fear" as "an acceptable explanation of popular allegiance to the state." Though many political theorists perceive public opinion as a rough equivalent to deliberative democracy, Schmeller explains that in the early American republic, public opinion signified something quite at odds with the oppositional politics of democratic deliberation. Closely tied to the technology of polling, the modern concept of public opinion envisions the public as a segmented entity, divided into discrete fractions opposing or supporting particular propositions. But republican ideology rested on the idea that the Revolution came from "the people," not merely from a majority of the public. Instead, republican public opinion was an expression of the people's one mind.[19]

Belknap was not politically naïve. He undoubtedly knew that a fraction (perhaps a large fraction) of Bay Staters did not share his antislavery views, just as not every individual (nationalist rhetoric aside) had supported the war against Britain. His reliance on the concept of public opinion made these voices of disagreement beside the point. Matters of public opinion were those which were beyond debate and dissent. In this context, the lack of a legislated abolition of slavery in Massachusetts helped to support Belknap's argument. Abolition wasn't a question to be deliberated in the General Court, but an emanation of public opinion. By vesting opposition to chattel slavery in the zeitgeist of Revolutionary Massachusetts, this historical explanation gave weight to the idea that antislavery sentiment was integral to the patriot cause. In this respect, Belknap's answers to Tucker's queries made slavery history, both by recording the former existence of the institution and by confirming that, by 1795, it was irrevocably past.

VIRGINIA: THE DREAM OF NATIONAL FREEDOM

Neither Tucker nor Belknap was interested in making slavery history solely as an academic endeavor. In the early republic, the writing of history was closely tied to the process of forging a new nation based on the principles of Revolutionary freedom. That the roles of actors and narrators in the Revolutionary project often coincided is evident from the list of correspondents to whom Belknap sent Tucker's queries, as well as from the biographies of Belknap and Tucker themselves. More than armchair observers of the Revolution's liberations, many of Belknap's informants were participants in the very processes they described. They included Samuel Dexter, a Governor's Councilor who received an emancipation petition from a group of black men in 1773; Nathaniel Appleton, author of Considerations on Slavery in 1767; and Prince Hall, founder of the African Lodge of Masons, who was widely regarded as the leader of Boston's black community. Unlike these three men, not all of the respondents were in the antislavery camp. James Winthrop, a judge who helped establish the Massachusetts Historical Society, added (rather gratuitously) in his letter to Belknap that the slave trade "manifestly tends to preserve life and to increase the quantity of productive labor in the whole world."[20]

Belknap himself was involved not only in researching slavery but also, ever so cautiously, in trying to end it. While anything but a social radical, he was sympathetic to the plight of people of color, and he was a particular ally of "respectable" black leaders like Prince Hall. Belknap aided Boston's black community most directly in 1788, when three black men were lured onto a ship in Boston Harbor and threatened with sale into Caribbean slavery. Outraged, Belknap led a group of local ministers in petitioning the state legislature to prohibit Bay Staters from engaging in the slave trade and to protect the state's inhabitants from being decoyed into slavery. Hall coordinated a second petition against the kidnapping, this one signed by free black men of Massachusetts. A group of Quakers had earlier submitted an anti-slave trade petition of their own. Eventually, the efforts of these three groups of petitioners succeeded in getting the men released (though not before they had been taken to Martinique and St. Bartholomew) and ultimately in securing a law ending the slave trade in Massachusetts. The next year, 1789, Belknap was elected a corresponding member of the Providence Abolition Society, a sister organization to the Quaker-dominated Pennsylvania Abolition Society, the oldest such group in the republic. However, Belknap soon took issue with the national scope of the organization's strategy and its alliances with Quakers.[21]

Belknap's rebuff of the Providence abolitionists is emblematic of the conservatism of Bay Staters' antislavery stance in the earliest decades of the republic. The Rhode Islanders, along with their allies in Pennsylvania, wanted to petition Congress to end the slave trade nationwide, accelerating a process that had already begun with various state-level prohibitions against importing bondspeople. But meddling with slavery and the slave trade in regions outside his own did not appeal to Belknap, nor, for that matter, to many others. As historian Matthew Mason explains, in the North at large and in New England in particular, "many were blinded to or at least apathetic toward the expansion of slavery in the South because abolition seemed like a done deal in their own backyard." There were economic and political reasons for New Englanders to shy from criticizing slavery in other regions. Even after general emancipation in Massachusetts and the enactment of gradual abolition laws in Connecticut and Rhode Island, the mercantile economy of southern New England remained intimately connected with Atlantic slavery. Not only were New Englanders heavily invested in the slave trade—even if they no longer imported slaves into their own region—but they also traded extensively with the slave-based economies of the West Indies and the American South. In Belknap's case, the reluctance to interfere with southern slavery took on a veneer of political principle. As firmly as he opposed slavery and the slave trade, Belknap thought it imperative that the compromises and principles that had unified the states be respected above all else. In his eyes, the Rhode Islanders' petition violated "one of the express stipulations" of the recently ratified Constitution, that Congress would not ban the slave trade before 1808. The Constitution was a "union and compact, formed on *certain conditions*," he insisted, complaining that the Quakers' zeal to press abolition on the nation at large would "violate these conditions, and set us again into a state of anarchy."[22]

The Providence Abolition Society's approach posed another problem for Belknap: "They are governed by their feelings, and they do not reason." Belknap approved of the way that the Revolution "called the democratic power into action" and "repressed the aristocratic spirit." The expansion of political power to a broader range of people advanced social equality, unity, and freedom. But as his reservations toward the Quakers suggested, good government would not necessarily proceed from the people naturally. Instead, they had to learn to control "feelings" and act on carefully formed judgments from conscientiously collected facts: "Government is a *science*, and requires education and information, as well as judgment and prudence." For Belknap, history too was a science, and one closely aligned with that of government. Both writing history and framing government required creating order out of anarchy and privileging reason over passions or interests. This emphasis on methodical, reasoned inquiry has led one of Belknap's biographers to call him "the founder of the 'scientific history' movement in the United States."[23]

Though very much a man of the American Enlightenment, Belknap spent most of his adult life outside the centers of intellectual activity. Born in Boston in 1744 to descendants of Great Migration Puritans, he spent nearly twenty years following his Harvard graduation—including the entirety of the Revolutionary War—in New Hampshire, where he ministered to the Congregational church in Dover. During that time, Belknap interviewed elderly residents of the state, corresponded with clergymen and local leaders, and scoured basements and attics of old homes and government buildings for documents, assembling the materials for what would become his three-volume *History of New Hampshire*, published between 1784 and 1792. His commitment to systematic research led him to write what scholars still admire as a judicious history, but it did not enamor him to his increasingly restive congregation. When offered a pulpit in Boston in 1787, Belknap jumped at the chance to return to New England's cultural capital. There he and other historical enthusiasts set up the Massachusetts Historical Society in the early 1790s.[24]

The historical society's constitution outlined the prerogatives of Belknap and his like-minded contemporaries: "The preservation of Books, Pamphlets, Manuscripts and Records…conduces to mark the genius, delineate the manners, and trace the progress of society in the United States, and must always have a useful tendency to rescue the true history of this country from the ravages of time, and the effects of ignorance and neglect." Embracing the

Enlightenment enthusiasm for collecting and categorizing, the society's primary mission was to gather and preserve historical documents. Initially, the Massachusetts Historical Society collected materials from across the nation, for the organization's establishment was rooted in a broader cultural nationalist movement that swept the country in the aftermath of the War for Independence. In the 1780s and 90s, poets praised "the rising glory of America," artists painted turning points in American history, and Noah Webster published his *American Spelling Book*. The *American Arithmetic* and *American Geography* would soon follow from other authors, while Belknap himself worked on his *American Biography* up to the time of his death.[25]

For Belknap and his cohort, the writing of history and the collecting of materials were tied to the formation of national unity and character. Perceiving each of the states as synecdoche for the nation, Belknap intended his magnum opus, the *History of New Hampshire*, to show the "genius" and "manners" of the whole United States. Furthermore, as the Massachusetts Historical Society's constitution disclosed, he and his colleagues were committed to the idea that there was a "true history of this country" and that excavating and narrating it would prove "useful." These assumptions underlay Tucker's questions about slavery in Massachusetts. In Belknap, the judge had found a correspondent who shared his perspective on history. His initial letter disclosed his hope that their correspondence might be a small step toward strengthening national unity. Ruing that he had "never visited the Eastern States," Tucker nevertheless expected that "a more frequent intercourse and intimate acquaintance would probably contribute more to remove local prejudices and cement the bond of union than any other project."[26]

Tucker put Belknap's history of Massachusetts slavery to use almost immediately after receiving it. The judge had a long personal familiarity with slavery. Born and raised in Bermuda, he came to the mainland to study law at the College of William and Mary in 1772. He twice married into families of the Virginia gentry, in both cases acquiring large estates of slaves. But Tucker had grave doubts about the institution that had built both the society to which he was born and the one that adopted him as a young man. When he began teaching at William and Mary in the early 1790s, among his lecture topics was the incompatibility of slavery with the principles of an enlightened society. When he sent his list of historical queries to Belknap in 1795, he was at work on a book based on his law lectures. The volume appeared in 1796 as *A Dissertation on Slavery: with a Proposal for the Gradual Abolition of It, in the State of Virginia*.[27]

Tucker's *Dissertation* sought to show that support for slavery was not ingrained in the minds of contemporary Virginians, even if it was deeply rooted in Virginia's soil. He noted that black slaves appeared in both Virginia and Massachusetts early in the colonies' histories, in 1620 and 1638, respectively: "Thus early had our forefathers sown the seeds of an evil, which, like leprosy, hath descended upon their posterity with accummulated rancour, visiting the sins of the fathers upon succeeding generations." The comparison to leprosy rendered contemporary white Virginians—including slave owners—as the victims, rather than the instigators, of the insidious disease that was slavery. Like other southern planters who critiqued slavery (most famously, Thomas Jefferson), Tucker worried intensely about the damage that slavery did to the ruling and slave-owning class. His *Dissertation* began with a warning that slavery was "an object of the first importance, not only to our moral character and domestic peace, but even to our political salvation." Present-day Virginians could not be blamed for originating the scourge of slavery, but it was imperative that they take responsibility for eliminating it. Otherwise, Tucker warned, they would be shirking "the principles of our government, and of that revolution upon which it is founded."[28]

As Tucker developed his comparison of slavery in the northern and southern states (drawing heavily on Belknap and a Connecticut correspondent, Zephaniah Swift, for his claims about the North), he dismissed any suggestion that the primary differences between the regions had to do with the mentality or culture of the people who lived in them. The differences that mattered to Tucker were material, encompassing both the climatic properties of the two regions and the physical characteristics of people of European and African descent. Articulating a common eighteenth-century assumption about black and white bodies, Tucker argued that Africans and their descendants were better able than whites to work in Virginia's hot climate. Citing Belknap and Swift, he added that white labor was more economically efficient in the North, since people of European descent were better adapted to harsh winters. "The great increase of slavery in the southern, in proportion to the northern states in the union," Tucker concluded, "is therefore not attributable, *solely*, to the effect of sentiment, but to natural causes; as well as those considerations of profit, which have, perhaps, an equal influence over the conduct of mankind in general, in whatever country, or under whatever climate destiny hath placed them."[29]

The early part of Tucker's *Dissertation* established slavery as a national problem. If it had been solved in some parts of the union, the problem at least had a past everywhere. Tucker's particular concern was that it not have a future in Virginia. While Tucker was a dispassionate jurist and historian, he did not shy away from moral judgment, calmly observing that Virginia's legal history "unavoidably led" its students "to remark, how frequently the laws of nature have been set aside in favour of institutions, the pure result of prejudice, usurpation, and tyranny." Adding another dimension to his earlier argument that Virginia slavery could not be blamed on any unique characteristic of Virginians themselves, he argued that slavery effectively held the ruling class in its thrall. The legal excesses of the slave regime, he concluded, "do not proceed from a sanguinary temper in the people of Virginia, but from those political considerations indispensably necessary, where slavery prevails to any great extent." In Tucker's view, the Revolution provided the people with the strength to break the political inertia that slavery created. "*Antecedent to the revolution,*" he argued, the Crown would have squelched any effort to end slavery. But now that Virginians had broken one set of chains, they were well prepared to sever another.[30]

The final section of the *Dissertation on Slavery* outlined Tucker's plan for emancipation. Demographics made it impossible for Virginia to emancipate all slaves "at a single stroke," as Tucker claimed had happened in Massachusetts. Instead, gradual emancipation offered a more palatable way to wean Virginians from the institution that had once seemed so well-suited to the local climate and economy, if not to the spirit of the people. Tucker cited the gradual emancipation laws of Pennsylvania and Connecticut as reasonable models for what he hoped might happen in Virginia. Like these northern statutes, Tucker's proposal was for a *post nati* emancipation law, affecting only those born after its passage. In Virginia's case, all women born after the law's enactment would be free, thereby eventually ensuring freedom to all their descendants, since slave status followed the condition of the mother. However, these women's freedom would not be immediate. Instead, in order to compensate "those persons, in whose families such females, or their descendants, may be born, for the expence and trouble of their maintenance during infancy," the women would serve their masters until the age of twenty-eight. The children of this first generation of "free" women would also serve as bound laborers, either in the family of the child's mother's master (if the mother was still in bondage) or for the local overseers of the poor (if the mother was free). These terms of service would end at the age of twenty-eight or twenty-one, respectively. As suggested by this proposal to bind out even those children who had two free parents, Tucker's plan placed very severe restrictions on free people of color. A free "Negroe or mulattoe" would not be permitted to vote, hold public office, own or serve as a trustee for real estate, bear arms, marry a white person, be a lawyer or juror, testify in a court case involving a white person, or make or execute a will.[31]

Tucker's claim that only by stripping blacks of nearly every imaginable aspect of political or legal agency could emancipation ever become popularly accepted seems to contradict his earlier assertion that "a very large proportion of our fellow-citizens" in Virginia decried the persistence of slavery in the state. Tucker's primary concern was the political and moral cost of slavery for the larger (and white-dominated) society. The existence of slavery might have made many freedom-loving whites uneasy, but the thought of living among a significant population of free people of color discomfited them even more. This tension created dissonance between the first part of the *Dissertation*, in which Tucker laid out the history of slavery in Virginia and his philosophical objections to it, and the second, more practical, part, in which he proposed abolition. The theoretical argument held that limiting a group of people's civil rights was a species of slavery. "Civil slavery," Tucker explained, prevails "whenever [natural] liberty is, by the laws of the state, further restrained than is necessary and expedient for the general advantage," as well as "whenever there is an inequality of rights, or privileges, between the subjects or citizens of the same state, except such as necessarily result from the exercise of a public office." He cited contemporary exclusions on black voting rights and militia membership as examples of the "civil incapacities" of free people of color under current law in Virginia and other states. But his emancipation proposal not only failed to eliminate these incapacities but also enshrined a more expansive set of them into law.[32]

At first glance, Tucker's regime of "civil slavery" seems markedly different from the emancipation experience in Massachusetts. Free people of color in Massachusetts had some of the legal rights that Tucker would have denied their counterparts in Virginia, including the rights to vote and hold real estate. That black Bay Staters should be guaranteed such rights had not been a foregone conclusion, however. The state constitution proposed in 1778 denied black men the vote, though the towns roundly rejected this draft, for varied reasons. In at least three towns, Spencer, Sutton, and Westminster, the disenfranchisement of men of color was one of the draft's problems. "Depriving of any men or Set of men for the Sole Cause of Colour from giving there votes for a Representative," the freemen of Spencer complained, was "an Infringment upon the Rights of mankind." Free, taxpaying black men deserved to vote, for "it is Our Fundamental Principle that taxation and Reprsentation [sic] Cannot be Seperated." Shaped, perhaps, by such responses to the 1778 draft, the constitution ratified in 1780 did not limit voting rights by race.[33]

Yet there were clear boundaries to the civil rights of people of color in Massachusetts, and they stemmed from the fact that many white Bay Staters were just as uncomfortable with the prospect of a multiracial republic as their Virginian counterparts were. In Massachusetts, Indians, blacks, and mulattoes were not allowed to marry whites, nor could they serve in the militia. In limiting these rights, state legislators were acting on the same antislavery sensibility that motivated Tucker's proposal: the primary problem with slavery was that it corrupted the society in which it existed, not that it harmed enslaved people. The pervasiveness of this sentiment adds a wrinkle to the "public opinion" argument. Belknap claimed that the people's opposition to slavery had been so strong as to render emancipation legislation unnecessary in Massachusetts. But another dimension of public opinion—popular prejudice—curtailed former slaves from fully realizing the promises of freedom. Looking back on the process of northern emancipation, Hosea Easton, a Massachusetts-born preacher of mixed African and Indian ancestry, bitterly noted in 1837 that "the system of slavery in its effects, is imposed on the injured party in two forms, or by two methods. The first method is, by a code of laws, originating in public sentiment, as in slave states. The other is, prejudice originating in the same, as it exists in free states."[34]

Though racial prejudice clearly plagued the union as a whole, it is nonetheless significant that Easton, writing in the 1830s, recognized a clear distinction between "free states" and "slave states." In contrast, in the mid-1790s, when Tucker wrote his *Dissertation on Slavery*, this line between "free" and "slave" was still in the making, as was its mapping onto "North" and "South." In writing to Belknap, Tucker lamented his unfamiliarity with "the Eastern States." Tucker's choice to reach out to a Bay Stater harkened back to the early years of the Revolution, when Virginia enjoyed a close relationship with Massachusetts, a province Virginians then regarded as just as much "eastern" as "northern." Moving into the last decade of the eighteenth century, Virginians didn't necessarily imagine their interests as clearly aligned with South Carolina and other future allies in the Confederacy. They could just as easily see themselves in coalition with the middle states and the Northwest. While the Constitutional convention and the Federal period saw frequent reconfiguration of interstate alliances, the crucial point is that these connections were there for the breaking and remaking. Antebellum sectional differences—the totalizing power of "North" and "South"—cannot be read back into the early years of the republic. Before the consolidation of a free North and slave South, it was conceivable to Tucker that Virginia might join the fraternity of free states, with the remaining slaveholding states to follow.[35]

But this sense that abolition was the common fate of all the states was fleeting—in Tucker's case, remarkably so. The Virginia legislature refused to entertain his proposal, which he put forward at a time when the post-Revolutionary enthusiasm for emancipation was dissipating alongside steady growth in the state's slave population. Up from 292,000 in the first federal census, Virginia slaves numbered 392,000 twenty years later in 1810. The ongoing revolution in Haiti also kept slave-owning Virginians on edge. Then, in 1800, the thwarting of a conspiracy near Richmond led by a slave named Gabriel confirmed fears of violent rebellion. By 1803 Tucker was wistfully imagining that freedpeople might be relocated to the newly purchased Louisiana, but he bitterly assured his readers that he had no expectation that such a plan would ever be enacted. Only seven years after his cautiously optimistic *Dissertation on Slavery*, he dismissed any sort of emancipation scheme as a "Utopian idea." Resigned to the persistence, even the growth, of slavery, Judge Tucker's legal decisions in the early nineteenth century increasingly entrenched the power of the planter class.[36]

Around 1820, Tucker mournfully revisited his *Dissertation on Slavery*. As the nation at large debated whether to allow slavery in what was to be its newest western state—Missouri—Tucker wrote in his private notebook of his hope that the nation would someday realize its Revolutionary potential and end slavery. His sons, on the other hand, vocally defended what they saw as the particular interests of the South when it came to the Missouri question; they even suggested that slavery might be good for the nation. "This generational shift," writes historian Phillip Hamilton, "signaled that the debate over slavery had taken an ominous turn away from discussions of compromise and natural rights and toward talk of irreconcilable differences, 'dissolution,' and 'exterminating civil wars.'"[37] The world in which a gentleman in Virginia and a clergyman in Massachusetts could compare notes about the history of slavery in their two regions was fast disappearing. Revolutionary-era Virginians and Bay Staters could share a sense that holding on to slaves in a free republic was hypocritical and even dangerous. By the turn of the century, these two commonwealths were beginning to diverge on the question of what the Revolution meant and what it demanded of the present. Virginia planters were assuming a self-congratulatory status as benevolent patriarchs. But Virginians weren't alone in taking a unique, even moralizing, pride in what had once been merely a matter of geographical difference. Bay Staters' sense of their local history was changing, too.

MISSOURI: THE COLOR OF CITIZENSHIP

The history of slavery in Massachusetts received little attention—at least in print—for twenty-five years after Belknap answered Tucker's queries. When the matter came up again, the impetus for revising Belknap's history was located well to the west, on a large expanse of land just north of the thirty-sixth parallel in the Louisiana Territory. The prospect of admitting Missouri to the union as a slave state, thereby throwing off the delicate balance of power in Congress and opening the possibility for slavery's westward expansion, set Bay Staters on edge. State legislators acted quickly to charge their Congressional delegation to take a strong stand against Missouri statehood. On behalf of the people of the Commonwealth, members of the Massachusetts legislature declared on February 23, 1820, "it is the duty of the people & Government of the United States by all constitutional means to prevent the extension of so great a Moral & political evil as Slavery." If the general opinion against chattel slavery had been but mutedly articulated in the Revolutionary period, the antislavery consensus was now a sweeping resolution from the state's representative political body.[38]

But the legislators' concerns were not directed solely toward Washington, Missouri, and the unorganized territory beyond. Indeed, as representatives to the Commonwealth's General Court, their powers and responsibilities were oriented toward matters much closer to home. The spread of slavery was the major issue in Congress for much of 1819 and 1820, but late in the year a second issue arose. The proposed constitution for the newly forming state of Missouri gave its legislature the power to make laws "to prevent free negroes and mulattoes from coming to and settling in the State." Northerners vehemently objected to this provision, arguing that it turned these people of color into a legally ambiguous class of persons: free people who were native-born but not citizens. If Missouri could restrict the rights of one kind of free person, what was to stop the state from withholding rights to all free people? Southerners countered that emancipation alone was not enough to convert property into citizens, so the restriction on the movement of free people of color was both limited and justified. Ultimately, both sides agreed to accept a Missouri constitution that included a promise to honor the rights of any incoming settler who was already a citizen of another state in the Union. But at a time when the relationship between national and state citizenship was unclear—indeed, the very meaning of "citizen" was ill-defined—the central question of the civic status of black Missourians continued unanswered.[39]

The ambiguous Missouri debate raised two questions for observers in Massachusetts: were people of color in Massachusetts citizens, and could people of color coming into the state from elsewhere become its citizens? Any freedpeople shut out of Missouri would have to find somewhere else to go. Many whites in the Bay State preferred it not be into their own cities and villages. Ever since Massachusetts had abolished the slave trade in 1788, local whites had feared an influx of out-of-state blacks drawn by the promises of free soil. On the same day that it outlawed the slave trade, the General Court passed another law to limit blacks from moving into Massachusetts. "No person, being an African or Negro, other than a subject of the Emperor of Morocco, or a citizen of some one of the United States," was to be permitted to stay in the Commonwealth for longer than two months, on pain of whipping. While a list of blacks warned out of the state on these terms survives from 1800, it is not clear if the 1788 law was regularly enforced. To some white Bay Staters, Missouri made such a law urgent again. Other states and municipalities had already restricted the rights of free people of color to move to or remain on their soil. Freedpeople could not stay in Virginia more than a year after they were emancipated; Georgia taxed free blacks twenty dollars a year and expelled those who couldn't pay; Ohio required them to post 500 dollars bond when they entered the state; the city of Washington required free blacks to register with the mayor's office each year.[40]

The proliferation of these laws worried Massachusetts legislators. On June 7, 1821, the House of Representatives appointed a committee "to take into consideration the expediency of making any alterations in the Laws of this Commonwealth concerning the admission into residence in this State of Negroes and Mulattoes." One week later, the three-member committee reported back with a "statement of facts" signed by Theodore Lyman, a young representative from Boston. After surveying other states' restrictions on freedpeople's residency, Lyman noted with alarm that from 1790 to 1810, the nation's free black population had increased at over three times the rate of the white population. Lyman concluded "that in the course of ten years, a great proportion of the free negroes of the South, will be driven northward to the New-England States," where their civil rights were relatively unrestricted. "Your committee," Lyman warned his fellow legislators, "do not think it necessary to make particular mention of the evils which will accompany this description of population." The committee listed only the "most apparent" of these dangers:

1. Increasing the number of convicts and paupers.
2. Collecting in the large towns an indolent, disorderly, and corrupt population.
3. Substituting themselves in many labors and occupations which, in the end, it would be more advantageous to have performed by the white and native population of the state.

Lyman asked that a committee investigate more thoroughly and report a bill the next time the General Court met. The House promptly reauthorized the same three members (Lyman, plus Nathan Chandler of Lexington and Joseph Bridgman of Belchertown) to perform the requisite research and draft appropriate legislation.[41]

The following January, Lyman's committee presented a sixteen-page report "concerning the admission into this State of free Negroes and Mulattoes," which the House soon published. The opening of the report was reminiscent of the "statement of facts" the committee had presented to the legislature the previous summer. The laws of other states, Lyman wrote on the committee's behalf, alerted Bay Staters to "the necessity of checking the increase of a species of population, which threatens to be both injurious and burdensome." The first fact in the 1822 report echoed the earlier report's tone of foreboding. As of January 1, 1821, disproportionately more blacks were in prison than whites; the same imbalance, Lyman warned, could in all likelihood be found in the poorhouses. While expressing a paternalistic pity for blacks—"that unhappy and degraded class of individuals, whose colour alone has exposed them to the cruelties and miseries of the slave trade"—the committee nonetheless saw it as their duty "to protect the population of this Commonwealth from all dangers and injuries, whether affecting morals or health, whether introduced from foreign countries, or from the sister States of these United States."[42]

While the opening of the report merely reiterated the assumptions of the 1821 "statement of facts," its conclusion was quite unexpected. The committee reneged on its charge to find a way to keep out people of color. The members begged to be relieved of their duty to draft a bill, and the other legislators acceded. Massachusetts would not follow Missouri in attempting to exclude free people of color. It is hard to know exactly what inspired this reversal. Perhaps constituents had pointed out the inconsistency between Massachusetts politicians' stances toward free blacks on the state versus the national level. Referring to the 1821 statement of facts, a Haverhill newspaperman pointedly observed that Lyman's committee was recommending "precisely the same provisions with regard to Free Blacks, which in the Missouri Constitution, was the cause of so strong an opposition to the admission of that state into the Union."[43] The January 1822 report did not explicitly mention Missouri and the controversies it had engendered. Instead, what intervened between the committee's initial expression of fear about an influx of people of color and its ultimate disavowal of any exclusionary law was history.

The Lyman committee's report, titled "Free Negroes and Mulattoes," was the most extensive history of Massachusetts slavery published since Belknap's in 1795. The committee's research led the three legislators to conclude that a law barring migrants of color was ill-suited to the history of Massachusetts. Initially, their research had revealed that such a statute already existed: the one passed in 1788 concurrent with the abolition of the slave trade. The report dismissed that law as having never been enforced (apparently, the committee was not aware of the published list of warnings-out from 1800). Lyman suggested that the reason the exclusionary statute had received little attention since 1788 was that it was an utter anomaly, "a law so arbitrary in its principle and in its operation so little accordant with the institutions, feelings and practices of the people of this Commonwealth." The remainder of the report elaborated on how history placed the Bay State firmly on the side of liberty and equality.[44]

Lyman's report articulated a historical identity for Massachusetts as a place where "the institutions, practices and feelings of the people" consistently favored universal liberty. In attributing such traditions and sentiments to "the people," the report reinvigorated Belknap's public opinion argument.[45] Whereas Belknap identified a discernible shift in public opinion away from slavery when Americans "began to feel the weight of oppression from 'our mother country,'" Lyman characterized antislavery sentiment as something endemic to Massachusetts from its colonial beginnings. Concerning an incident in 1646 in which the General Court ruled a slave trader guilty of "man-stealing," Lyman wrote: "It is the earliest public manifestation of the sense which our ancestors had of the freedom and personal rights of every man, whatever might be his country or complexion."[46]

Lyman's report cannot be read merely as wishful history. As he did in relating the man-stealing incident, he was careful in other instances to modify his sweeping statements with details and nuances that limited the grandeur of his claims. Yet the overwhelming sense that his narrative creates is that antislavery sentiment was always present and expanding in Massachusetts and that the Commonwealth held pride of place in introducing universal freedom into the Atlantic world. In 1701, at a point when the slave population was beginning an upward swing, one item on the Boston selectmen's agenda was to promote the importation of white servants instead of African slaves. No actual policy seems to have followed from this agenda item, but Lyman speculated that it marked the first time in history that a group of people had recorded their opposition to slavery. He concluded that Bay Staters ought to take pride in this piece of their past: "The greatest emphasis may most deservedly be placed upon this record, and the highest and truest compliment be paid to the generous and just feeling, which prevailed at so early a period in this State."[47]

The Lyman committee's most powerful evidence for the strength of anti-slavery public opinion in Massachusetts came from the 1760s and 70s. Lyman mentioned "political writings of the day" in which "the rights of the blacks are blended with the whites." He also noted the General Court's efforts to abolish slavery in 1767 and 1774, antislavery votes in local town meetings, an abolitionist petition authored by black men in 1773, and slaves' lawsuits against their masters. Belknap had also recorded all of these anti-slavery measures, but in contrast to his predecessor's more measured recounting, Lyman heaped praise on his Revolutionary-era forebears. Of the jurors in the freedom lawsuits, who, acting on public opinion, had allowed liberty to prevail, he wrote: "As a manifestation of public feeling, and as productive of the most valuable results, it is not in our power to bestow too great commendation upon the sublime and eternal principles to which these juries appealed." He then boasted that these decisions put Massachusetts ahead of Britain and every state in the country in establishing legal freedom for all on its soil.[48]

As the report drew to a close, Lyman made a bold and deceptive statement: "The people of this Commonwealth have always believed negroes and mulattoes to possess the same right and capability to become citizens as white persons." At one level, this claim is impossible to contest, for there was no obvious way to determine what the public collectively thought. But a series of restrictive statutes passed in the eighteenth century, from a prohibition on interracial marriage to limitations on the free assembly of people of color to the exclusion in 1788 of blacks born out of state, formed a strong case that the Massachusetts whites who made those laws hadn't regarded people of color as their equals. The 1822 report was no sweeping call for racial equality, and Lyman himself was no social radical.[49] It is difficult to parse exactly what he meant when he suggested that people of color were as able as whites to "become citizens," but it is easy to contest the implication that black Bay Staters had never been held to a second-class status under the law. Nevertheless, Lyman's rose-colored view of Massachusetts history served potential immigrants of color well in that it didn't turn them away at the state line. Apparently, his committee had come to believe that the sympathies of the people and the Commonwealth's historical tendency toward liberty outweighed the state's interest in restricting the flow of migrants, even those regarded as potentially dangerous. In the interest of preserving this interpretation of Massachusetts history, the committee chose a course of action that at least left the door open for equal citizenship.

Lyman's report suggests that historical narratives have the potential to shape what their tellers do. Scholars have long recognized that narratives are deeply embedded in the historical contexts that produce them. Often, accounts of the past are interpreted as reactions to or justifications of pre-existing agendas or actions. But tales of the past can also push action in unexpected directions.[50] At times New Englanders' visions of their region as a free (read: white) republic prompted them to seek the removal of former slaves and other people of color.[51] In other cases—as the Lyman report suggests—New England's historical idealism actually made such exclusionary measures less palatable. As outside observers, we might ever be aware of how an author's own subject position and social context mediate his account of the past, and at our most skeptical moments we might even agree with Julian Barnes that history is "autobiographical fiction pretending to be a parliamentary report." But we are able to be skeptics in these cases only because we are outsiders to the narrative being produced. The critical point is that those who narrate history see themselves as accountable to something outside themselves. Masquerade or not, that sense of accountability to the past is what made Lyman's use of history so powerful in his own "parliamentary report." When his interpretation of the past clashed with the nature of the law he was expected to make, it was the historical narrative that won out and set his committee's course of action—a move that edged Massachusetts another step away from Missouri.[52]

MASSACHUSETTS: THE POWER OF PUBLIC OPINION

In light of Lyman's contemporaries' interest in the colonial and Revolutionary past, the historical emphasis of the report makes sense. Beginning in the wake of the War of 1812, Americans—Bay Staters foremost among them—enthusiastically looked backward. The historically inclined benefited from the preservationist work of historical societies in the early republic, and they participated in a wave of commemorative activity that reached a zenith in 1824 and 1825, when the Marquis de Lafayette toured the country to mark the semicentennial anniversary of the Revolution. Print culture teemed with anecdotes and lessons about all aspects of the American past. William Lloyd Garrison's abolitionist newspaper, the *Liberator*, periodically published primary sources relating to the history of slavery, many of which had recently been discovered as historical enthusiasts stumbled upon long-locked trunks, attics, and libraries. As Bay Staters rediscovered documents and artifacts, they turned out a growing number of historical publications, including scores of booklength local histories.[53]

Those men (and a small number of women) who wrote state and local histories in the early and mid-nineteenth century prized what they viewed as historical "truth." Believing that the truth of history was transparent in the sources, compilers of local histories transcribed long extracts from documents, which they often strung together with very little interpretive or connective material. In his study of local histories, David Russo explains that "the histories produced after the Revolution, and especially after 1815, were formed in part out of a rejection of myth, folklore, hearsay, anything that was not factual or incontestable." No fact was too trivial to record, for one could not judge at one moment what might be useful information the next. To modern readers, then, nineteenth-century local histories can be maddeningly tedious and confusing to read. Generally lacking in explicit interpretive schemes (on the assumption that "the documents and records of the past speak for themselves"), their organization is often either relentlessly chronological, detailing events year by year with little attention to the relationships among them, or capriciously topical, with material appearing to be placed in the order the researcher had discovered it.[54]

This dutiful attention to documentary fact gave nineteenth-century local historians an admirable, though for them sometimes painful, comprehensiveness. Because slaves turned up in the documents local historians used, slaves appear in many local histories. "However disagreeable it may seem to many, we have to record the fact that the 'peculiar institution' did exist in the town previous to the Revolutionary War," wrote a historian of Plymouth, listing the names of slaves and slave owners who figured into town records. The systematic approach of these historians located slaves in myriad places.

As they paced through graveyards, antiquarians found headstones with inscriptions like "Here lies the best of slaves, / Now turning into dust; / Caesar, the Ethiopian, craves / A place among the Just." As they interviewed the oldest residents of their towns, they heard stories about devoted servants and loving masters—and about recalcitrant slaves and abusive owners. As they flipped through lists of baptisms, they inevitably found the word "negro" after certain names. As they traced a family's finances, they discovered slave bills of sale. Such evidence made the history of slavery in Massachusetts impossible to ignore: "It may seem to some singular to find anything in a town history in Massachusetts, relative to the subject of human slavery. And yet, it is a well known and undeniable fact, that, previous to the Revolution, slavery existed in all the colonies, not even excepting our own." Sometimes owning up to this fact provoked an emotional reaction. "Strange as it may appear," confessed one antiquarian in 1859, "Norton was once a slaveholding town; and our pen blushes with shame when we say that some of the masters, as well as their slaves, were members of the church."[55]

What was so "disagreeable," so "singular," so "strange" about the history of slavery in Massachusetts? Belknap had not used such language in 1795. On one level, it makes sense that someone writing about events that happened in his own lifetime would not judge them strange, whereas a historian some decades later might find them unnerving. But the foreignness of slavery to the mid-nineteenth-century Bay State authors did not stem merely from temporal distance. They were also responding to a shift in the cultural and political geography of the nation. In the earliest years of the republic, Belknap and Tucker, the New Englander and the Virginian, could correspond about slavery as a concern that affected both their regions. By the second quarter of the nineteenth century, this national unity of purpose had given way in New England to what historian Harlow Sheidley calls "sectional nationalism." This idea presumed that "the survival of the Revolutionary legacy…depended on the nation's continued loyalty to New England's culture and its political leadership."[56]

The rhetoric of slavery and freedom shaped sectional nationalism through the debates over the War of 1812. Slavery was a central rhetorical figure in these debates, even when the speakers held little concern for the plight of actual bondspeople. Echoing Revolutionary language about the colonies' political enslavement to Britain, New Englanders warned that the South, in its eagerness to expand slavery westward, was engaged in a bid for tyranny over the North. Fears of the South's growing territorial and political clout encouraged some New England Federalists to contemplate secession. As historian Matthew Mason argues, the principles behind this move were more disunionist than abolitionist. Nonetheless, the rhetoric served to tie Northernness in general and New Englandness in particular to what was supposedly a *national* ideal: American freedom.[57]

Although the disunionist sentiment subsided with the failure of the Hartford Convention in 1815, New Englanders nonetheless eagerly embraced their sectional distinctiveness and grafted it onto a nationalist narrative as the republic continued to grow. This idea of New England as the epitome of America was not confined to those in the upper echelons of the Federalist, National Republican, and Whig parties that successively took on the mantle of Yankee conservatism in the first half of the nineteenth century. Urbanites and rural folk, reactionaries and radicals all tapped into the discourse of "Yankeedom." Historian Bruce Laurie notes that particularly in the villages of New England, a strong regional identity could lead either to extreme nativism and parochialism or to antislavery and egalitarianism. In some corners, these seemingly contradictory impulses turned up simultaneously. At its core, Yankeedom was a historical idea. While not all Bay Staters who embraced the "Yankee" label would have approved of the politics of the *Massachusetts Abolitionist*, most would have agreed with the newspaper's founding editorial from 1839:

> MASSACHUSETTS! Her very name is the synonym of freedom! Her founda-
> tions were laid by men derived from their native land, for their devotion to the
> rights of man. For conscience's sake, our pilgrim fathers landed on these then
> barbarous shores, and, by their labors, their sufferings, and their prayers,
> consecrated them as the perpetual home of free men, and free principles. It
> has been the boast of our citizens that they were the sons of such sires. In the
> great struggle for national independence, they asserted their ancestral rights
> unto blood.

This strong association between freedom and northern (more particularly New England, and more particularly still Massachusetts) identity explains why a local history of slavery was so difficult to imagine.[58]

Nineteenth-century Bay Staters' close identification with their local past sometimes foundered on evidence of local slavery. In these cases, writers adopted various strategies of distancing and mitigation. One of the most common claims was that Massachusetts slavery had existed only "in a mild form." For these historians, the relative inoffensiveness of local slavery was especially evident when compared to the South.[59] Another rationalization of slavery brushed it off as part of the culture of the colonial era: "Slavery was then considered neither illegal nor immoral."[60] Here nineteenth-century Americans' ambivalence toward the Puritans came into play. Sometimes they represented slavery as one of the various atrocities that Puritans brought to New England; witch trials and persecution of Quakers were others. Those who sought to minimize the significance of colonial slavery explained it and other Puritan sins as examples of excessive devotion to Old Testament prac-tices or, more generally, the darkness of the less-civilized past. At the same time, many mid-nineteenth century New England antiquarians viewed themselves as inheritors of the Puritan legacy. They justified Puritan slavery as mild and kind, with benevolent masters respecting biblical limits on their power.[61]

A revealing variation on the argument about New England slavery's minimal severity was the contention that a harsh slave system simply could not survive in the region. Slavery, wrote local historian Oliver N. Bacon in 1856, "never prevailed to any extent in Natick. The soil and climate were unfavorable to the existence of this class of persons, and the 'peculiar institution' quickly died out within its limits." The idea that people of African descent could not withstand cold winters had a long history, while the claim that the "soil" of Massachusetts was unsuitable for slavery referred to the fact that large pools of agricultural labor were impractical in the rocky New England landscape. Essex County historian E. Vale Smith made a similar claim about the unfavorable "climate and soil," adding that slavery in Massachusetts "was so limited, in regard both to time and numbers in Newbury, as to have had no material influence on the character of the people." Echoing her, Newton's historian declared that slavery was "never congenial with New England society, or New England character, and consequently never took root, or acquired permanency, among the Puritans or their descendants."[62]

The claim that slavery was incompatible with the "soil" of Massachusetts evoked not only the material conditions that happened to exist in the state but also something more profound, simultaneously more personal and more cosmic. From a modern view, the places people inhabit are morally irrelevant: to be on sand or clay or peat makes no difference to one's character. For nineteenth-century Bay Staters, the ground they stood upon was drenched in too much history for this perspective to hold. As they saw it, no slavery could take root in the soil that had nurtured the Liberty Tree and its gardeners. This sense that free soil somehow ennobled the people who lived on it was ubiquitous in the political discourses of abolitionism and sectional nationalism. It was especially powerful during the controversy over the Fugitive Slave Law in the 1850s, when the *Liberator* editorialized, "every fugitive slave shall instantly be transformed into a freeman as soon as he touches the soil of Massachusetts."[63]

Those who devoted any attention to the history of slavery in Massachusetts acknowledged that the local soil had not always had this magical effect. The vagaries of the abolition process made it difficult to determine exactly when the transformation had taken place. Many nineteenth-century local historians drew on Belknap's history in explaining emancipation, but without having observed the transformations of the 1770s and 80s firsthand, they lacked the nuanced interpretation of their predecessor. Belknap's complex interplay between public opinion, ordinary people's activism, and legal reform became simplified into a discrete and immediate emancipation. If they explained emancipation at all, local historians usually identified the constitution of 1780 as the act that abolished slavery. Under the heading "People of Color," Thomas Gage declared in his *History of Rowley*, "on the adoption of the State Constitution, in 1780, they [i.e., slaves] all became free; and their number was soon much reduced."[64] Despite the vagueness of its "free and equal" clause, some writers took for granted that the first article of the constitution's declaration of rights was intended to abolish slavery.[65]

For his part, Lyman had mentioned both the constitution of 1780 and the Quok Walker decision of 1783, but he leaped from these dates to a perplexing conclusion: "It may therefore be properly considered that Slavery was effectually abolished in this State just before the declaration of independence." Lyman did not point to any particular occurrence around 1776 that could be construed as eliminating slavery from Massachusetts. But in aligning local emancipation with the national Declaration of Independence, he fed into another favored explanation for abolition in Massachusetts: the agent of emancipation was simply "the Revolution." If we understand the American Revolution as John Adams eventually did, as a transformation in the sentiments of the people, then attributing emancipation broadly to the Revolution was another way of making the public opinion argument. It was especially effective because it further exalted the already heroic Revolutionary generation and provided an appealing explanation for how slavery had made its way to New England in the first place. Slavery was the invidious legacy of the "British Colonial Government," one local historian determined, with another concluding (perhaps drawing on Lyman) that "by 1776, public opinion had virtually emancipated the slaves of Massachusetts."[66]

Like these brief passages on slavery and emancipation in local history volumes, longer nineteenth-century accounts of slavery's history in Massachusetts also followed the contours of Belknap's argument. Interest in the Bay State's experience with slavery and abolition intensified with the rise of the abolitionist movement after 1830. Before the Beverly Lyceum in 1833, Robert Rantoul, Sr., a prominent Essex County politician, began his presentation on "Negro Slavery in Massachusetts" by noting that in recent years, "by the collision between the Colonization society and the Anti-slavery society, the subject of African bondage has been made a subject of interest in almost every village." With large portions of his talk lifted directly from Belknap, Rantoul offered what he called "a more dispassionate examination of the subject than the partisans of either of these societies would help us to." Narrating not only the local history of slavery but also the institution's development from ancient times to the present, Rantoul portrayed Massachusetts slavery as a marginal institution, present for a time but never firmly grounded in law. Charting the numbers of slaves in various Massachusetts counties in the eighteenth century, he mused, "it is difficult to reconcile the fact that there were so many slaves in Massachusetts with the laws that are found upon the statute book."[67]

The confusion for Rantoul and many other nineteenth-century readers of colonial law originated with the "Body of Liberties" of 1641. At first glance, this early Bay Colony document seemed to prohibit slavery: "There shall never be any bond slaverie, villinage or Captivitie amongst us." The following clause, however, legitimated the institution by outlining circumstances in which permanent bondage was permissible: when the enslaved "strangers" submitted voluntarily or were captured in "just warres," and when masters treated them in accordance with biblical directives. This one short paragraph about slavery has been interpreted both as the earliest articulation of Massachusetts abolitionism and as the first legal document to sanction slavery in the British American colonies. The Body of Liberties was thus an early manifestation of the ambivalence that many white Bay Staters would come to feel toward the institution of slavery. Although repugnant in theory, bondage nonetheless seemed an acceptable fate for certain classes of "strangers," under certain legal restrictions.[68]

While Rantoul proudly presented himself as a measured moderate in good Massachusetts tradition, he wrote his history at a moment when a small cluster of his fellow Bay Staters (eventually to include his own son) were taking a more radical stand against slavery. The principle behind the "moral suasion" phase of the abolitionist movement, spearheaded by Garrison in the 1830s, was that the only effective way to end slavery was to convert the minds and especially the hearts of the citizenry. When challenged to explain how the proliferation of antislavery literature would effect any change in the world, one moral suasionist insisted that "appeals to the heart of the community are not lost! They fix themselves silently in the popular memory; and they become at last a part of the public opinion, which must, sooner or later, wrench the lash from the hand of the oppressor!"[69] The discourse of public opinion thus assimilated abolitionism into the progress of civilization. Early in the paper's career, the *Liberator* hopefully editorialized, "we feel satisfied from the change that has taken place in public opinion on other subjects, that a change equally great will take place on the subject of slavery." Moral suasionists believed that in contrast to the divisiveness of political pressure or active force, appeals to public opinion could effect a peaceful transition from slavery to freedom. Little surprise, then, that the *Liberator* had republished Belknap's responses to Tucker's "Queries."[70]

The sense that the most sublime and effective way to end slavery was by appealing to public opinion or moral sensibility made emancipation in Massachusetts an especially valuable historical case study, even after the dominant forces of abolitionism had abandoned the moral suasion campaign. In 1857, Emory Washburn wrote that "much interest has been felt, of late years, to know when, and under what circumstances, slavery ceased to exist in Massachusetts." A one-time governor of the state who had a long and distinguished career as a law professor at Harvard, Washburn added that none other than Daniel Webster had once asked him about how emancipation had happened locally. The "generally received notion," Washburn argued, was that the state constitution of 1780 had been the immediate cause, but not the driving force:

> Could we arrive at the true history of the state of public sentiment,—a power often quite as strong as the law, and always, in some measure, an exponent of the law itself,—we should, I think, find that the Constitution, with its Bill of Rights, was literally a *declaration* of what the people regarded as already their rights, rather than an exposition of any newly adopted abstract principles or dogmas to be wrought out into a practical system by any course of future legislation under a new regime.

Washburn went on to say that the judges and juries who found for the plaintiffs in antislavery lawsuits were mere "exponents of public sentiment," and the "free and equal" clause in the state constitution ratified "that all-pervading sense of the community." Echoing Lyman some thirty years earlier, Washburn concluded that "the historic fame of Massachusetts should be fully known and understood": "descendants of Africans had the rights of free citizens in Massachusetts, years before the Constitution of the United States had been framed, or even conceived of."[71]

As Washburn was preparing his paper on the "extinction of slavery in Massachusetts" to present to the Massachusetts Historical Society, the justices of the Supreme Court of the United States were investigating a similar set of questions in the *Dred Scott* case. Washburn's claim that Revolutionary-era Bay Staters had accepted blacks as "free citizens" was roundly contradicted by Chief Justice Roger B. Taney's determination that the nation's white founders, North and South, had no intention of extending the privileges of citizenship to people of color. Washburn's and Taney's conflicting visions both attest to the significance that nineteenth-century Americans vested in the public sentiment of their Revolutionary forebears. Their fundamental disagreement shows how the consensus that both of them projected back onto the Revolutionary generation was nonexistent in their own world. Taney undoubtedly knew that his decision would only intensify the sectional rift. For his part, Washburn's emphasis on the power of antislavery public opinion in Revolutionary Massachusetts might be read as nostalgia, an elegy for an apolitical solution to the problem of slavery that had no chance of repairing the divisions then plaguing the nation.

For manifold reasons, the "public opinion" argument was attractive to nineteenth-century historians who narrated the end of slavery in Massachusetts. It used ideas and language consonant with Revolutionary notions about the relationship between the people and the state. At a time when slavery was becoming an increasingly divisive issue in national politics, the public opinion explanation for emancipation presented a way out of slavery that skirted violence and discord. Anyone who seriously contemplated the differences in regional slave systems could hardly argue that public opinion would change as readily in the South as it had in New England, but these historical contrasts did not stop Bay Staters from taking pride in their state's early abolition. The argument also had the benefit of a compelling basis in fact. Documentary evidence of challenges to slavery supported the idea that sentiments had changed in the Revolutionary period. At the same time, the lack of any single, clearly identifiable person or event that ended slavery (such as the passage of a gradual emancipation law) enabled historians to diffuse responsibility for emancipation across the entire populace. In short, the argument that Belknap put forward in 1795 and that his successors advanced well into the nineteenth century perfectly melded the narrative of emancipation with Bay Staters' understanding of the American Revolution as a product of the "genius of the people."

In the last few decades, many historians have adopted a perspective on agency and causality that is, for all its theoretical edginess, remarkably close to the approach that Belknap took in 1795. In particular, cultural historians have drawn on social theorist Jürgen Habermas's articulation of the "public sphere" in order to expand the set of actors who are recognized as having "agency" and the range of actions that count as "political."[72] The concept of the public sphere helps us to understand how, through the power of public opinion, ordinary people can make history. The problem with the public opinion argument is that its standards of proof are remarkably slippery. "Public opinion" in eighteenth-century terms meant a universal opinion, not an aggregate of individual opinions—but when was opinion ever universal? If there were always dissenting perspectives, where was the threshold at which the consensus of the public shifted? Once public opinion did change, how long did it take for legal, political, or social transformation to follow? And if material changes were slow in coming, could the supposed verdict of public opinion then be called into doubt? These unresolved questions show that there are limits to the analytical power of "public opinion." Still, the concept continues to hold considerable influence over our historical imaginations, in part because it does have explanatory value within those limits, and in part because it, like "agency," is an integral part of the "revolutionary idiom" of modern historiography. Twenty-first-century historians have inherited this language not only from Habermas but also from earlier

generations of historians who narrated the revolutions of the late-eighteenth
and nineteenth centuries, even as they were living through those upheavals
themselves.[73]

In considering slavery's end in Massachusetts, the historian T. H. Breen
has argued that the explanatory power of public opinion was lost after
Belknap, to be replaced by a "heroic legal narrative" that assigned most
responsibility for emancipation to judges and lawyers.[74] But Lyman, Rantoul,
Washburn, and many a local historian clearly found the public opinion explanation appealing in the nineteenth century. To the extent that they discussed
the emancipation lawsuits, they stressed that judges, lawyers, and juries were
simply echoing public sentiment. At a time when articulating the meaning of
New England's past was critical to framing the region's future and its place in
the nation at large, it made sense for narrators of state and local history to be
drawn to an argument that made freedom the common heritage of all Bay
Staters. The public opinion argument was effective because it packaged antislavery not as a contentious political issue but as an organic part of local
Revolutionary ideology, making it seem as though the Revolution had solved
the problem of slavery in Massachusetts. This broad attribution of agency
allowed the substantial portion of the public that opposed (southern) slavery
in the nineteenth century to share in what they saw as the true Revolutionary
spirit. The public opinion argument made the "people of Massachusetts,"
writ large, into the heroes of the Revolution and the heralds of liberty in a
way that a more limited legal narrative could never do.[75]

2

Heroes and Paupers

The Revolution made all Americans heroes, but from the beginning it was clear that some were more heroic than others. Over a hundred Americans died at the Battle of Bunker Hill on June 17, 1775, but what sealed the day's place in history was the fall of one man, Joseph Warren, the Boston physician who had just been designated a general in the newly formed Continental Army. "Our dear Friend Dr. Warren is no more but fell gloriously fighting for his Country—saying better to die honourably in the field than ignominiously hang upon the Gallows," Abigail Adams wrote to her husband shortly after the battle, adding, "the tears of multitudes pay tribute to his memory." The tears and the memories kept flowing. One historian writes that on June 17, 1775, Warren became the "first great celebrated martyr to the cause of American liberty...nearly at once he was transformed from a local figure into a national hero." Technically speaking, the Battle of Bunker Hill was a military loss for the Americans. But even though they failed to hold onto Bunker (actually Breed's) Hill, an army that had only recently been cobbled together had shown it could inflict considerable injury on His Majesty's troops. Furthermore, men from Massachusetts had fought alongside men from Connecticut and New Hampshire, an early indication that the military struggle to come would extend beyond provincial boundaries. As further evidence of the diversity of the nation that was just beginning to take shape, the battle engaged New Englanders of all colors and social backgrounds—including dozens of men of African and Native ancestry.[1]

Black men's participation in the Battle of Bunker Hill is as factually true as Joseph Warren's. In painstaking research, George Quintal, Jr., has identified 103 men of color in fourteen regiments and forty-six companies that fought at Bunker Hill. One of them, Caesar Bason, was killed in the battle. But all facts, like all heroes, are not created equal. Some things happen only to linger, as E. H. Carr memorably put it, in "the limbo of unhistorical facts about the past." It is possible to find dark faces in early illustrations of Revolutionary events, and it is possible to identify the names of people of color—designated by various creative spellings of "Negro," "Indian," "mulatto," and "colored"—in military records, but, as Carr notes, "the facts speak only when the historian calls on them."[2] For the most part, from the Revolution through the War of 1812, those who took it upon themselves to create representations of the past— whether in pictures or words, objects or spaces—chose not to "call on" the fact of black participation in the Revolutionary War. At a time when Bay Staters were preoccupied first with fighting a war and then with building a new nation, what were the facts that mattered instead? And how did the choice of which facts to elevate to historical significance relate to ideas about who belonged in the newly free Commonwealth?

The exclusion of veterans of color from historical memory overlapped with a tendency to celebrate heroic officers rather than ordinary soldiers, whether white or black. But for black veterans, many of whom had counted on their Revolutionary service to stake their claims to freedom, the selective memory of the early national period represented a particularly grave lost opportunity. Too often, commemorative culture presented black men's service to the Revolutionary cause as servitude to Revolutionary officers. Without an independent footing in the postwar economy, many black soldiers descended into poverty after completing their service. While rank-and-file white veterans also suffered economic hardship, black servicemen's struggles were especially acute, symptomatic of the troubles afflicting freedpeople as a whole. In post-emancipation Massachusetts, local officials refused to acknowledge the uniquely precarious financial footing of former slaves, and they tried to exclude freedpeople from poor relief. Even though people of color continued to reside in nearly every town, their ambiguous portrayal in representations of the Revolution and their exclusion from the localized conception of citizenship denied that they belonged in the Commonwealth in any meaningful way. These problems become evident through a juxtaposition of Bunker Hill's place in the early nation's commemorative culture against that of the Boston Massacre, an event that the postwar republic did its best to forget. As the Commonwealth of Massachusetts sought to rebuild itself as part of a free and orderly new nation, Joseph Warren quickly proved to be a far more appealing patriotic martyr than Crispus Attucks could ever be.

FORGETTING CRISPUS ATTUCKS

Even as the Revolutionary War was barely underway, commemorative culture was already creating meanings for its events and characters. Immediately after the Battle of Bunker Hill, almanac writers in Massachusetts and beyond identified June 17 as a key date on the Revolutionary calendar.[3] As early as 1777, Congress approved funds for a monument to Warren. The martyr of Bunker Hill had two kinds of republican credentials: a patriot's willingness to die for the nation and a virtuous citizen's independence and gentility. A physician turned charismatic patriot leader, at the time of the battle Warren was serving as president of the Massachusetts Provincial Congress and had recently been elected a major general in the Continental Army, though he had not yet received his official commission. Perceiving his medical and political skills as too valuable to sacrifice, his fellow officers tried to convince him to take command and stay out of the action at Bunker Hill. Warren instead insisted on fighting alongside ordinary soldiers, and in remaining on the redoubt while others retreated around him, he was shot. Though the details of his death are murky, it is likely that it (like his martyrdom) was instantaneous.[4]

Warren's fortunes in historical memory are worth comparing with those of another early martyr of the Revolution, Crispus Attucks. The event that ushered Attucks into history, the Boston Massacre, had an uneven presence in historical memory in the years of the Revolution and early republic. Like the Battle of Bunker Hill, the violent confrontation between soldiers and civilians that took place in King Street on March 5, 1770, attracted a massive response from the public and the press when it first happened. Three days after the shootings, the city of Boston buried the dead in what might well have been the largest funeral in the British colonies up until that time. As the four hearses made their way past the town hall in King Street, "the Theatre of that inhuman Tragedy," a large yet orderly crowd formed: "an immense Concourse of People, so numerous as to be obliged to follow in Ranks of six, and brought up by a long Train of Carriages belonging to the principal Gentry of the Town." The anger and sorrow of the populace did not dissipate when the crowds dispersed. Within a few weeks, Paul Revere's print of the "Bloody Massacre," depicting a neat row of British soldiers firing into a crowd of civilians, went on sale; it would become one of the iconic images of the Revolution. In the years that followed, patriot almanacs singled out March 5 as they would later do for June 17.[5]

Annually from 1771 through 1783, Bostonians commemorated the Massacre with public orations. Historian Bernard Bailyn has called these addresses "some of the most lurid and naïve rhetoric heard in eighteenth-century America," but they served the prerogatives of the early 1770s and the war years well.[6] The orators emphasized the freedoms to which American colonists were entitled, both as men and as Englishmen. In particular, they railed against the dangers of standing armies, a line of argumentation appropriate to the occasion they were commemorating. In 1770, the British soldiers who had occupied Boston for nearly a year and a half were a widely detested presence. The killings on March 5 showed why. As Joseph Warren explained in his commemorative address of 1775, "when the people on the one part, considered the army as sent to enslave them, and the army on the other, were taught to look on the people as in a state of rebellion, it was but just to fear the most disagreeable consequences. Our fears, we have seen, were but too well grounded." Warren's speech—delivered just 103 days before his death on Bunker Hill—would become a significant piece of his legacy, with its language of slavery and freedom eventually taking on resonance beyond the imperial conflict between Britain and the colonies. "That personal freedom is the natural right of every man, and that property, or an exclusive right to dispose of what he has honestly acquired by his own labor, necessarily arises therefrom, are truths which common sense has placed beyond the reach of contradiction," Warren expounded in 1775, and abolitionists enthusiastically quoted him for their own purposes decades later.[7]

The Boston Massacre orators had little to say about the people who had died in the event they were commemorating. Attucks's name came up only once in the thirteen addresses, and then only because John Hancock gave a brief nod to the victims in 1774. After that year, no orator mentioned the names of the Massacre dead. The gentleman hero of Bunker Hill, Joseph Warren, was eulogized in the addresses of 1776, 1778, and 1781, even though he had not been involved in the Massacre itself, but rather in commemorating it in the years before his own martyrdom. It is unsurprising that the Massacre's victims, all of whom ranked among the city's "lower sort" (among them were a teenaged apprentice and an Irish immigrant, as well as Attucks, the runaway slave) did not receive the same kind of commemorative attention as Warren, the well-to-do and well-loved political leader. But it is telling, given the relentless attention to color in other contexts, that Attucks was not racially marked in these commemorations. In the early memorials of the Boston Massacre—from the epitaph that appeared on the victims' gravestone, to the caption below Paul Revere's print, to Hancock's speech in 1774—Attucks simply appeared as one in the list of names of those killed.[8] The black-and-white versions of Revere's print betray no evidence that one of the victims of the massacre was a man of color. Some of the hand-colored versions of the engraving do show one victim with darker skin or hair than the others: the lower half of his body truncated by the edge of the frame, this figure is largely obscured by other victims and onlookers, and he is hardly the focal point of the scene.[9]

Neither Attucks's color nor his politics figured significantly into the earliest representations of the event in which he died. This is not to say that his race or his specific actions and intentions were unimportant in 1770, as Bostonians were trying to sort out just what had happened on the night of March 5. The lawyers and witnesses in the trial of the British soldiers saw his color clearly. They routinely referred to him not by either of his aliases

(Crispus Attucks or Michael Johnson) but as "the Molatto."[10] Attucks was by no means the only person of color involved in the events of March 5, 1770. In one of the skirmishes preceding the violence on March 5, a black drummer led a group of British soldiers in a tangle with ropeworkers. Looking on from a doorway, a Boston justice of the peace called out to the man, "You black rascal, what have you to do with white people's quarrels?" Describing another incident, a witness recalled that an unnamed "Negroe Boy" had been in the room to overhear one of the defendants boast that "he never would miss an opportunity of firing upon the Inhabitants" of Boston. Like this "Negroe Boy," the slaves who lived in about one out of every ten households in the city would have often overheard "white people's quarrels." And they would have found themselves pulled into them, as did three black men who testified in the trials: Andrew, slave of patriot merchant Oliver Wendell; Jack, slave of Dr. James Lloyd; and Newton Prince, a free West Indian pastry-maker.[11]

The testimony of Andrew, Jack, and Newton Prince was not automatically trusted. Andrew was followed on the witness stand by his master, Oliver Wendell, who was asked to testify to his slave's "general character for truth." Pronouncing it to be "good," Wendell also admitted, "He is a fellow of a lively imagination, and will sometimes amuse the servants in the kitchen, but I never knew him to tell a serious lye." Not everyone believed him. Andrew's account suggested that the soldiers had acted in self-defense against an unruly mob, but the prosecutor dismissed this claim and the witness along with it: Andrew's "unaccountable flights of Fancy may be ornamental in a Poet...but, will never establish the Credibility of an Historian." Even after the trial, patriots continued to suspect blacks of being in league with liars (at best) or Loyalists (at worst). On the first anniversary of the Massacre, the patriot *Massachusetts Spy* published an acrostic poem on the name "ANDREW"; the "A" line read, "As Negroes and L—rs in judgment agree!"[12]

If those who saw the events of March 5 as a genuine "massacre" assailed the reliability of the King's most significant black witness, those who defended the soldiers' actions sought to make the "Molatto" victim as unsympathetic as possible. From this perspective, people of color were not onlookers to "white people's quarrels" but instigators of them. In his closing statement, the soldiers' defense attorney, John Adams, managed to get both his clients and the white patriots of Boston off the hook by turning Attucks into a scapegoat. First describing how "Attucks with his myrmidons" tried to rally the crowd into attacking the soldiers, he then asked the jurors to put themselves in the defendants' position:

> Now to have this reinforcement coming down under the command of a stout Molatto fellow, whose very looks, was enough to terrify any person, what had not the soldiers then to fear? He had hardiness enough to fall in upon them,

and with one hand took hold of a bayonet, and with the other knocked the man
down: This was the behaviour of *Attucks;*—to whose mad behaviour, in all probability, the dreadful carnage of that night, is chiefly to be ascribed. And it is in
this manner, this town has been often treated; a Carr from Ireland, and Attucks
from Framingham, happening to be here, shall sally out upon their thoughtless
enterprizes, at the head of such a rabble of Negroes, &c. as they can collect
together, and then there are not wanting, persons to ascribe all their doings to
the good people of the town.

By this account, Attucks was scary-looking, a man of color, and an out-of-
towner who, helped along by a foreigner (an Irishman, no less), set out
looking for violence on the night of March 5. In so doing, he brought his
death upon himself and dishonor on the respectable people of Boston. By
painting the civilians who participated in the fray as "a motley rabble of
saucy boys, negroes and molattoes, Irish teagues and out landish jack tarrs,"
Adams made it possible for the elite and middling white patriots of Boston to
accept the acquittal of the soldiers accused.[13]

Adams's successful case in the Boston Massacre trials indicates why early
commemorations of the event avoided saying much about the victims. As a dead
body, Attucks was politically useful, his corpse a symbol of the violent excesses
to which a standing army would inevitably be driven.[14] Had he been remembered as a political actor, however, he could have been a threat to elite patriots
who sought to limit the social implications of their revolution in government.
Adams's closing arguments, which positioned Attucks and the other supposed
instigators of the violence as good-for-nothing outsiders, and the commemorative addresses, which focused on the rights of Englishmen rather than the radicalism of ordinary Bostonians, were central to the efforts of Whig leaders intent
on "taming" both the Revolution itself and the earliest memories of it. "In
Boston," explains historian Alfred Young, "the process of controlling the memory
of the Revolution began even as the events were taking place, indeed, almost
before they were over."[15] By the time the war years ended, the Boston Massacre
had outlived its usefulness. A commemoration oriented around the dread of
British soldiers had little meaning as Americans were celebrating their military
victory over the King's army, and memorializing mob activity had little appeal
for political leaders seeking to reestablish social order in the wake of the upheavals
of war. After 1783, Boston selectmen opted to replace their annual observance of
the Fifth of March with citywide celebrations of the Fourth of July.[16]

This shift from a primarily local holiday to a national one was well suited
to the period of nation-building. The change in dates also represented a shift
in priorities, at least for the patriot leadership. Whereas the early Boston
Massacre commemorations had highlighted Whig fears of political slavery,
nationalist festive culture after the war was oriented around containing the
potential dangers of individual liberty. Historian David Waldstreicher argues

that "by fostering an idea of the nation as extralocal community and by giving ordinary people the opportunity for local expression of national feeling," nationalist celebrations, as well as accounts of them that appeared in print culture, "literally and figuratively papered over the disturbing class resentments (expressed in the antiaristocratic language of the Revolution) that had energized much of the populace in the first place."[17] Similarly, the hope of freedom that had motivated many black patriots did not figure into commemorative representations of national independence. As July Fourth observances took on a partisan political slant during and after the ratification of the Constitution, people of color were largely excluded from the parades and feasts that were cultural manifestations of political conflicts seen, once again, as "white people's quarrels."[18]

THE FAITHFUL SERVANT ON THE FIELD OF HONOR

Though commemorations of the Boston Massacre were eliminated in the Federal era, the Battle of Bunker Hill continued to hold an undisputed place in the canon of Revolutionary events, not least because remembering it could instill patriotic gratitude, bourgeois respectability, and republican virtue in the populace at large. In 1785, the Connecticut-born artist John Trumbull selected Bunker Hill as the subject of one of his earliest history paintings, not only because of the event's historical import, but also as a way of "paying a just tribute of gratitude to the memory of eminent men, who had given their lives for their country." Completed in 1786 and copied many times in the decades that followed, Trumbull's painting of the battle placed Joseph Warren at center stage, where the citizen-soldier acted out what he had allegedly told Elbridge Gerry a few days before: "*dulce et decorum est pro patria mori.*" Significantly, the primary title that Trumbull gave his painting was not "The Battle of Bunker Hill" (as it is sometimes known in shorthand) but *The Death of General Warren.*[19]

The central drama of Trumbull's painting is both horrific and tender. There is a fury to the image: a tangle of bodies, some vital, some injured, some in red coats and some in the more varied garb of patriot militiamen. From the right billow smoke and flames, reminding viewers that June 17 would come to be known as the day that Charlestown burned. Against the black and navy and red that fill most of the canvas with fire, smoke, and uniforms, a patch of white stands out where Warren languishes on the arm of another soldier. A third coatless figure hovers above these two, with his gun slanted toward an overzealous British grenadier. But pale Warren and his white-shirted protectors are not the only heroes in this scene. As the grenadier plunges forward with his bayonet pointed toward Warren's torso, a British officer, Major Small,

John Trumbull, *The Death of General Warren at the Battle of Bunker's Hill*, 1786. Oil on canvas. Yale University Art Gallery, Trumbull Collection. *Courtesy of the Yale University Art Gallery*

grasps the weapon to hold the soldier back. Trumbull depicted this small gesture of mercy as an example of the ideal of disinterested virtue that formed the backbone of both American republicanism and English gentility.[20]

While Trumbull strived to make the figures and faces in the battle scene as lifelike as possible, at the heart of his composition was an effort to dispense a kind of artistic justice.[21] Trumbull told his friend Benjamin Silliman that the grenadier plunging toward Warren at the center of the canvas "was a pictorial liberty—analogous to the *licentia poetae*." This liberty enabled the painter to pay tribute to the British officer whom he depicted as protecting Warren: "Col Small was distinguished in his humanity and kindness to American prisoners and therefore was made by the artist to do a deed of mercy." Silliman asked Trumbull if the scene at the far left of the picture, where a British soldier stabs the throat of an American who is desperately reaching upward, was "literal *history*." Trumbull's answer was "*no*—but such things happen in battle and my patriotic feelings were highly excited to exhibit the cruelty of the victors."[22]

Although most of the characters in the painting have their attention on Warren, two other figures seem to be retreating from the scene in the bottom right corner of the canvas. In front is a well-dressed white man with three plumes in his hat, blood visible on his chest and bandaged hand, and his sword drawn as he takes a cautious step back from the hill. Immediately behind him is a black man. The man's body is mostly obscured, but his head and the gun he is carrying are visible over the white man's shoulder. Would Trumbull have considered this figure's appearance a "pictorial liberty" or "literal history"? At the very least, given the probability that more than a hundred people of color fought in the battle, the man at right and a second dark face at left (nearly obscured by a flag-waving arm) stand in for a significant presence on the battlefield. It is less clear that either of them was meant to represent a particular individual. In an early description of the painting, Trumbull called the white man standing in front of the more prominent of the two black figures "a young American, wounded in the Sword Hand, and in the Breast…attended by a faithful Negro."[23] Silliman, Trumbull's close friend, identified the white man as Lieutenant Thomas Grosvenor of Connecticut, who was a slave owner. Nineteenth- and twentieth-century viewers of the painting, however, have frequently labeled the black man behind Grosvenor not as his personal slave, but as one of two African Americans known for their service at Bunker Hill.[24]

Peter Salem and Salem Poor—the similarity in their names has led them to be confused or even conflated with each other—are each sometimes credited with having fired the shot that killed British Major Pitcairn. In his history of Bunker Hill, prepared in conjunction with the semicentennial of the battle, Samuel Swett recorded that "Salem a black soldier" was one of several patriots who shot Pitcairn. A few years later an abolitionist editor identified the shooter as Peter Salem.[25] Other accounts from the second quarter of the nineteenth century reported merely that Pitcairn was shot by "a negro soldier" or "a son of Africa." In his authoritative *History of the Siege of Boston*, first published in 1849, Richard Frothingham did not mention a black soldier's involvement in the death of Pitcairn. Frothingham disdained the oral history and local lore that formed the basis of other nineteenth-century accounts of the battle, including Swett's. Instead, he built his book around written documents contemporary to the events he narrated, noting that "less scepticism as to tradition, and the admission of a larger portion of personal anecdote, would have made [the history] more amusing, but it would have been less reliable."[26]

The story about an African American shooting Pitcairn seemed to take hold in print only decades after the Revolution. One version was recorded— but not published—in 1787, when historian Jeremy Belknap wrote in his personal notebook, "A negro man belonging to Groton, took aim at Major Pitcairne, as he was rallying the dispersed British Troops." Peter Salem was from Framingham and Salem Poor from Andover. A third relatively well-known black soldier said to have been at Bunker Hill, Barzillai Lew, was from Groton; celebrated for his musical talent, he served in the Revolution as a fifer.[27] No source argues that Lew specifically was the one who shot Pitcairn, and no published accounts of the Battle of Bunker Hill seem to have taken up

Belknap's version of the British officer's death. Belknap's note is tantalizing nonetheless in that it hints at everything we don't know about the myriad ways that people made meanings out of this particular piece of the past. If we apply to Trumbull's painting the same standard that Frothingham used in assembling *The History of the Siege of Boston*, any claim that the man on the right represents Peter Salem, Salem Poor, or an anonymous black soldier who shot Pitcairn is untenable. Contemporary documentary evidence simply does not corroborate it. But neither can we dismiss the stories as total fabrications of a later era. If we question Frothingham's suggestion that "tradition" and "anecdote" serve only to make history more "amusing," we might wonder whether oral culture sustained memories of a black soldier at Bunker Hill, until a resurgent interest in ordinary people's participation in the Revolution put variants of the tale into print and public memory some fifty years later.[28]

Trumbull, whose extensive autobiographical writings suggest he was hardly a man of few words, never said that he intended his painting to illustrate a story about a black man shooting Pitcairn. In a subscription paper for engravings of his *Death of Warren* and *Death of Montgomery*, Trumbull proclaimed that his paintings would "assist in preserving the Memory of the illustrious Events which have marked this Period of our Country's Glory, as well as of the Men who have been the most important Actors in them." His medium, he argued, was significant, because "Historians will do Justice to an Æra so important; but to be read, the Language in which they write, must be understood;—the Language of Painting is universal, and intelligible in all Nations, and every Age." Here Trumbull was careful to distinguish the commemorative purpose of his art from the work that historians did. As his embrace of "pictorial liberty" suggests, Trumbull did not bind himself to the facts of history in his representations of the past. Through a visual medium that he perceived as comprehensible to all, he brought reminders of past events before audiences who could then give the heroes of those events the gratitude and admiration they deserved.[29]

While history and memory were distinguishable in Trumbull's view, they were not in the "fundamental opposition" that, according to scholars, characterizes their relationship in modernity.[30] David Ramsay, who compiled his *History of the American Revolution* around the same time as Trumbull painted *The Death of Warren*, carefully recounted the events of the Battle of Bunker Hill, but he also listed the many virtues that made Warren a hero.[31] The historian's version had a dispassionate air that contrasted with the tumult and emotion on the artist's canvas, but at base the two representations complemented each other's message. Moreover, Trumbull's painting, just like Ramsay's history, could be understood differently by different people. Contrary to Trumbull's own claims, the language of painting was hardly universal. Once they entered the eyes and minds of viewers, his images had the power not only to preserve memory but also to create it. Trumbull's *Death of Warren*, which became the most familiar image of the battle, not to mention one of the best known images of the war, staked black men's ground on Bunker Hill. If the painting's man of color was constant in his presence *to* viewers, however, he was hardly consistent in his meaning *for* viewers. Even if the artist intended to depict black men as humble servants of whites, the painting had the potential to reinforce and perhaps even generate stories about African American heroism on Bunker Hill.

This much can be said for sure: works of art do not speak for themselves. But a close look at the painting and related sources, alongside a broader sense of the social and political context in which they were produced, can illuminate both what Trumbull sought to represent in the mid-1780s as well as what contemporary viewers might have seen in *The Death of Warren*. Moving from left to right across the canvas, we see the brutality of a British soldier, Warren's last moments coupled with Small's noble gesture, Pitcairn falling into his son's arms, and Grosvenor and the black man edging out of the picture; there are probably half a dozen smaller dramas visible among these four. The painting is more than the sum of its parts, however. The drama of the whole scene comes through the relationship of the different vignettes to each other. In his own explanation of the painting, Trumbull linked the scene surrounding Warren to the retreating figures at right. Grosvenor, he wrote, "has begun to retire...but seeing his General fall, hesitates whether to save himself, or, wounded as he is, to return and assist in saving a life, more precious to his Country than his own." This description accords with art historian Patricia Burnham's argument that the entire painting was an "homage to an institutionalized system of deference in society." In the canvas's visual moral accounting, Grosvenor became worthy of gratitude and respect because he showed willingness to sacrifice his own interests for those of his superior.[32]

Paired with Grosvenor, the black man at the far right of the canvas appears to be acting out another element of the deferential order. He is a faithful, if perhaps somewhat fearful, servant who literally has his master's back. Trumbull's preparatory studies for the painting confirm this link between the man's servitude and his blackness. Apparently, Trumbull had not initially planned to include a black man in the pair of retreating figures. In the studies, neither man has noticeably darker coloring than the other, and both are carrying guns. With each man holding a gun of his own, it is apparent that each is an independent actor, serving the republic on his own terms: two guns, two soldiers, two citizens. In the final painting, however, the difference in skin tone is obvious, and the black man is standing behind the white. Most importantly, in the final version, the black man is holding a gun, while the white man brandishes a sword. With only one gun and one sword between them, it becomes possible to see the black man as a servant, carrying one of his master's weapons while the master makes use of the other.[33]

John Trumbull, study for *The Death of General Warren at the Battle of Bunker's Hill*, 1785. *Courtesy of the Historical Society of Pennsylvania*

Detail from John Trumbull, study for *The Death of General Warren
at the Battle of Bunker's Hill*, September 1785. Brush and black
wash, pen and brown ink. *Courtesy of the Yale University Art
Gallery, bequest of Susan Silliman Pearson*

Nothing that Trumbull wrote about *The Death of Warren* or sketched in
preparation for it explains why he ultimately made one of the figures black or
whether, in doing so, he decided he also had to change the weapons each was
holding. But Trumbull's intentions need not limit what we see in this painting.
They surely did not constrain how eighteenth- and nineteenth-century audiences saw it. By the 1850s, in conjunction with the circulation in print of a

story about a Negro shooting Pitcairn, the black man in Trumbull's painting
had come to represent African American heroism in the Revolutionary War.
On Web sites and book covers, this figure serves a similar purpose today. But it
was not always so. Over time, the meanings of this figure, like the stories that
all history paintings tell, "shifted, multiplied, and collided."[34] However the
man in Trumbull's painting would come to be read, viewers in the late eighteenth century very plausibly viewed him as belonging to another man. Even
if he was participating in the struggle for national independence, his personal
state of dependence persisted so long as he carried another man's rifle.

In Trumbull's painting, Grosvenor's body almost completely obscures the
black man's, making the two figures inseparable. They appeared together in
later reproductions and reworkings of the painting.[35] Whether or not
Trumbull intended it to be so, this image is a powerful symbol of the ways in
which the histories of white Americans are fundamentally inextricable from
those of Americans of color, and vice versa. But Trumbull painted over the
fact that in the decades after the Revolution, enslaved men and women were
stepping out from behind their white masters. That move did not automatically give them pride of place in a reimagined canvas of social relations.
Instead, as the legal and social history of the period shows, many white Bay
Staters in the early republic sought instead to imagine that blacks were
simply out of the picture.

THE VAGRANT FREEDMAN IN THE SETTLED VILLAGE

While in a London studio Trumbull was sketching a deferential relationship
between black and white New Englanders, back in Massachusetts the legal
regime that supported black men's dependence on their white masters was
unraveling. In the mid-1780s, with a series of emancipation lawsuits behind
them and rough economic times enveloping them, slave owners found it
increasingly difficult to hold on to their human property and to support
extra members of their households. For their part, in thousands of households across the Commonwealth, African Americans were testing the limits
of Revolutionary promises of freedom. For men of color, participating in the
military during the war years had been critical to establishing their personal
liberty. Despite Trumbull's positioning of the black man as Grosvenor's loyal
servant, many enslaved New Englanders who served on the patriot side in
the Revolution did so to escape slavery, whether as runaways who found the
army an agreeable alternative to bondage or as substitutes who fought in
their masters' places in exchange for manumission.[36]

Military service gave black men a chance to be free, and even, perhaps, to
be heroes. One candidate for heroism was Salem Poor. In the nineteenth

century, some writers would herald Poor as the man who shot Major Pitcairn at Bunker Hill. No record contemporary to the Revolution corroborates that claim, but a written document from 1775 did cement Poor's status as an especially honorable soldier. In December 1775, fourteen officers submitted a petition on his behalf to the Massachusetts House of Representatives:

> The Subscribers begg leave to Report to our Honble. House (Which Wee do in Justice to the Caracter of so Brave a Man) that under Our Own observation, Wee declare that A Negro Man Called Salem Poor of Col. Fryes Regiment. Capt. Ames. Company in the late Battle at Charlestown behaved like an Experienced Officer, as Well as an Excellent Soldier, to Set fourth Particulars of his Conduct would be Tedious, Wee Would Only begg leave to say in the Person of this sd. Negro Centers a Brave & gallant Soldier. The Reward due to so great and Distinguisht a Caracter, Wee Submit to the Congress.

Regrettably for later historians, the petitioners found it unnecessary to relate exactly what Poor did on the hill that day. Still, their high esteem for Poor's military performance could hardly have been clearer. That such a "petition for bravery" is a rarity in the archives of Revolutionary Massachusetts puts Poor's valor in even sharper relief. Poor, who had bought his own freedom six years prior, seems through his actions at Bunker Hill to have definitively crossed the line from serving a master to serving his country, thereby completing the transition from slave to citizen.[37]

To give this extraordinary document a context, it helps to lift Poor from the realm of "Brave & Gallant" heroes and to situate him in the broader history of slavery and its aftermath in eighteenth-century Massachusetts. The petition is vague not only in "Particulars of his Conduct," but also in Poor's (or his advocates') intentions in going before the legislature. While researchers have been able to assemble only a few details of Poor's biography, what is known of him suggests that his overall experience was hardly out of the ordinary for a slave turned free man in Revolutionary New England. Though the circumstances of his birth are unclear, he was probably sold in Salem as an infant, around the year 1742. After that, two dates stand out in his life before Bunker Hill. In 1769, he paid twenty-seven pounds to his then master, John Poor of Andover, to secure his freedom. In 1774, the Andover town meeting denied his request to provide support for his wife and children. This last detail raises the possibility that what motivated Poor and his allies to submit the petition was not only a desire for abstract recognition of heroism, but also real economic need. The most immediate challenge for freed slaves was to find a way to support themselves. The request of Poor's wife and children for maintenance from the town suggests that Poor struggled to make ends meet. Military service provided an economic opportunity—however meager—for black men, as well as for poor whites. Perhaps Poor hoped that a little extra money would be the "Reward due" for his courage and commitment at Bunker Hill. Unfortunately, the petition was withdrawn, suggesting that the legislature was reluctant to take action on his behalf.[38]

To suggest that there could have been an economic motivation behind Salem Poor's petition is not to diminish the significance of his military heroism. It does, however, expose the inadequacy of the Revolutionary discourse of liberty and independence to comprehend the complexity of the experience and status of former slaves. During the time that Salem Poor was a slave, he was legally a dependent in his master's household, but in his efforts to scrape together the money to free himself, he was also acting independently. After he became free, he no longer had claims of dependency on his master, but being an independent man in republican terms meant not only having personal freedom but also the means to support dependents of his own. If, in 1769, Poor had been able to keep his twenty-seven pounds to provide for his family down the road, rather than pay his master for his freedom, perhaps his wife and children would not have had to seek maintenance from the town of Andover. This dilemma was a common one for black participants in the patriot cause. Even as they invested themselves in the fight for the nation's independence, they lacked the means to extricate themselves from the dependent status that kept them from being equal citizens. A group of black men—including military veterans—acknowledged this problem in 1780 when they petitioned the legislature for tax relief: "We take it as a heard ship that poor old Negers should be Rated [i.e., taxed] which have been in Bondage some thirty some forty and some fifty years and now just got their Liberty some by going into the Serviese and some by going to sea and others by good fortan."[39]

While we know little about Salem Poor's economic and social circumstances during and after the Revolutionary War, the experiences of another slave-turned-soldier underscore the precariousness of free blacks' economic well-being and civic belonging in early national Massachusetts. Edom London's early life gives the lie to any suggestion that New England slaves belonged as members of their masters' families.[40] Over a twenty-year period, from about 1757 to 1777, London had eleven different masters. He told a court in 1806, "When I was a small Boy I lived with Capt. Samuel Bond of Lincoln who was the first Master I have any Recollection of." Bond sold him to a minister in Weston, whose daughter inherited London at her father's death. Since the daughter was married to Colonel Oliver Partridge of Hatfield, London became Partridge's property and lived with him for seven years. Partridge sold London to John Ingersoll of Westfield in 1767, in exchange for another "Negro with his Family." After three years with Ingersoll, London was sold in quick succession to a master in Longmeadow, Massachusetts, and then to another in Simsbury, Connecticut. Four years later, he returned to

Massachusetts: briefly as the slave of William Bond of Lincoln, then as the property of Thomas Cowdin of Fitchburg. In 1775, Cowdin sold London to Jonathan Stimpson of Winchendon. Looking back thirty years later, London didn't give an exact date for this sale, but he noted that it took place "the next Week after Lexington Fight." No doubt sensing that the world around him was changing, he didn't wait for his ninth master to bring him to yet another new town: "The Night after [the sale] I absconded from Fitchburg and enlisted into the Eight Months Service at Cambridge."[41]

By his own account, Edom London "remained in the Army for almost the whole of the Time during the War." He served, among other places, at Bunker Hill. London might have intended his "absconding" to join the army to be an assertion of his freedom. But if he thought of himself as a free man, his master—and the laws of the province of Massachusetts—did not. Before his eight-month term of service was out, he was sold again, this time to Thomas Sawyer of Winchendon, who was also in the army. After spending a short time with Sawyer "at Boston & the Towns adjoining & a few Weeks at Winchendon," London changed hands again. He lived with Daniel Goodridge, also of Winchendon, for not more than five weeks before enlisting for a three-year term in the Continental Army. "Mr. Goodridge received the whole of my Bounty and some Part of my Wages," London reported. Goodridge more or less concurred: "I secured a small Part of his Wages, when he was in the army, and he has not lived with Me since."[42]

Stopping here, Edom London's biography could serve merely as confirmation that chattel slavery thrived in Massachusetts in the years leading up to the Revolution. As the many masters who discarded him recognized, Edom London certainly was movable property. He was also profitable property, as Goodridge must have appreciated when he received his slave's military wages and bounty. Moving into the post-Revolutionary period, this Bunker Hill veteran's story becomes a tale not of the deprivations of slavery but of the limitations of freedom. By 1804, London had returned to Winchendon and was unable to support himself. The local Overseers of the Poor paid for his needs—room and board, a shirt, shoes, a pair of overalls. They also began looking for ways to get someone else to pay for the growing roster of expenses associated with supporting an aging, infirm man. Ultimately, they sued the town of Hatfield, where London had lived from 1760 to 1767 as a slave in the household of Oliver Partridge. Thus this impoverished old man became the subject of one of the major legal cases that decided the status of former slaves in Massachusetts.[43]

The strategy that the Winchendon town fathers used in dealing with Edom London's case, and that Hatfield employed in refuting it, was based on the colonial idea of legal "settlement." Legal historian Kunal M. Parker explains that in eighteenth-century Massachusetts, "instead of citizenship, the legal concept of 'settlement' or 'inhabitancy' determined the individual's rights of access to, and presence within, territory as well as the individual's claim on the community's resources by reason of age, illness, disability, and poverty." Each municipality was obliged to provide for the deserving poor who "belonged to" the town. Just what it took to acquire settlement in a town changed over the course of the eighteenth century. For much of the colonial period, one came to belong to a town by virtue of having been born there, marrying someone with a settlement there, or simply living there for a given period of time without being asked to leave.[44] Rules and practices regarding settlement became more restrictive over time, as towns tried to limit the number of people whom they were legally obliged to support. Those who moved into a community where they lacked settlement could be officially requested to leave. This "warning out," usually targeting the poor or other undesirables, was the town's way of declaring that it had no obligation to support individuals it regarded as legal strangers.

So long as slavery had existed in Massachusetts, laws of settlement had not applied directly to slaves. Slaves belonged to their masters as property, and masters belonged to towns as legally settled inhabitants. Owners were expected to provide for all their slaves' needs. The law required a master who emancipated a slave to put up bond to the town as insurance against the freed slave becoming a burden on the local system of poor relief.[45] This system worked well enough so long as the number of freed slaves in the Commonwealth was small. But as the institution of slavery unraveled after the Revolution, the situation became stickier. As the dispute between Winchendon and Hatfield in Edom London's case shows, towns did not eagerly embrace their responsibility to treat former slaves the same as their impoverished white inhabitants. *Winchendon v. Hatfield* thus turned on the question of how to determine whether a freedperson had settlement in a particular town. Chief Justice Parsons affirmed that a slave "could not acquire a settlement in his own right" but did have "a derivative settlement from his master." The judge equated this status of slaves to that of other household dependents, namely wives, who derived settlement from their husbands, and minors, whose settlement came through their fathers.[46] Each time Edom London changed hands, he took on a derivative settlement through his new master but lost his settlement through the former. According to this logic, by selling London out of Hatfield, Oliver Partridge absolved the town of any responsibility to provide for him later.

While Winchendon's efforts to foist London's support onto Hatfield ultimately failed, that the town's overseers of the poor even attempted the lawsuit highlights the vulnerability of freedpeople's claims to "belong" in the towns where they lived. Later in the nineteenth century, Winchendon's historian, Abijah Martin, wrote, "as [London] did service in the war of independence, it is to be hoped that the maintenance was cheerfully rendered." Martin's comment suggested that military service, specifically in the Revolutionary War, demanded civilians' monetary expression of gratitude. But during the period in which *Winchendon v. Hatfield* and cases like it were making their way through the courts, this sense of the republic's obligations to its ordinary "suffering soldiers" lacked the urgency that it would take on in the wake of the War of 1812.[47]

As London's experience shows, for an ordinary black soldier, not only was military service insufficient to earn grateful recognition, but it also failed to keep him out of abject poverty and dependence. The black men who petitioned for tax relief in 1780 complained that although "many of our Colour (as is well known) have Cheerfully Entered the field of Battle in the defence of the Common Cause," decades of enslavement had left them "without an equal chance with white people." Eighteen years later, another group came before the legislature, lamenting that "tho born here, they…cannot divest themselves of the idea, that they are still strangers in a foreign land, a land…they & their children are destined to serve, but not enjoy." These men—and a few women—used a relatively new term to capture their degrading treatment: "They are treated as a different *race* of beings." As the vocabulary and ideology of race became grafted onto the preexisting logic of civic belonging, black Bay Staters were left without a place in the villages of the republic. Mourning their outcast status, the petitioners in 1798 asked that the General Court give them money to leave Massachusetts and settle in Africa.[48]

The legislature did not grant this petition. Indeed, although African colonization piqued the interest of some Massachusetts blacks in the early republic, a mix of choices and circumstances kept many freedpeople in the state and even the towns where they had spent much, if not all, of their lives.[49] Local history volumes like Martin's provide the names of freed slaves living all across the state, many of them with stories like London's. Because demographic studies have told us that free blacks moved to cities after emancipation, historians looking at the post-Revolutionary period expect to find blacks in urban seaports, such as Boston, Salem, and New Bedford, where job opportunities and community ties were most promising.[50] But freed slaves and their descendants continued to make their homes in all corners of the Commonwealth. In 1810, the Bay State's population of people of color was spread across 240 towns, with about half of those towns home to fewer than ten individuals of color. Even when they left town, whether by death, voluntary migration, or involuntary removal in accordance with pauper laws, people of color left their marks on the landscape. Well into the nineteenth century, locals remembered the names of the former slaves associated with certain places throughout their towns. There was Mingo's Field in Hanover, Peter's Ridge (former home to "'Black Peter,' a negro") in Haverhill, and Cato

Farm in Canton. In Groton, "the rise of ground, near the place where the Pepperell road leaves the main road" was named "Primus Hill" after the father of Bunker Hill veteran Barzillai Lew.[51]

Though many such place names seem innocuous and even picturesque, some could evoke memories of racism and suffering. In 1790, Philip Allen and his family, former slaves of James Packard, were warned out of Goshen, but ninety years later, a local antiquarian reported that "the lot of land he owned and occupied, still retains the name of 'Nigger pasture.'" Near the turnpike in Framingham, there was Prince's Meadow, cultivated by Prince Young, an African-born slave said to have refused his master's offer of freedom by saying, "Massa eat the meat; he now pick the bone." This line hints at slaves' awareness of the interdependence of masters and slaves and the uneasy economic footing of freedpeople in the early republic. In Leicester, Massachusetts, Peter Salem Road honors the Bunker Hill patriot sometimes said to be depicted in Trumbull's painting. The irony is that although Salem lived for many years in the town after the war, in his old age he was removed to Framingham, the town in which he had last been a slave. According to a local historian, Salem had been a beloved figure in Leicester, but the "precarious livelihood" he earned by making baskets and bottoming chairs could not sustain him. Lacking a legal settlement in the town, he had to turn to Framingham's overseers of the poor.[52]

Such nineteenth-century accounts of freedpeople as impoverished wanderers echo the contemporary trope of the "disappearing Indian," that tragic and romantic figure who enabled white Americans to see conquest of Native lands as necessary and inevitable. These resonances in the representation of "Indians" and "African" Americans are hardly coincidental. Racial categories and labels were—and are—highly artificial. Many nineteenth-century New Englanders designated as "colored" or "mulatto" (or even "black" or "negro") were descendants of Nipmucs, Wampanoags, Narragansetts, Pequots, and other Native residents of the region that would come to be called New England. Crispus Attucks is often identified as the first African American casualty in the Revolutionary War, but it is his Native ancestry that is better documented. Many black soldiers—including, quite possibly, the two best-known veterans of Bunker Hill—had connections to New England Indians. Because the region's peripatetic basket-makers and chair-bottomers were generally Indians, Peter Salem's familiarity with these crafts suggests he had Native roots. Nancy Parker, the wife of Salem Poor, is identified in Andover town records as a "mulatto," but local lore claimed that she was "the last remnant" of an Indian village located near present-day Lawrence, Massachusetts. "Remembered by the very old settlers as a tall, wild-looking, but harmless and industrious Indian woman," Nancy made a living by going house to house spinning yarn and thread for local farmers.[53]

Obscuring the heritage and identity of Native people, nineteenth-century record-keepers' tendencies to lump people of color together under labels such as "black" and "colored" facilitated the apparent disappearance of Indians from the New England landscape.[54] With aboriginal people supposedly gone, "white" (that is, European-descended) Americans could step in to proclaim themselves "natives." In other words, racialized terminology contributed to the effort to designate who belonged in the early republic and who didn't. It didn't matter if a black veteran could claim ancestors who had inhabited the local landscape for generations before Europeans set foot on it. Settlement, and the privileged civic status that came with it, was for independent white men. Parker argues that local government practices and judicial decisions regarding the legal settlement (or lack thereof) of people of color erased them from the "landscape of claims," situating them literally and figuratively outside the territory of those who could make demands on the state.[55] Despite these efforts, people of color remained on the physical landscape, even if only in one household in town, and even if only in memory. A small presence in terms of numbers, a scorned presence in terms of law, and a subordinate presence in commemorative culture, people of color nonetheless *were* present, and present with a past.

THE MAN WHO SLEPT WITH GEORGE WASHINGTON

If the commemorative culture of the early republic paid little heed to men and women of color, it could not stop them from perpetuating their life stories on their own. When one Revolutionary veteran, Primus Hall, died in Boston in 1842, his obituary noted that he "was well known, particularly to the younger portion of our citizens, to whom he was in the habit of recounting scenes of the Revolutionary War." Our access to what must have been a rich oral historical culture in post-Revolutionary Boston is, regrettably, profoundly limited. This storytelling culture might well have sustained memories of Crispus Attucks, Peter Salem, and Salem Poor in the generations before print and public celebrations remembered them. Primus Hall's own Revolutionary memories are recorded only in two affidavits he made in the 1830s, when he sought a military pension from the federal government. In this testimony, Hall reported that he was born in Boston in 1756, the son of a servant, Delia Hall, and a free man, Prince Hall, who would go on to become a leader of Boston's black community. As an infant, Primus was bound out to an Essex County shoemaker, Ezra Trask. Finding himself ill-suited for the cordwainer's trade, at the age of fifteen he secured from his master "freedom with full liberty for me to transact any of all business of every kind." He worked as a farmer and truckman in and around Salem until 1776, when he enlisted for a year in the Fifth Massachusetts Regiment. The war brought Hall first to Winter Hill, where his company waited out the Siege of Boston. The men then marched to New York, where they fought at White Plains and Harlem Heights, then on to New Jersey, for the Battles of Trenton and Princeton. On a second enlistment, Hall served at Saratoga and witnessed Burgoyne's surrender.[56]

Hall continued his career in another capacity in 1781, when he became a steward to Quartermaster General Timothy Pickering, a well-known conservative Whig (and later Federalist politician) from Salem. In a letter to his wife, Pickering recounted the circumstances of Hall's hiring: "I have luckily met with a likely negro fellow who has lived several years in Salem....He desired to live with me as a Servant....He said he would not have tendered me his service, but that I was a *New England man,* & *he knew my character.*" Clearly Hall knew how to charm or persuade a fellow son of Essex County. Was Hall's allusion to Pickering's origins and character a clever appeal to his potential employer's ego, or did he sincerely believe that a "New England man" with a certain "character" would make a better boss? Evidently both he and Pickering understood that to be a "New England man" distinguished one somehow. Noting that he would not have deigned to be a servant for just anyone, Hall willingly attached himself to Pickering. Significantly, it was the employee who proposed the arrangement to the employer. New England men, it seems, understood that servants need not be servile. Pickering accepted Hall's offer on the spot, and he assured his wife that the family's new servant was "so intelligent as to be capable of learning any thing." Hall spent much of the summer of 1781 shuttling letters and supplies back and forth between Philadelphia (where Pickering was posted) and Newburgh, New York (where Pickering's wife, Rebecca, was living).[57]

Hall's work for the Pickering family gives us another way to view the "faithful Negro" standing behind his purported master in Trumbull's painting of the Battle of Bunker Hill. While Trumbull intended viewers to see Lieutenant Grosvenor's humble servant as part of a larger tableau idealizing social hierarchy, Hall's experience as a servant to a military officer shows how people of color could have understood this apparent display of deference quite differently. Hall's choice to work for Pickering might best be read as a carefully calculated step in this former bondman's upward mobility. After the war, Hall established himself as an independent tradesman (a soapboiler) in Boston. With a particular interest in educational matters, he was also a leader in the city's free black community. A school for black children met in his home for a period before settling into larger quarters at the African Baptist Church, which Hall helped to found. Later he advocated the establishment of a college for the higher education of blacks, and he protested the substandard educational facilities for Boston's children of color. Hall also took public stands against slavery and the slave trade, beginning as early as 1788, when he and other black men submitted a petition to the state legislature, and continuing through the 1830s, when he became a supporter of Garrisonian abolitionism.[58]

Hall became a property owner and political actor in Massachusetts during the same years that cases like Edom London's were working their way through state and local courts. Taken together, Hall's and London's stories illustrate the differing fortunes and common problems that free people of color encountered in early national New England. After the war, some black veterans (such as Hall) went on to start their own families, set up shop in their own trades, and purchase their own land and homes—all those things that a good male householder did in the early republic. Others, like London, succumbed to a difficult postwar economy, an increasingly virulent system of racial prejudice, and a collective amnesia on the part of whites who imagined that slavery had never happened in Massachusetts. None of this is to say that racism and historical denial did not affect someone like Hall, who was relatively successful at navigating the challenges of being a free person of color in a republic that increasingly associated liberty with whiteness.[59]

Memories of Hall that appeared in print after his death reveal the persistence of the idea that black men's primary role in the Revolution was a servile one. An anecdotal account of him appeared in several publications, beginning with *Godey's Lady's Book* in 1849.[60] This item described George Washington's visits to his quartermaster general, Timothy Pickering, during the time when Hall was working for the latter. On numerous occasions while in camp, when Washington felt he needed exercise, Hall set up a sort of jump rope for him, fastening one end to a stake and holding the other taut at his own chest. This anecdote gave an amusing picture of the nation's founding father engaged in play "with true boyish zest." It revealed little about Primus Hall, other than that he seemed to be at General Washington's beck and call.[61]

The *Godey's* article also related an anecdote that brought the race and status dynamics between Hall and Washington to a more intimate level. One night, Washington's meeting with Pickering ran so late that he preferred not to return to his own encampment. Hall assured the general that an extra blanket and straw were available for him to sleep on. Thus the two officers settled down on their beds of straw, while Hall "worked, or appeared to work, until the breathing of the prostrate gentlemen satisfied him that they were sleeping." Without space to lie down himself, Hall sat on a box and "leaned his head on his hands to obtain such repose as so inconvenient a position would allow." In the middle of the night, Washington woke up and was surprised to spot the servant propped in such an uncomfortable posture. "Primus!" he cried, "what did you mean by saying that you had blankets and straw enough? Here you have given up your blanket and straw to me, that I may sleep comfortably, while you are obliged to sit through the night." "Don't trouble yourself about me," Hall assured the general, who responded by protesting that there was room for two under his blanket. The servant demurred again, but the general persisted:

> "I say, come and lie down here!" said Washington, authoritatively. "There is room for both, and I insist upon it!"
> He threw open the blanket as he spoke, and moved to one side of the straw. Primus professes to have been exceedingly shocked at the idea of lying under the same covering with the commander-in-chief, but his tone was so resolute and determined that he could not hesitate. He prepared himself, therefore, and laid himself down by Washington, and on the same straw, and under the same blanket, the General and the negro servant slept until morning.[62]

This is arguably a story about Primus Hall, a model free black man of the young republic. As such, it was retold in two compendia assembled by prominent abolitionists. At the height of the antislavery crusade, William Cooper Nell included it in *The Colored Patriots of the American Revolution*. After the Civil War, white abolitionist Lydia Maria Child put the story in her *Freedmen's Book*, an anthology of writings by prominent African Americans (including Phillis Wheatley) and biographical sketches of laudable individuals of African descent. While the anecdote's inclusion in *The Freedmen's Book* added Hall to the roster of exemplary African Americans, the story appeared under nearly the same title as in *Godey's*: "Anecdote of General Washington." In the end, the general was the hero of the tale, and Hall merely played the role of the agreeable servant.[63]

It is not clear how this story originated, or why it named Primus Hall as the black man who shared a bed with the father of the country. Hall was known around Boston for regaling anyone who would listen with tales of his Revolutionary exploits, and the bed-sharing incident could have been one of his own stories. But it's unlikely that it was the whole story, because Hall's own recorded versions of his Revolutionary service emphasize his involvement in the "actual" work of war, rather than his obsequious service for the war's officers. Petitioning Congress in 1836, Hall described his role in the war:

> Your Petitioner served as a Soldier...and was in actual Service. Nineteen months and a half as a private soldier and was in several Skirmishes and Battles with the Enemy, particularly at White Plains...and at Trenton and Princeton in New Jersey when the Hessians and British were taken at those places. At the latter place He made Prisoners of two of the Enemy with his own hands after pursuing them over half a mile.

In addition to this congressional testimony, Hall gave two accounts of his military service as part of his application for a federal military pension.

Washington's name came up a number of times in his narrations of his military career. When his first year of service expired shortly after the Battle of Trenton, Hall explained, "to the earnest request of General Washington he volunteered for the further term of six weeks, and during said service he was at the taking of Princetown, and soon thereafter marched to Morristown in New Jersey and there received an honorable discharge from the Army signed by General Washington." By mentioning his presence in battles that Washington had overseen, by suggesting that he had enlisted at Washington's request, and by noting that he had received a discharge signed by the general himself, Hall emphasized that his relationship to Washington had been one of a soldier to officer. In contrast, the blanket-and-straw anecdote suggested that Hall related to Washington as a servant (or slave) to a master.[64]

How had Primus Hall's Revolutionary service become a matter of congressional debate? In 1835, the War Department's commissioner of pensions, James Edwards, had rejected his application for a military pension, on the grounds that Hall had served not as a "soldier" but as a "waiter, or in some other civil capacity."[65] To justify his claim, Hall and his pension agent marshaled testimony from his neighbors and comrades-in-arms in support of his case. Some of the men who went to battle with Hall evidently didn't make the same distinction that Edwards did between servant and soldier.[66] Veteran Ebenezer Hart remembered frequently seeing Hall during wartime. "I distinctly recollect said Primus as a *steward* to Col. Pickering in the Quartermaster Department at Yorktown," he said. He added, however, that "it is, and has been matter of notoriety that said Primus was engaged in the public service as a *soldier*." Other witnesses portrayed Hall more clearly as a soldier among soldiers, thus obviously entitled to a pension. John Brown reported that he and Hall had enlisted in Danvers at the same time, before being discharged together at the end of the three-month tour. Throughout his time in the army, Brown noted, Hall "was much esteemed by the officers & men, as a brave & faithful Soldier in the service of his Country." Thomas Thorp's testimony was particularly compelling. Thorp repeatedly used the pronoun "we," calling attention to all the things he and Hall had done together, including enlisting in the same company, marching to New Jersey, and reenlisting at the same time: "Primas was with me during the whole period of thirteen and a half months & in all the above named Battles And at Morristown in New Jersey we received our discharges and returned to our Native state in the winter of 1777." Despite all they had shared in battle, some fifty years later Thorp, a white man, was receiving a pension and Hall was not.[67]

None of the affidavits Hall filed with the pension office—his own or any of his witnesses'—mentioned the pursuit and capture of two British soldiers whom Hall would later describe in his congressional petition. Whether this incident actually happened or was an embellishment to tantalize the House committee reviewing Hall's case, it was effective. Overruling the pension commissioner's decision to reject Hall's claim, Congress passed a bill declaring him "justly entitled to a pension for a faithful service of eighteen months as a revolutionary soldier, not merely in camp duty, or the ordinary performance of military obligations, but in the field of battle, where his bravery and good conduct are proved to have been such as would have done honor to any man."[68]

Financially, Hall was well off for a man of color; it is probably safe to say that he didn't pursue a pension solely for the money. Having his military service recognized for what it was—service to the nation, and not to an individual master—mattered enough to him to pursue the matter all the way to the halls of Congress. Yet none of Hall's activism, whether on his own behalf or in support of the black community in Boston, merited mention in his obituary. The *Boston Transcript* noted that Hall, "a respectable colored citizen, and a revolutionary pensioner of the U.S.," enjoyed talking about his presence at turning points of the war. This obituary continued, "for about two years [Hall] was in the military family of General Washington, of whom he spoke with that fervor of attachment which was common to all who were personally acquainted with that great man. He has departed full of years, to meet, we trust, the reward of a good and faithful servant." The abolitionist *Liberator* reprinted this obituary but added an acerbic note to the *Transcript's* editor: "With multitudes of such instances of the devotion to liberty of the race to which this 'respectable colored citizen' was more particularly identified, you would join in the huge enormity of the southerner in enslaving, and in the vile prejudice of the northerner in insulting him." The mainstream press could praise Hall's faithfulness as a servant and his association with Washington, but Hall's work on behalf of the "liberty of the race" would at best pass unnoticed and at worst be scorned.[69]

Though these obituaries and anecdotes about Primus Hall stem from the mid-nineteenth century, they draw on a tendency evident in Revolutionary commemorative culture from its very beginning: the elevation of a few individuals with recognized social authority to the status of heroes. At first glance, placing a man of color alongside these heroes disrupted that pattern by raising questions about what a black man was doing at the edge of Trumbull's painting or in a revered general's tent at a Continental Army encampment. The short and literal answer was "serving." But was he serving his country or his master? If he was serving the nation through participation in the military or display of patriotic commitment, then he was entitled to the rights of a dutiful citizen. If he was serving another man, he could hope for the master's gracious protection and support, but he relinquished all claim to belonging and acting in the republic on his own terms. The problem of who or what was the source of black men's obligations and concomitant privileges lay behind every appearance, real or representational, of a black man in the Revolutionary War.

Even if the published anecdotes about Primus Hall were more about George Washington than about Hall himself, it is significant that these stories appeared in print in the second quarter of the nineteenth century. With a string of fiftieth anniversaries of Revolutionary events in the 1820s, Americans enthusiastically looked backward on their nation's founding years. By that point, popular interest in the Revolution generated efforts to honor ordinary men who had participated in the fight for freedom, in addition to valorizing the manly sacrifice and genteel leadership of the Warrens and Washingtons of the war. In the 1830s, the rise of an organized antislavery movement cast Revolutionary claims to freedom and equality in a new light, such that by the following decade, there was a sizeable audience to whom it mattered that Washington would willingly share his bed with a black man. This audience would turn its gaze back to Bunker Hill—and see things there that John Trumbull never would have imagined.

3

Movements and Monuments

In the summer of 1843, an unnamed black writer recorded an incident he had witnessed at the celebration of the completion of the Bunker Hill Monument on June 17. While watching President John Tyler and other dignitaries in the grand parade, he noticed "three strange looking colored men" on Boston Common. Curiously, as other onlookers "were forcing their way towards the President, [these men] kept as far from him as possible." "Continually gazing around them," the three seemed overwhelmed by their surroundings. When the parade ended, the writer headed for Bunker Hill in Charlestown, where he enjoyed the music of the chorus and bands and gazed upon the crowd, sons and daughters of New England "congregated to reap the fruits of sacred liberty, which was nourished and cultivated by the tears and blood of their fathers and my fathers." At the ceremonies that followed, Tyler, a Virginian and a slaveholder, "presided as a sort of high priest of liberty." The high point was Daniel Webster's speech, punctuated by thunderous applause, until an unexpected interruption wrested the crowd's attention away:

> A tremendous commotion took place—the ladies screamed, and every body was thrown into the greatest excitement. Presently these three strange looking men whom we saw on the common, rushed by, pursued by as many constables, all dressed up in Liberty's ribands.—"Stop them! stop them!" they cried; and the poor fellows being followed so closely, they took shelter behind the monument. Webster was compelled to stop speaking. The constables came up, and dragged them out, while they clung to the consecrated stone and wept, and pointed to the American Constitution that was hung to it, and begged to be protected. It was all in vain. *They were three of the thirty slaves of John Tyler*, who had taken the advantage of their master's absence, and ran away. They were chained, and hurried away from the ground and the Constitution....

Here ends this writer's account, save for one last line: "All this might have happened, though it did not."[1]

Perhaps this story is evidence only of one antislavery writer's overactive imagination. But we can also read it as richly suggestive of the contentiousness and potency of historical memory in the second quarter of the nineteenth

century. Abolitionists throughout New England condemned Tyler for allegedly bringing a slave to hold his umbrella at the Bunker Hill Monument dedication ceremony. As it turns out, the umbrella-holding slave was something
else that "might have happened, though it did not." No definitive reports survive of the presence of any slaves at the Bunker Hill ceremonies of 1843,
either as servants or as fugitives. But abolitionists persisted in seeing slavery
there anyway. For all that the Bunker Hill Monument was supposed to represent American nationalism—the tagline from Webster's speech was "this
column stands on Union"—its dedication in 1843 brought the country's
political, sectional, and racial divisions into sharp relief.[2] If partisan alliances
were increasingly taking on a sectional cast, the fracturing of national identity along racial lines was not strictly a southern phenomenon. The black
writer who attended the Bunker Hill celebrations distanced himself from the
multitudes of white New Englanders at the ceremony, stating that "their
fathers and my fathers" had spilled blood there, rather than giving praise to
a common set of "our" ancestors. That this author chose to set his drama
about the nation's divisions on the grounds of an early battle in the War for
Independence shows how symbolically powerful he understood such a site
of memory to be.

Between the War of 1812 and the middle of the nineteenth century, as
patriotic commemorations were multiplying, abolitionist activism devel-
oping, and sectional divisions intensifying, the American Revolution was
hardly an abstract idea. Memories of the Revolution were accessible to
Americans through sensory experience. When completed, the monument on
Bunker Hill was a visual reminder of patriotic principles, standing so tall that
it was said to be visible from the homes of three hundred thousand New
Englanders.[3] Surrounding the monument, however, some observers saw real
or imagined figures who represented the betrayal of those ideals: three desperate fugitives, a slave with an umbrella, a despised chief executive, a sellout
statesman. Still others heard the monument speak, though it seemed to have
wildly different messages for different listeners. In addition to its visual and
aural power, the 220-foot shaft of granite was memory made tangible. Visitors
climbed inside of it. In the story about Tyler's slaves, the runaways "clung" to
it. Many people marveled at how long it would undoubtedly last, but they
also wondered what it would mean if it fell.[4]

Many New Englanders reveled in the synesthetic possibilities that the
monument and the events surrounding it generated. However, the sensory
overload of the commemorative fervor sickened a small but vocal group of
abolitionists. Celebrating American freedom at a time when American slavery
was at its peak struck abolitionists as the grossest hypocrisy. For reformers of
a pacifist bent, any glorification of war was noisome. Some of the most radical
abolitionists went beyond critiquing the militaristic dimensions of the nation's

founding and shunned the American Revolution itself. In the wake of emancipation in the British Empire, American abolitionists of the late 1830s and
1840s wondered if the Revolution might have placed them on the wrong side
of the imperial divide. One writer for the *Liberator* mourned the irony that
Joseph Warren, the martyr of Bunker Hill, had died at the hands of the British
for the principle of freedom, only so that a few decades later Britain could
make "herself the illustrious exemplar of the principle by proclaiming a
Jubilee for her 800,000 slaves." Many abolitionists rejected the nationalistic
spirit of patriotic commemorations, preferring to think of themselves as
linked together in an "antislavery international," a world community of
Christians, or a transatlantic network of cosmopolitan humanitarians. The
Liberator's motto, proudly emblazoned under the paper's masthead from 1831
onward, declared, "our country is the world—our countrymen are mankind."
Ratifying this sentiment, the New England Anti-Slavery Convention voted in
1844 in favor of William Lloyd Garrison's call for disunion instead of compromise with slaveholders.[5]

For some abolitionists, the offensiveness of the Bunker Hill Monument
and the festivities surrounding it concerned something even more
fundamental than what freedom meant, whether war was ever justified, and
whether the nation-state was compatible with ideals of justice. The problem
that the 220-foot monument made tangible was the significance of history
for the contemporary world. The most radical opponents of slavery tended
to criticize elaborate commemorations of past events and heroes, while those
who feared society's deviation from tradition were most enthusiastic about
erecting monuments, writing hagiographies, and orchestrating commemorations. At the same time, radicals frequently sought historical precedent for
their ideas and tactics, and conservatives were often ambivalent about what
to do with what the past had bequeathed them. The questions all these nineteenth-century Americans asked themselves were who belonged to history,
and to whom did history belong?

The Bunker Hill Monument anchors this chapter on memory in an age
of reform. As they molded stone into what they believed the past signified
and demanded, those who imagined and then built the monument were
making history in one sense. But history is made not only in granite but
also through gesture: the fugitive's determined footsteps over cobble-
stones at dusk, the daring flourish of a petitioner's hand across a page, the
hearts that leap and the heads that nod and the fists that shake when an agi-
tator speaks. When they are planned, organized, channeled to a single
purpose, these small movements become *a* movement, and when the
movement changes the world around it, that's history. In the events and non-
events of June 17, 1843, these two ways of making history—movements and
monuments—collided.

HISTORY IN PARCHMENT AND STONE

Patriotic fervor and historical curiosity surged in the late 1810s and 20s, as the Revolution's semicentennial followed in the wake of the War of 1812. Around the country, citizens planned monuments to the heroes and ideals of the Revolution. The most elaborate of these centered around Bunker Hill. The elite men who comprised the Bunker Hill Monument Association envisioned an impressive monument that would instill in its visitors a sense of republican duty and decorum. At the same time, as a growing number of ordinary people clamored to participate in commemorative activities on their own terms, it became important for the Monument Association to harness the "democratic desire to commemorate common men's sacrifices." The Bunker Hill Monument would not only be a shrine to Joseph Warren, but a memorial to all the American men who had given their lives on June 17, 1775.[6] The designers struggled to determine the most appropriate shape for such a monument. It was clear that a statue of an individual hero was not appropriate for this collective memorial.[7] Initially, some members of the association were drawn to a column, which traditionally represented victory. Ultimately, they settled on an obelisk, a symbol of death, as the form best suited to elicit the patriotic gratitude that Bunker Hill demanded of its visitors. The smooth, symmetrical sides of the monument gave it a republican dignity, eloquent in its reticence. Horatio Greenough, who submitted the winning design, declared, "The obelisk has to my eye a singular aptitude in its form and character to call attention to a spot memorable in history. It says but one word, but it speaks loud. If I understand its voice, it says Here! It says no more."[8]

Would those who visited Bunker Hill get the message? For years, the men behind the monument agonized over whether saying "Here!" was saying enough. In 1823, before construction began, one of the early planning committees proposed that the monument "contain the names and dates of the distinguished characters and events which originated the independence of the country." The decision over what to inscribe on the monument was repeatedly delayed, until, in 1848, a committee led by Daniel Webster and Edward Everett (another leading Massachusetts Whig) took up the issue in earnest. The committee gathered ideas for memorial tablets at various locations around the monument complex, marking where Warren fell, where the remains of the breastwork were still visible, and where Lafayette laid the cornerstone and Webster addressed the crowd in 1825. On the side of the monument itself, they proposed a marble tablet with gold-leaf letters declaring it the location of the redoubt. Absent from the proposed inscriptions was a list of the names of those who had died (aside from Warren). Francis C. Gray, who worked with the committee to draft inscriptions, asked,

"Is there not a just and proper pride in assuming that the names of those distinguished there and the leading events of the day must be known to all who can read the inscriptions?" Among Gray's proposals were inscriptions reading, "Honor to the men of Massachusetts Connecticut and New Hampshire who fell here fulfilling their duty to their country and mankind" and "The names of those who fought here belong to history and will outlast this stone."[9]

In debating the suggested inscriptions, the association focused less on the content of the proposals than on the very "impropriety of placing any inscription on the outside of the Monument," as Webster put it in an impromptu resolution. The assembly quickly approved Webster's resolution that the blank face of the monument be preserved. The statesman rushed to write down this decision on a slip of paper headed by the decree, "a record of the history of this structure, with the names of the principal originators, contributors, & agents, inscribed on Parchment is herein deposited, for the information of after times." It seems ironic that the members of the Monument Association found it necessary to preserve accounts of their own activities even as they decided that the events they were commemorating required no written record, and that they carefully recorded their own names even as they resisted listing the names of the men who had fought and died. The men who made up the Bunker Hill Monument Association were used to having their names in the public eye. The roster of long-serving directors was a who's who of Brahmin influence: Appleton, Lawrence, Peabody, Saltonstall, Shaw, Thorndike. The decisions about how (not) to inscribe the monument reveal these elite men's understanding of history and their own place within it. At one level, building the monument was about honoring the sacrifices of their forebears. At another, this commemorative activity was this group's way of asserting that they, too, belonged to history—and vice versa. As Everett explained, "It is the order of nature that the generation to achieve nobly, should be succeeded by the generation worthily to record and gratefully to commemorate." If the Revolutionaries made history with blood, in the second quarter of the nineteenth century their sons and grandsons made it out of parchment and stone.[10]

This new generation's historical status wasn't so assured as that of the martyrs of 1775. Whereas those who died at Bunker Hill would be remembered even when the 220-foot granite obelisk had eroded, those who built the monument felt they had to keep careful accounts of their own contributions to the nation. They fulfilled their own place in history not merely by recording what had happened in the past but also by allowing the past to inform the sensibility of their current generation—in effect, keeping the past present. On the day after the Bunker Hill anniversary in 1849, Everett proposed a resolution that received the unanimous support of the Monument

Association's board of directors: "that the great object for which the obelisk was erected on Bunker Hill is monumental, and not historical, and that it is not expedient that any record of names, dates, or events connected with the battle should be inscribed upon it." Everett's distinction between the "monumental" and the "historical" underscores his sense that inscribing the monument with specific facts would serve to anchor the structure in historical particularity. In contrast, if left uninscribed, the significance of the monument would be so profound and universal that it would transcend the temporality—the "names, dates, or events"—of ordinary human experience. The monument was inspired by a historical event, but its builders saw it as standing for something outside the messiness of history.[11]

This commemorative agenda suited the politics of Everett and his peers, who sought to maintain a hierarchical social order resembling the system of deference perceptible in Trumbull's *Death of Warren*. The Bunker Hill Monument raised that conservative interpretation of the Revolution to new heights. In arguing that "monuments are the most conservative of commemorative forms," historian Kirk Savage explains that "while other things come and go, are lost and forgotten, the monument is supposed to remain a fixed point, stabilizing both the physical and the cognitive landscape." The monument's physical presence, permanent and overpowering, literally dwarfed any human actors who might assemble around its uninscribed face. In literary scholar Russ Castronovo's terms, then, "under the aegis of monumental history, the political citizen is forgotten."[12]

Yet the events that Everett, Webster, and their associates were commemorating in this "most conservative" of ways happened in the context of great change, including transformations initiated and encouraged by people at the margins of traditional political agency. Modern historians continue to argue about just how revolutionary the American Revolution actually was. There may be no resolution to this debate, but perhaps the most important point to take from it is that the Revolution did have revolutionary possibilities. In the decades in which the Bunker Hill Monument Association was meeting to plan and build their memorial, diverse collections of Americans were coming to see the radical potential of remembering the 1770s. In tracing the vicissitudes of Revolutionary memory, historian Alfred Young notes that Americans in the first decades of the republic did not commemorate the popular protests that preceded the Revolutionary War, such as the action against the Stamp Act in 1765 or the destruction of tea in Boston Harbor in 1773. Even in the 1820s, as the fiftieth anniversary of the War for Independence and the aftermath of the War of 1812 piqued interest in the Revolutionary period, the commemorative emphasis was on military gratitude. As Young explains, "Elites who had never been comfortable with prewar events—controversial, ambiguous, menacing—felt more at home commemorating the war, when ostensibly there was a consensus between people and leaders, soldiers were under hierarchical command, and battles were clear-cut, as they are only in retrospect." But as the labor movement began to strengthen, particularly into the mid-1830s, people lower on the social scale than those who funded the Bunker Hill Monument began to claim that the Revolution belonged to them, too. For these Bostonians, the monument-in-progress on Bunker Hill stood not for a dream realized some sixty years earlier but, as one working-class activist put it, for "unfinished independence."[13]

Young and others have shown that political leaders and cultural elites worked hard to curb the radical potential of Revolutionary memory. One of their strategies was to co-opt the memory of ordinary participants in the Revolution for the purpose of preserving, rather than critiquing, the existing social order. Another was to perpetuate their version of the Revolution's meaning in as many public forums as they could create or find. The careful balancing act between democratization and elite control was evident in the ceremonies surrounding the Bunker Hill Monument's ground-breaking in 1825. All the surviving veterans of Bunker Hill were invited to lead the parade on the fiftieth anniversary of the battle, when the Marquis de Lafayette came to town to lay the cornerstone of the monument. While soldiers of all ranks were allowed to participate, the event was carefully scripted by members of the Monument Association. The remainder of the parade was a tightly organized procession of political dignitaries, military officers, clergymen, professors, and members of historical societies.[14]

The ordinary soldiers who marched must have had many a good story to tell of their experiences in the war. One local writer, Samuel Swett, took advantage of their presence and wrote an account of the Battle of Bunker Hill based on interviews with the veterans. Boston's cultural elite, the men who filled the rosters of the Bunker Hill Monument Association and the Massachusetts Historical Society, dismissed these oral histories as "boastful, inconsistent, and utterly untrue,—mixtures of old men's broken memories and fond imaginings with the love of the marvellous." A committee of the Historical Society pronounced the reminiscences "wholly worthless for history."[15] Instead, the elite custodians of Boston's history turned to one of their own to interpret the battle for the crowd assembled at Bunker Hill. At the monument's ground-breaking on June 17, 1825, it was Daniel Webster who spoke for all, in the first of his two Bunker Hill addresses. Politically, Webster was a complicated figure. Unabashedly committed to unionism, he nevertheless viewed what was best for the nation as so close to what was best for New England and its mercantile interests that he could alienate anyone who did not share his sectional or economic loyalties. Abolitionists skeptical of partisan politics altogether had still other reasons to distrust him. But when it came to articulating the significance and demands of New England's heritage, Webster was without rival. He had cemented his reputation for historical oratory five years earlier, at Plymouth's bicentennial of the pilgrim landing, and his Bunker Hill address of 1825 would become one of the most beloved speeches in American history.[16]

Webster used his two addresses at Bunker Hill (in 1825 and 1843) to bring his interpretation of the past to audiences of unprecedented size.[17] Neither speech mentioned slavery. Instead, Webster's historical vision identified the threat to liberty as originating *outside* the Anglo-American world. In 1843, he succinctly described how history had set the United States on a distinct path from its Latin American neighbors: "England transplanted liberty to America; Spain transplanted power." Webster drew here on the Jacksonian political lexicon that positioned power—meaning tyranny, corruption, and governance by coercion and fear—as liberty's "other." In his version of American history, English liberty came to America in two installments and along two different paths. The first was "the spirit of commercial and foreign adventure," which traveled with Walter Ralegh and his "daring" and "high-spirited" successors to Virginia. The second was "religious liberty drawing after it or bringing along with it, as it always does, an ardent devotion to the principle of civil liberty." This, Webster explained, was what the mother country had delivered to New England. The Revolution forged links among Massachusetts, Virginia, and their sister colonies in Anglo-America, which all came to prize free markets and free conscience in a way that Spanish America, with its historical ties to a gold-hungry monarchy and a repressive papacy, could not. Webster cast his nationalism in an international context by showing how the differences between the United States and its New World neighbors overshadowed any divisions within the nation. In other words, American exceptionalism supplanted American dissent.[18]

Emphasizing that this history of freedom knit all Americans together, Webster suggested in 1825 that the monument was superfluous, because "the record of illustrious actions is most safely deposited in the universal remembrance of mankind." The monument promised to "show our own deep sense of the value and importance of the achievements of our ancestors…and to foster a constant regard for the principles of the Revolution." As his frequent use of the first person plural indicates, Webster assumed a collective consciousness of the national past that linked him to every member of his audience. The events surrounding the Battle of Bunker Hill were "familiarly known to all." Indeed, "if we ourselves had never been born, the 17th of June, 1775, would have been a day on which all subsequent history would have poured its light." This statement implied that the nation's history transcended the significance of any individual person. Yet the fact that Webster and his listeners, through their birth on American soil or to American parents, had been positioned to claim the legacy of the Revolution ennobled them: "We are Americans. We live in what may be called the early age of this great continent; and we know that our posterity, through all time, are here to enjoy and suffer the allotments of humanity. We see before us a probable train of great events; we know that our own fortunes have been happily cast."[19]

Benedict Anderson has observed that "it is the magic of nationalism to turn chance into destiny." Nineteenth-century Americans hadn't chosen to be born into the American tradition, yet the fact that they were designated—whether by God, fate, or the mysterious forces of history—to inherit the legacy of the Revolution was a source of pride for them. To be sure, this privileged status entailed certain duties. As Webster elaborated in his address marking the completion of the Bunker Hill Monument in 1843, foremost was the obligation to subordinate political divisiveness to national spirit: "Woe betide the man who brings to this day's worship feeling less than wholly American! Woe betide the man who can stand here with the fires of local resentments burning, or the purpose of fomenting local jealousies and the strifes of local interests festering and rankling in his heart." According to Webster, those born into American history did not need him to explain what their heritage signified and demanded. Calling the monument "itself the orator of the occasion," he declaimed, "the powerful speaker stands motionless before us. It is a plain shaft. It bears no inscriptions…it looks, it speaks, it acts, to the full comprehension of every American mind, and the awakening of glowing enthusiasm in every American heart." To be American was to have a certain set of capacities—to be able to hear a slab of granite, to see it move, to read messages of freedom on its blank face.[20]

At every turn, Webster emphasized the uniformity of national feeling: "Among the seventeen millions of happy people who form the American community, there is not one who has not an interest in this monument, as there is not one that has not a deep and abiding interest in that which it commemorates." Claims like this one (which glossed over the fact that three million of the nation's "happy people" lived in bondage) and Webster's silence on the subject of slavery in general made his speech ring hollow and hypocritical in abolitionist ears. Indeed, the eighteen-year gap between Webster's two Bunker Hill speeches, marking the cornerstone and then the completion of the monument, indicates a broader lack of consensus about how to remember the Revolution. Waning public support for the project in the late 1820s and 30s stalled the Monument Association's fundraising efforts, and without the money raised by a huge craft fair organized by local women in 1840, the monument would not have been completed. The average Bostonian did not share this enthusiasm for lavishing time and money on monuments. For the small number who took an active stand against slavery, the problem was not simply the monument's expense but also how it seemed to freeze the process of history before it had reached its fulfillment.[21]

MAKING GOOD THE PROMISE

What Webster did not comprehend was that for those on the margins of American society, American history was not an inheritance but rather a work in progress. In the same years that elite Bostonians were struggling to raise funds for the Bunker Hill Monument, opponents of slavery were configuring themselves into a new abolitionist movement, one that was small in numbers but ardent in its commitment and strident in its approach. The most urgent cries against American slavery in the 1810s and 20s had come from the mid-Atlantic and Northwest states, places with greater proximity than New England to the slaveholding South. In those border states, the visibility of the internal slave trade (especially the trade in "term slaves," or bonds people promised future freedom under gradual emancipation statutes) and the kidnapping of free people of color violated the emerging consensus that the Northern states were free soil. In Massachusetts, whites had largely sat out this phase of antislavery activism, though under the leadership of William Lloyd Garrison, that apathy shifted to make Boston a center of abolitionism in the 1830s. Garrison began publishing *The Liberator* in 1831 and established the Massachusetts Anti-Slavery Society the next year. Over the succeeding decade, his followers became increasingly vocal in their attacks on slavery and American society more broadly. More conservative abolitionists balked at Garrison's contempt for the churches, which he saw as too reluctant to criticize slavery, and his linkage of abolitionism with other radical reforms, especially women's rights. Garrison's insistence that the American political process was irredeemably corrupt wearied other sets of abolitionists, most notably those who would go on to establish the Liberty Party (based in New York) and other politically partisan antislavery groups. By 1840, both Garrison's feminism and anti-clericalism, as well as his intransigence with respect to his strategy of moral suasion and "nonresistance," had forced a schism in the national organization, the American Anti-Slavery Society.[22]

In the fall of 1842 and spring of 1843, however, Boston abolitionists celebrated a significant and rare triumph, secured despite the ongoing bickering between Garrisonian and Liberty Party factions.[23] The chain of events that brought antislavery Bay Staters this victory began in Virginia, on the night of October 4, 1842, when George Latimer, the twenty-two-year-old slave of Norfolk storekeeper James B. Gray, met up with his wife, Rebecca, a slave in another local household. Together, the two crept onto a vessel in Norfolk harbor, where they huddled in a chamber of ballast for nine hours. According to an advertisement Rebecca's mistress later published in a local newspaper, the twenty-year-old woman, "self possessed, and easy in her manners," was "obviously *enceinte*." Did the couple time their escape so that their child would be born on free soil? They had planned carefully for a journey of several stages: from Norfolk to Frenchtown, Maryland, thence to Baltimore and Philadelphia, and finally to Boston. What George Latimer did not anticipate was that on his very first day in Massachusetts, he would run into a Virginian, William Carpenter, who used to work at his master James Gray's store. Carpenter immediately sent word to Gray that his slave was in Boston. Gray then set out for Boston himself, arriving in the city on October 18. Once there, he had Latimer committed to the Leverett Street jail while he hired a lawyer to help make his case that Latimer was his property.[24]

In the weeks that followed, "Latimer" was on the tongue of every abolitionist in Boston. Antislavery Northerners were already alert to the legal dilemmas posed by fugitive slaves. Earlier in the year, the Supreme Court had dealt a major blow to abolitionists with its decision in *Prigg v. Pennsylvania*. By denying due process to a black family in Pennsylvania seized as runaways from a Maryland owner, *Prigg* affirmed the constitutionality of the federal Fugitive Slave Law of 1793 and invalidated Pennsylvania's personal liberty statute of 1826. Much to the shame of Massachusetts abolitionists, the opinion of the court was authored by a Bay State man and Harvard professor, Justice Joseph P. Story. The one loophole that Story's opinion left for antislavery activists was similar to the modern concept of "unfunded mandates": while state and local authorities could not interfere with the enforcement of the federal law, neither could they be required to expend their own resources to carry it out. Capitalizing on this idea, abolitionists protested Latimer's imprisonment at city expense.[25]

Abolitionist outrage crystallized at a massive meeting on October 30, held in Faneuil Hall, the site of some of the American Revolution's greatest political theater. The resolutions on the table that night directly linked Latimer's cause to "all the glorious memories of the revolutionary struggle." Driven by those memories, the assembly resolved "That Massachusetts is, and of right ought to be, a free and independent State; that she cannot allow her soil to be polluted by the foot-print of slavery, without trampling on her bill of rights, and subjecting herself to infamy; that she is solemnly bound to give succor and protection to all who may escape from the prison-house of bondage, and flee to her for safety." No longer could slavery be dismissed as a southern problem, best solved by those who lived among the plantations and slave markets of New Orleans and the Mississippi Delta, Charleston and the Chesapeake. George Latimer's pursuers had brought slavery to Massachusetts.[26]

Like their Revolutionary predecessors, Latimer's advocates appealed to white New Englanders' fears of enslavement to outside interests. Under the headline "The White Slaves of the North," the editors of *The Latimer Journal and North Star*—a short-lived newspaper published thrice weekly during the Latimer uproar—mused, "The idea has extensively prevailed that Massachusetts is a *free* state. It was but the other morning we awoke and found ourselves slaves." They argued that jailing Latimer at public expense and putting the courts at Gray's disposal bound Bay Staters to slave-owning Southerners. The justice system that permitted these corruptions betrayed the principles of Anglo-American liberty in general and the Bay State's heritage in particular: "Judges seem to sit on their benches only to shout in chorus... 'Great is the Slavery of the Southern States.'...let a Southerner claim a Negro—no matter if it be even within the shadow of Bunker's Hill, and the whole bench turns pale."[27]

From the abolitionists' perspective, New Englanders' willing compliance with unjust federal laws was even more demeaning in its slavishness than the literal bondage that Latimer was trying to escape. A parodic song called "The Slave's Attorney" began by recounting how Massachusetts patriot Elbridge Gerry had nobly fought for justice and freedom; it then turned to ridiculing Gerry's grandson and namesake, Elbridge Gerry Austin, who was serving as the slave owner Gray's lawyer in the Latimer affair:

> Oh, fortunate slaveholder!—seeing it was his
> To win on the chances fate offers to few.
> For 'tis rare in the land of the pilgrims, I wis,
> While hunting for one slave, to light upon *two*.
> Yet, grandson of G****, though low in yon cell,
> At the word of thy lips, may poor Latimer be,
> Loaded down with the chains from thy fingers that fell,
> 'Tis degrading to *him* to compare him with *thee!*[28]

The writer of this song shared with the members of the Bunker Hill Monument Association a concern that the present was not living up to its obligations to the past. For the Monument Association, that realization prompted commemorative activity, including parades, monuments, and orations. For the Latimer activists, honoring the pilgrim and patriot ancestors demanded bringing their brand of courage and resolve into the present-day struggle for liberty. Urged another pro-Latimer song, "Make good the promise your early days gave, / Boston boys! Boston boys! rescue the slave."[29]

To those committed to the abolitionist movement, the commemorative extravaganzas popular in nineteenth-century Boston looked silly at best, hypocritical at worst. The *Latimer Journal* published a pitch-perfect parody of the "orders of procession" distributed at events like the grand Bunker Hill

Day celebration of 1825. If Latimer was to be returned to slavery, the *Journal* argued, the rendition should happen in style, with a parade of city officials, musicians, and merchants marching "with their eyes bandaged with cotton, and their mouths stopped with sugar and tobacco." Latimer himself would be "heavily ironed, escorted by a guard of honor, consisting of fourth of July Orators and Readers of the Declaration of Independence from the earliest times," while his master James Gray, at whose whim the justice system lay prostrate, would take the place of honor as "HIS IMPERIAL ROYAL HIGHNESS, (His train borne by the Judges of the United States, and State Courts)."[30]

Latimer's plight inspired not only outraged parodies, but also calls for action. Abolitionists—especially the African Americans among them—debated how to rescue Latimer forcibly from his captors if the court ruled he should be sent back to Virginia.[31] As lawyers for both sides engaged in complicated legal wrangling, abolitionists continued their public relations battle, focusing on the case's implications for the status of Massachusetts as a "free state."[32] Their efforts paid off. Cowed by public pressure, the sheriff decided there was no justification for holding Latimer in jail and released him. Lacking the support of the criminal justice system, Gray soon gave up his fight to win Latimer back, and after some negotiation, he agreed to manumit Latimer for 400 dollars. On November 18, about six weeks after he had first sneaked away from Norfolk, George Latimer was officially a free man, not to mention a famous one. Garrison's biographer Henry Mayer argues, "The abolitionists had never before had so telling an effect upon public opinion, and the mass movement had never before secured so rapid an antislavery victory." Mayer doesn't mention that open hostility between Garrisonians and local Liberty Party leaders, the latter responsible for the most effective fundraising and legal counsel in the Latimer crusade, was still simmering.[33] But these tensions among abolitionists make it all the more impressive that Latimer nonetheless ended up with such widespread public support. Ever since the early days of the movement for immediate abolition, the political mainstream in Massachusetts—comprised of people who disliked the idea of slavery but were reluctant to interfere with what they saw as a southern problem—had regarded abolitionist activists as dangerously radical. In the Latimer case, by appealing to the sacred heritage of freedom that Bay Staters vested in their own ground and their own institutions, abolitionists edged the mainstream closer to their point of view.

With Latimer's help, Massachusetts abolitionists soon began spending the political capital they had amassed during his ordeal. They redoubled their petitioning campaign, christening their latest memorial to the state legislature "The Latimer and Great Massachusetts Petition." Anyone who believed that slavery had not been a problem in Massachusetts since its dismantling in the 1780s would have been startled by the petitioners' language. Demanding a stricter set of personal liberty laws, the petitioners declared that they were "earnestly desiring to free this commonwealth and themselves from all connection with domestic slavery and to secure the citizens of this state from the danger of enslavement." The "free and equal" clause in the state constitution, the precedent of the Quok Walker cases, the vague promises of Revolutionary freedom: these were not enough. Massachusetts had to take an unambiguous stand against slavery within her bounds. Demonstrating this sense that freedom was central to the Bay State's heritage, and that threats to that freedom were currently very real, a handwritten roster of activists was labeled "List of those who are determined to do their share towards saving Massachusetts from Slavery, by circulating the Mammoth Petitions in Boston. Let there be at least *500 true sons & daughters* of the State in our very midst!"[34]

What did it take to be a true son or daughter of Massachusetts in the 1840s? Did it demand that one pay reverence to Revolutionary heroes by erecting a monument, or did it require adding one's name to the cause of the abolitionist movement? From the fall of 1842, when George Latimer arrived in Boston, into the spring of 1843, when Massachusetts passed a new personal liberty law, it seemed possible to reconcile the movement and the monument as two sides of a common pride in the Bay State's heritage of freedom. In prohibiting state officers from aiding in the arrest or detention of alleged runaway slaves, the Massachusetts Personal Liberty Law of 1843 reached farther than any such statute had before. Indeed, the state went as far as it could go without violating the Constitutional parameters laid out in *Prigg v. Pennsylvania*. The success of the "Latimer and Great Massachusetts" petition seemed to indicate that antislavery sentiment (if not abolitionist radicalism) was widespread. With all its signatures, the completed petition was two feet wide and over half a mile long. It weighed 150 pounds. The first signatory was "George Latimer, a native American, lately a slave in Norfolk, Virginia, now a citizen of Massachusetts"; 64,526 names followed his. The *Latimer Journal* claimed that Latimer's name headed the list "in order to prove that the colored man in our opinion is a citizen." Little wonder that abolitionists became furious when, just a few weeks later, a black man appeared on Bunker Hill as a slave.[35]

THE PRESIDENT'S PARASOL

Abolitionist Bostonians were still giddy over the Latimer victory when they learned that John Tyler was coming to town for the dedication of the Bunker Hill Monument. The Garrisonian contingent prepared to turn the festivities surrounding the monument into another occasion to champion their movement. At the opening of the New England Anti-Slavery Convention in May, with George Latimer on the platform at the front of the hall, the delegates formed a committee charged with calling on Tyler and asking him to emancipate his slaves. To publicize that plan, especially if the president refused to meet with them, the activists also approved a letter justifying their demand that Tyler set his slaves free. Authored by Garrison on behalf of all the convention's participants, the "Address to John Tyler" confessed that the presence of slavery on their nation's soil "fills us with grief and shame as American citizens." Juxtaposing the president's professed beliefs—in the self-evident truths of the Declaration of Independence, the ideals of justice and liberty propounded in the preamble to the Constitution, the golden rule of Christianity, and the patriotic heroism associated with Bunker Hill—against the simple fact that Tyler owned slaves, the address's refrain was "yet you are a slaveholder!"[36]

This interpretation of the American Revolution, setting slaveholding at odds with the republic's foundational principles, was spelled out even more clearly in a second address the New England Anti-Slavery Convention approved in May 1843. The "Address to the Slaves of the United States," also written by Garrison, exhorted bondspeople that they were "as entitled to life, liberty, and the pursuit of happiness as those who cruelly enslave you." Southern masters, though "descendants of those, who, in 1776, threw off the British yoke, and for seven years waged war against a despotic power," were now proving themselves to be "hypocrites and liars." In an address that itself quoted a substantial portion of the Declaration of Independence, Garrison told the slaves that each time their owners read the Declaration aloud or claimed to abide by its principles, they were effectively declaring "that it is both your right and your duty to wage war against them, and to wade through their blood, if necessary, to secure your own freedom." Garrison was ambivalent enough about bloodshed not to see such a violent outcome as desirable; he intended to demonstrate the hypocrisy of slaveholders rather than to instigate insurrection. "Should you attempt to gain your freedom in the same manner" as Patrick Henry and Joseph Warren, Garrison cautioned the slaves, "you would be branded as murderers and monsters, and slaughtered without mercy!" Such a violent reprisal against those fighting for their God-given rights would only prove what the Garrisonians knew to be true, that the country had fallen far off the path that the Revolution had set. The abolitionists' militantly antislavery version of American history permitted them to see their movement as the necessary fulfillment of Revolutionary ideals.[37]

As Bunker Hill Day approached, the *Liberator* encouraged readers to "make hay while the sun shines" and "improve the opportunity to scatter profusely, among the great multitude this week, the Addresses to the Slaves and to President Tyler, asking him to give liberty to his slaves." By spreading the word to a city full of celebrants, the abolitionists' cause could benefit from the commemorative festivities, even if their plea to Tyler went unheeded. Indeed, Tyler offered no official response to the address directed to him. According to abolitionist Anne Warren Weston, Wendell Phillips "had heard indirectly & without being at all sure of its truth that the President had said in regard to receiving the A.S. Committee 'he held no Slaves as President of the United States, & as John Tyler it was nobody's business.'" Abolitionists recognized no such distinction between the president's public and personal affairs, but even aside from his household arrangements, Tyler's public policies gave them sufficient reason to despise him. The "accidental President" was widely regarded with contempt in a state dominated by Whigs, whose party he had betrayed shortly after assuming the presidency at William Henry Harrison's death. New Englanders and abolitionists were especially fearful of Tyler's rumored plans to annex Texas as a slave state. Opposition to Texas annexation and support for personal liberty laws in the North were both manifestations of the impulse to contain slavery to the existing southern states. In this context, Boston abolitionists capitalized on the president's visit to assert that they would brook no slavery on their ground. Tyler's refusal to meet with them came as no surprise. "We have got just what we expected from him—nothing," Garrison wrote, adding that he had sought only moral victory: "[Tyler] has got our Address, and so has the country, and our great purpose is accomplished."[38]

The abolitionists' address to Tyler received wide publicity, if not broad support. The *Liberator* printed excerpts from newspapers from Virginia, Tyler's home state, which called on the president to "act with the firmness which becomes a Southron" and ignore the petitioners. The *Richmond Enquirer* declared the abolitionists' action "a gross breach of the hospitality which is due to the President of the republic—and the wise and liberal gentlemen of Boston should have kept down this unseasonable and offensive effervescence." Portsmouth, Virginia's newspaper was less delicate in its response. The *Old Dominion* noted that one member of the committee appointed to hand-deliver the address to Tyler was a fellow Virginian, none other than George Latimer, whom the newspaper called "the negro who was stolen from his master by the abolitionists of Boston." The writer concluded, "We hope the President will be accompanied by some southern friend who will on the spot cowhide the scoundrel who may attempt to introduce to him Latimer or any other negro for the purpose mentioned" (that is, presenting the address).[39]

City leaders had hoped that the festivities of June 17, 1843, would banish political controversy of this sort, at least temporarily. The Bunker Hill

Monument was finally to be dedicated, eighteen years after its construction had begun. The city was festooned with banners and bunting, and people crowded the streets and into every convenient window to watch an elaborate parade of dignitaries. As Tyler rolled by in his carriage, men cheered and women waved their handkerchiefs. Any animosity toward the president seemed to dissolve into the patriotic unity of the occasion. Veterans of Bunker Hill and other Revolutionary battles marched to the rhythms of fifes and drums and accepted the enthusiastic adulation of those assembled along the route. Later, Webster, who not long before had resigned as Tyler's secretary of state, spoke before an enormous crowd at the foot of the monument. One observer noted rapturously, "The whole scene was the most grand that can be imagined....into the great area were crowded thousands & thousands of a free, happy & well ordered people, celebrating their national jubilee; & upon the platform...stood the great man of the age, with a voice, action & presence almost god-like." To top it off, the weather was absolutely beautiful.[40]

The day before the monument dedication, a nor'easter had maintained a steady drizzle on Boston as Tyler and his entourage toured the city. At times, the rain was so bad that Mayor Martin Brimmer personally held an umbrella over the presidential pate. The dismal weather on June 16 made the sky seem all the brighter when a clear morning dawned on Bunker Hill Day. According to one report, the sun was so bright during the ceremony at the battlefield that the president had one of his slaves stand behind him, holding a parasol to shield him from the light. This image infuriated antislavery folk. "What a fine figure," the *Nantucket Telegraph* wrote in disgust, "fighting for freedom, with a SLAVE holding a shade over him!!" On a day when New Englanders wanted to commemorate their region's signal place in the history of American freedom, Tyler had implicitly reminded the crowd that the future of the nation was largely in the hands of *his* kind—Southerners and slave owners. A writer for the *Woonsocket Patriot* sniffed, "To a northern freeman, the fact that the Chief Magistrate of this great republic is an owner and buyer and seller of GOD'S IMAGE, is certainly repulsive enough; but that that functionary, when visiting us, must needs bring him one of his 'chattels personal' to taunt our eyes with, is an insult and an indignity we cannot and will not allow to pass unnoticed and unrebuked."[41]

The complicating factor in this commemorative controversy was that when these well-intentioned and infuriated New Englanders criticized the president for bringing a slave to Bunker Hill, their outrage was oriented around a man who wasn't there. In its first issue following the ceremonies of June 17, the *Liberator*, the same newspaper that would later reprint various other papers' accounts of Tyler's umbrella-toting slave, closed its own rant about the celebration with this curious observation: "President Tyler had the effrontery to bring with him a *slave*, on his 'pilgrimage' to Bunker Hill! and but for his (the slave's) indisposition on the 17th, would have been on those 'hallowed' heights."⁴² If there had been no slave at the president's side that day, what exactly *had* happened, and why had there been so much anger? Were those who railed against Tyler's actions merely capitalizing on what "would have been"? Did a slave's illness keep him from serving not only as an aide to his master, but also as an abolitionist icon? As the slave fades out of the picture, we're left with an umbrella hovering in midair. Did the mayor take hold of it, as he had in the carriage in the rain the day before? Did the president carry his own parasol? Did Tyler, Southerner that he was, just put up with the glare and heat of a summer afternoon? Or does the umbrella itself disappear into our muddle of minor facts and misperceptions about the past—hardly worth the vitriol it at least temporarily provoked?

The possibility that the president had a slave at his side on June 17 was so horrifying that some antislavery folk reported it almost with glee. Evelina Smith wrote to Caroline Weston from Hingham:

> Events are daily occurring both to arouse and encourage Abolitionists. The financial state of our country, the glaring inconsistances which the pro-slavery party must find themselves in every day, the strike, which the people are making in Ireland in England & many other places for more freedom, all must have an effect upon the emancipation of the slave. Think of the absurdities committed in Boston on the 17. The President insulting us by bringing a slave here at this late day, and more when he came professedly to worship at the shrine of freedom. Think of the great Webster being crippled in his speech by a knowledge of the state of things here and at the South. He was evidently crippled, I think, for his speech was a poor affair. How long will these men submit to such things for their own sakes, if they care nothing for the slave.

Smith put the small "absurdities" of Tyler's slaveholding and Webster's speech in an almost apocalyptic context. Against the spreading of emancipation on the world stage, the gaffes of these two politicians, both colluders with the slave power, revealed that the despicable institution of American slavery could not stand much longer. As one abolitionist writer warned on the eve of Bunker Hill Day, the Lord was asking, "Shall not my soul be avenged on such a nation as this?" In June of 1843, many Americans, of various political and religious stripes, could see apocalypse just around the corner. Those of a Millerite bent would be disappointed when the world would not end later that year, as they had first predicted, nor the next, as they revised. But if the day of judgment was slow in coming, something had changed in the last decade or two, and that something made a man with an umbrella a powerful symbol of the changes that still needed to take place.⁴³

Was he only that—a symbol, a figment of antislavery imagination? As it turns out, there *was* a black man at Tyler's side on Bunker Hill Day, though contrary to many press reports, he was not a slave. In a private letter to her sisters, Anne Weston explained whom all those infuriated abolitionists had seen at the monument dedication on June 17:

> Tyler's black servant (a free man & Virginian) came to the Liberator office & saw Garrison. He seemed an intelligent man & said he had read the Liberator for several years. He had 7 copies of the Address to the slaves given him. He says the man who entered Boston behind the President's carriage was a slave, not owned by Tyler but hired of somebody. He has beside two free black servants, our informant & another. The other accompanied him to Bunker hill & carried the parasol over his head. So you see they did not actually venture to take a slave on to Bunker Hill. You may state these facts, but not our informant's authority as his visit to the Liberator Office is private.[44]

Given the context, Weston's account of Tyler's attendants makes sense. Beyond the public relations problems associated with bringing a slave to Bunker Hill, taking a slave to Boston would have been foolhardy in the wake of the Latimer fugitive slave case. Indeed, the hired slave who accompanied Tyler's carriage into the city had apparently been promised his freedom after the trip as an inducement not to run away. When a black abolitionist tried to convince the man to abscond in Boston, he explained that family ties compelled him to return to Virginia.[45]

For whatever reason, the presence of this man who trailed the president's carriage—and who actually was a slave—did not attract much public attention. It is understandable that abolitionists thought the free servant with the umbrella was in bondage, given that Tyler was widely known as a slave owner. Reading the *Liberator* today, one gets the feeling that abolitionists almost wanted a slave to be on Bunker Hill that day, in order to underscore everything they already believed about the hypocrisy of the president and the commemoration as a whole. In that sense, the man with the umbrella wasn't an individual person at all, but a symbol of something larger, as loud in his silence as the Bunker Hill Monument itself.

What did this man represent? In the immediate aftermath of the Revolution, John Trumbull had painted a black presence on Bunker Hill. In those early years of the republic, it was easy enough to accept that the black man in Trumbull's canvas was a white man's servant. Not until the 1820s, when new questions about who counted in American history emerged, and the 1830s, when the abolitionist movement developed in full force, did people of color take on anything more than supporting roles in popular historical memories of the Revolution. The story that a black man had shot Major Pitcairn finally emerged in print in 1825.[46] In the ensuing years, black men on and near Bunker Hill became incrementally more visible, whether they were sneaking away to freedom in the shadow of the new monument or standing at the president's side at commemorative ceremonies. Their presence was a noticeable challenge to the narrative that the Bunker Hill Monument was built to honor, about a nation forever united and a liberty irrevocably won.

The historical critique that abolitionists launched against the Bunker Hill commemorations was not a wholesale refutation of the Revolution. Garrison recognized the symbolic power of Boston's historical landscape in the very first issue of the *Liberator*. He exalted to "lift up the standard of emancipation in the eyes of the nation, within sight of Bunker Hill and in the birth place of liberty."[47] Garrison embraced the Revolutionaries' language, approvingly quoting long passages from Jefferson in his "Address to the Slaves." If such praises for the founders smacked of opportunism—Jefferson was excoriated for his slaveholding in other issues of the *Liberator*—so be it.[48] Boston abolitionists frequently held up Warren as one of their precursors in the struggle for liberty, without mentioning (perhaps because they were not aware) that the martyr of Bunker Hill had been a slave owner.[49] The clash at Bunker Hill in 1843 was not about anything so simple as whether or not it was worth remembering the Revolution at all. Instead, the contest was between two distinct ways of understanding the past in relation to the present and future. Should the present generation build a monument to history, fixing its meaning for all time and all comers? Or should the past animate the present, pushing the living to revitalize the ideals of the dead?

In a long and merciless critique published in the *Liberator*, one abolitionist excoriated Webster's address of 1843 as "too purely historical for such an occasion." Instead, this writer sought "not merely a retrospect of the past, but a sober, careful, faithful survey of the present condition of the country; not only a picture of what had been achieved by revolutionary valor and self-sacrifice, but a description of what remained to be done by other and higher instrumentalities." Both this writer and Daniel Webster shared the sense, inherited from their Revolutionary forebears, that it required careful vigilance to keep a republic strong. In the abolitionist's view, however, Webster's deep admiration for the past failed to distinguish the parochialism and myopia of the Revolutionaries from those aspects of their ideology and action that were truly emancipatory. As a result, Webster couldn't see what was right in front of him: "another struggle, mightier than of old, for the emancipation of three millions of people from servile chains, is going on in the land ... It is a struggle to secure to all the full enjoyment of those rights, which the patriots of 1776 fought and bled in vain to establish; not limited by any geographical boundaries, nor actuated by any local considerations." For abolitionists, Webster's efforts on Bunker Hill to extol the universality of American freedom and patriotism were meaningless when they could see a slave's umbrella hovering just a few feet away.[50]

THINKING THE UNTHINKABLE

On June 17, 1843, the most visible black man on Bunker Hill stood tall and still, like the monument, keeping the president in the shade. Anne Weston's letter introduces us to this man's companion, who found his way to the *Liberator*. The first man's presence sparked coverage from the press and commentary from ordinary people; the second man's activity had to be kept secret. Still, in some small way—in the information this free black man exchanged with abolitionists, in the messages of hope he brought back to Virginia, in his self-assured movement through a city caught in the frenzy of commemoration—surely he too was making history. He was certainly answering a call that had gone forth from Boston to the port cities of the Atlantic seaboard, and then farther yet into the plantation South, some fourteen years earlier. David Walker's *Appeal... to the Coloured Citizens of the World* (1829) had set out another argument about fulfilling the Revolution. Like Garrison, Walker called for movement, rather than fixing and revering the past in the form of a monument. What distinguished Walker was that well before Garrison authored his "Address to the Slaves"—indeed, before Garrison had even initiated his campaign to change the hearts and minds of (white) Northerners—Walker spoke directly to people of color throughout the nation to demand that they act in their own behalf. Ultimately, Walker's ideas are significant to the controversy surrounding the Bunker Hill dedication because they are a measure of what wasn't said in 1843, either in the ceremonies themselves or in the Garrisonian press.[51]

Though he spent his early life in the Carolinas, by 1825 Walker had settled in Boston, where he quickly established himself in the black community's rich organizational life. He enrolled in the African Lodge of Masons, helped to found the Massachusetts General Colored Association, and joined the May Street Church, then under the charismatic black minister Samuel Snowden. While his work in religious, fraternal, and antislavery circles made him a respected figure among Boston's people of color, it was with the publication of the *Appeal* that Walker became known (if not always respected) on a much wider scale. Directed "to the Coloured Citizens of the World, but in Particular, and Very Expressly, to Those of the United States of America," Walker's *Appeal* is often read as a call to violent slave rebellion (fearful whites both North and South certainly interpreted it as such in the nineteenth century). But as Peter Hinks, Walker's biographer and exegete, observes, "The biggest problem Walker addressed was the one of the individual psyche: how to transform the consciousness of individual blacks mired in the paradox of powerlessness amid power into personalities unified around an awareness of their own strength, integrity, and freedom."[52]

It was in revising Jefferson's *Notes on the State of Virginia* that Walker most clearly articulated his belief that black, as well as white, Americans had to change their behavior in order to bring an end to slavery:

> When I reflect that God is just, and that millions of my wretched brethren would meet death with glory—yea, more, would plunge into the very mouths of cannons and be torn into particles as minute as the atoms which compose the elements of the earth, in preference to a mean submission to the lash of tyrants, I am with streaming eyes, compelled to shrink back into nothingness before my Maker, and exclaim again, thy will be done, O Lord God Almighty.

The beginning of this passage echoed Jefferson's prophecy that American slavery would eventually occasion divine judgment: "I tremble for my country when I reflect that God is just: that his justice cannot sleep for ever." Jefferson's rumination on a "revolution of the wheel of fortune" was vague on the role of human agency in bringing about this change. It was clear to him that "supernatural interference" would play a role in abolition. In contrast, an emancipation initiated by slaves was "unthinkable history," both in the sense that he did not want to contemplate what such a revolution would entail and that he could not imagine that blacks were capable of instigating such "an exchange of situation." In revising Jefferson, Walker turned quickly from the assurance of God's justice to the equally important acknowledgment of black agency and resolve. It was indeed God's will that all men be free, but it was only through the self-sacrifice and self-assertion of "colored citizens" themselves that God's will would be done.[53]

Walker's engagement with the Jeffersonian text proved him well-versed in American political discourse. Even as he concerned himself with the condition of people of African descent across time and space, Walker saw himself as an American. In the longest chapter of the *Appeal*, a devastating critique of colonizationism, he insisted, "This country is as much ours as it is the whites, whether they will admit it now or not, they will see and believe it by and by." A few pages later, Walker corrected himself: "America is more our country, than it is the whites—we have enriched it with our *blood and tears*." We can read Walker's *Appeal* as a response to the vision of the American past and future propagated by Daniel Webster and his ilk. Walker's allusion to "blood and tears" called into question the idea that to be American was to enjoy a fortune "happily cast," as Webster put it in his first Bunker Hill address. For Walker, American history offered not a legacy to be preserved but a promise to be redeemed. Black people's historical investment in the United States— even if it had been unwilling, even if it had cost individuals their dignity, their happiness, and their very lives—meant that they should count as Americans. Indeed, their sufferings only made it all the more important that they stay in the country to claim their due. In this respect also, Walker was responding to the politics of Webster and other New England Whigs involved in the American Colonization Society, which aimed to settle freed slaves in Africa, thereby (in the view of Walker and other anticolonizationist abolitionists) skirting the problems of racism and inequality within the United States.[54]

It is little surprise that a militant black voice like Walker would be at odds with the political and commemorative priorities of a leading New England conservative like Webster. But how should we read Walker's *Appeal* alongside the Garrisonian critique of Webster and Tyler that emerged around the dedication of the Bunker Hill Monument? The comparison is tricky, because unlike the Boston-based abolitionists of the 1830s and 40s, Walker did not draw on local historical memory. His upbringing in the South and relatively short time in Boston supplied him with a cultural vocabulary distinct from that of people immersed in the significance of Bunker Hill, Faneuil Hall, Lexington and Concord. Furthermore, Walker died in 1830, so he never witnessed the publication of the *Liberator*, the proliferation of antislavery societies and abolitionist factionalism, the Latimer case, or the completion of the Bunker Hill Monument. Still, in the years after his death, the *Appeal* remained an inspiration to black activists, some of whom (like Walker's Boston friend Maria Stewart) perpetuated in their own writings and speeches Walker's ideas about the necessity for blacks to act in their own behalf.[55]

Neither in 1843, when they criticized the Monument dedication, nor in 1842, when they rallied with their Liberty Party rivals to secure the freedom of George Latimer, did Garrison and his followers say much about blacks (especially enslaved blacks) as historical actors. The Revolutionary discourse of the Latimer crusade, both in the Garrisonian *Liberator* and the Libertyite *Latimer Journal and North Star*, was aimed primarily at getting a predominantly white public to act in the liberty-loving spirit of their ancestors, the likes of John Adams and Elbridge Gerry. "Boston boys, Boston boys, rescue the slave!" could have been intended as a call to action for free Bostonians both black and white, but undoubtedly many listeners attached implicit racial labels to the subject and object of this refrain: it was Boston's *white* boys who would rescue the subjugated *black* slaves. This racialization of agent and victim reflected a broader chauvinism on the part of white abolitionism, as well as the particular priorities associated with Garrison's moral suasion approach. Coming out of a Christian perfectionist world view, Garrisonians privileged the purification of the individual soul, the conversion of individual hearts and minds against slavery and other worldly corruptions, over the practical result of abolition. "If we never free a slave, we have at least freed ourselves in the effort to emancipate our brother man," explained white abolitionist Wendell Phillips.[56]

Historians Jane Pease and William Pease have drawn on remarks like Phillips's, and the understandably dim view that many black abolitionists took toward such an attitude, to argue that there were effectively "two abolitionisms" in the antebellum United States, one white and one black. Whites, drawing on the Revolutionary history that "was their goodly heritage and present reality," were positioned to perceive "slavery and freedom as polar absolutes." Meanwhile, blacks, who even if legally free experienced daily the compromised status that came with color, instead understood slavery and freedom as "terminal points on a continuous spectrum."[57] Surely this interpretation is overdrawn: there were more than two abolitionisms in nineteenth-century America, and the lines dividing the different ideologies and factions were hardly strictly black and white. Yet there is something to the argument that people of color, who experienced firsthand the slavery of the South or the limited freedom of the antebellum North, perceived more acutely a need for direct action against slavery.

The "Address to the Slaves" distributed during the Bunker Hill celebration of 1843 evidenced Garrison's preference that the cry for emancipation be raised by northern abolitionists, not southern slaves. Much of his address detailed the work of the slaves' "warm, faithful, sympathizing, devoted friends"—those who "call themselves abolitionists"—who were tirelessly endangering their own lives and fortunes for the good of the slaves. Conversely, those Northerners who refused to join the antislavery camp, who committed themselves instead to a compromised Constitution and Union, were those most responsible for keeping the American balance of power far south of the Mason-Dixon line. "It is solely by the aid of the people in the North, that you are held in bondage," Garrison preached to the slaves, promising to reform northern attitudes through "appeals, warnings, rebukes, arguments and facts, addressed to the understandings, consciences and hearts of the people." He counseled slaves "to be patient, long-suffering and submissive...trusting that, by the blessing of the Most High...you will yet be emancipated without shedding a drop of your master's blood, or losing a drop of your own." Garrison did acknowledge that thousands of slaves had taken their fate into their own hands by escaping north, and he noted that abolitionists were prepared to help runaways in any way they could. But he also cautioned that the way was dangerous for fugitives. Moreover, the risks of violent resistance were too great to be tested: "Every attempt at insurrection would be attended with disaster and defeat, on your part, because you are not strong enough to contend with the military power of the nation."[58]

In mid-August of 1843, two months after the Bunker Hill celebration in Boston, Henry Highland Garnet issued his own "Address to the Slaves" at a gathering of black activists in Buffalo, New York. The militancy of his address made it controversial even before an all-black audience. Garnet's first priority, as Walker's had been fourteen years earlier, was to break down the psychological inertia that slavery created in those it subjugated. While Garrison was convinced that northern complicity kept slavery thriving, Garnet argued that slaves themselves maintained the institution by submitting to it: "Brethren, the time has come when you must act for yourselves.... You can plead your own cause, and do the work of emancipation better than any others." The closest Garnet came to offering a concrete proposal for how blacks could accomplish the "work of emancipation" amounted to a labor strike, a decision of the three million slaves to "cease to labor for tyrants who will not remunerate you," even if such refusal meant almost certain death. While Garnet preached "RESISTANCE! RESISTANCE! RESISTANCE!" in no uncertain terms, he hedged on calling directly for violence, cautioning that "a revolution with the sword...would be INEXPEDIENT." If the political exigencies of the early 1840s stopped Garnet short of openly calling for a violent uprising, the people he mentioned near the end of his address—Denmark Vesey, Nat Turner, and Joseph Cinque, the leader of the *Amistad* revolt—confirmed his admiration for those who struck at the beating heart of the slave power.[59]

No one talked about Vesey, Turner, or Cinque amid the Bunker Hill furor of the summer of 1843. Nor did they say much about the armed black men who had fought in the cause of American liberty, such as Crispus Attucks or Peter Salem. Instead, when a black man appeared on Bunker Hill in the 1840s, he held an umbrella, not a gun. In doing so, he symbolized how the institution of slavery threatened to corrupt the freest ground in America, not how people of color could themselves rid the nation of that corruption. But in their effort to save George Latimer from captivity in 1842 and their vitriol against the celebrations of June 17, 1843, abolitionists presented a critique of the concept of history that Webster and his cohort were trying to construct on Bunker Hill. If the monument-builders privileged the idea of history as a received narrative, abolitionists perceived history as a story that was still being written—indeed, that they, through their activism, were in the process of writing. As a broader range of actor-narrators became ever more assertive, both the story and the process would become more complicated yet.

One of the actor-narrators in Boston's black community was a historian and activist named William Cooper Nell. By 1848, the thirty-one-year-old Nell had already devoted half his life to abolitionism and civil rights advocacy when he wrote a forward-looking editorial in Frederick Douglass's newspaper, the *North Star*, under the headline "The Morning Dawns!" The cadences of Nell's opening lines perfectly captured the mood of the day: "The times are revolutionary: society is progressing; the theme is freedom for all, the problem for nations to solve is, How shall Republics become truly free?" Nell's vision was portentous but hopeful. "The struggle between freedom's allies and freedom's foes, is now waxing warm on American soil," he warned. Then he sketched out the stark differences between the two parties in the coming battle:

> The Conservative fails to appreciate the truth stamped on every page of history, that reforms once begun among an injured but determined people, have never retrograded; and taking counsel of his fears, instead of his hopes, holds himself aloof from the labors of those who are actively engaged in the elevation of the weak... while on the contrary, the Reformer, animating his courage by a glance at the past, his heart encouraged by such a constellation of glorious examples, yields obedience to that inspiration.

Nell wondered how his contemporaries would read "the truth stamped on every page of history." Would they be guided by their fears or their hopes? Would "a glance at the past" inspire progress, or leave the viewer "satisfied with things as they are"? With his labels of Reformer and Conservative, Nell put an ideological spin on the difference between movements and monuments.[60]

In this contest, Nell opted for movement, for a history that animated courage and pushed reform relentlessly forward. Inverting what he claimed to be the "Conservative" approach, he chose hope over fear. And so did his allies, who in ways both minute and grandiose, at times carefully recorded and at others nearly imperceptible, kept abolitionism in motion for decades. It was hope, ultimately, that spoke louder than anger in Walker's *Appeal*, which told Americans of color that their country could still be theirs, despite the abject misery of their present situation. It was hope, in spite of fear, that propelled George and Rebecca Latimer from Norfolk to Boston in 1842. The next year, hope motivated a black servant to sneak away from the presidential entourage to visit Garrison. And it was hope that kept abolitionists talking about the American Revolution even when many feared that the ideals of the Declaration of Independence and the Massachusetts constitution might never be fulfilled, not even on their own hallowed soil.

Hope also caused William Cooper Nell to reinvigorate a name that had once struck fear into the hearts of white Bostonians. His 1848 editorial marked the first time that Nell mentioned Crispus Attucks in print: "The page of impartial history bears testimony to the fact that the first martyr in the American Revolution was a colored man by the name of Attucks, who fell in King street, Boston." Nell's writing moved effortlessly back and forth from this kind of historical detail to calls for revolutionary action. For him, memory and aspiration were perfectly intertwined. Nell is best known today as the man who literally wrote the book on blacks in the Revolutionary War (*The Colored Patriots of the American Revolution*, published in 1855). His efforts in the 1850s would generate memories of Attucks as a Revolutionary martyr and militant. In the 1830s and 40s, however, this kind of public representation of black agency was overshadowed by appeals to a generic (white) sense of Yankeedom. Black activists were asserting themselves in the streets and in the press, but in the shadow of Bunker Hill, the black man was a slave, a victim, a symbol. Yankee culture confined the memory of individual New Englanders of color to other kinds of spaces, more private and less explosive than the Revolutionary battlefield.

4

Tea and Memory

The table is elegant and practical without being obtrusive. Its top unfolds to create a larger surface, while a compact drawer keeps cards or game pieces out of the way below. Its trimmings are few but carefully sculpted. Confident curves arch across the apron front. Four graceful cabriole legs, almost impossibly long, extend toward four bony claws, each gripping a ball of mahogany. The table appears to be a typical piece of high-end eighteenth-century furniture, but neither its representative Chippendale features nor its likely manufacture by a Charlestown cabinetmaker is what earned it a proud spot in a display room at the Massachusetts Historical Society. Instead, what distinguishes this piece—what might well have caused its succession of owners to preserve it with care over the course of more than two centuries—is its association with the most famous woman of color in Bay State history, Phillis Wheatley.

Family lore recorded in 1992 claims that a relative of General Israel Putnam purchased the table after Wheatley's death, when her property was sold to pay her debts. The table then passed down to succeeding generations of Putnam's female descendants.[1] Though there is no documentation that connects the table to Wheatley, the Massachusetts Historical Society now identifies it as her writing desk. Perhaps the label was inspired by the graceful—though differently shaped—table at which Wheatley is seated, pen poised, in the frontispiece portrait from her *Poems on Various Subjects*. In any case, the air of mystery associated with this object is fitting. Most of what we know about Wheatley's life comes from a few well-rehearsed facts and the embellishments of historical memory. Nevertheless, it is worth noting that the facts were continually rehearsed and the memories freely embellished, for unlike Crispus Attucks, Wheatley was never a forgotten figure. Her literary production and her fame as a prodigy out of Africa ensured that activists, writers, and thinkers would continue to wonder over her, offering her up as an example of the intellectual potential of people of color or deriding her accomplishments as slavish imitation of true art. Especially after her biography was published in Boston in 1834 (a full fifty years after

Phillis Wheatley's writing desk. Mahogany folding tea table
attributed to Benjamin Frothingham, Jr., Charlestown,
Massachusetts, circa 1760. *Courtesy of the Massachusetts
Historical Society*

her death), Wheatley came to signify something else: the possibilities and
limitations of free black respectability in the new republic. The author of
this detailed memoir of the poet's life was Margaretta Matilda Odell, a collateral descendant of Wheatley's mistress. Like the table, the memoir bespoke
a woman of a certain refinement and a careful restraint.[2]

The table and the memoir represent the efforts of white New Englanders
to lay claim to the memory of a woman of color. Phillis Wheatley is only the
best known of a number of respectable black Bay Staters whose legacies were
appropriated by white people, including neighbors, friends, employers, and,
most strikingly of all, former masters and their relatives. Especially preva-
lent in the second quarter of the nineteenth century, white-authored memoirs, obituaries, and anecdotes of freedpeople engaged white Bay Staters'
nostalgia for the "deference politics" of a previous generation. Men and
women of color in late eighteenth- and early nineteenth-century
Massachusetts had forged social and economic connections to well-placed
whites, manifested in the political sphere in the black electorate's support
for the Federalist party. This alliance created a patronage system that gave

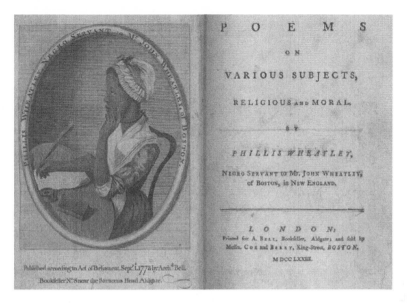

Title page and frontispiece from Phillis Wheatley, *Poems on Various Subjects, Religious and Moral*. London: printed for A. Bell, 1773. *Courtesy of the Massachusetts Historical Society*

free people of color access to jobs and social protection, while it confirmed the Federalist elite's sense of organic social order. That order broke down as the regional and national political economy transformed with industrialization and territorial expansion.[3]

When nineteenth-century white writers reminisced about former slaves, they perceived in this first generation of free black Bay Staters a model for black agency and respectability that accommodated racial hierarchy to the ideals of the Revolution. There was a gender dimension to these representations of black agency, which emphasized humility and deference (traits associated with femininity) as desirable for both women and men of color. These representations also downplayed social connections among people of color, thereby minimizing the significance of their activity within domains not controlled or influenced by whites. Whereas contemporary black reformers perceived respectability as an aspirational politics—elevating the status of people of color by adhering to rigorous standards of personal conduct—many white writers contained the possibilities of "uplift" by representing conformity to racial etiquette as compatible with and even necessary to black respectability.[4]

Memories of individual people of color emancipated in Massachusetts constitute an important counterpoint to the historical sensibility created and perpetuated at Bunker Hill and the Commonwealth's other revered sites of the Revolution. In these public spaces of national significance and local pride, historical memory positioned slavery and inequality as foreign to Bay State soil. The biographies of former slaves disrupted that myth by placing people of color in the spaces of everyday New England life. It is therefore fitting that memories of Phillis Wheatley should be made material in a table. The taking of tea around such a piece of elegant furniture was one of the most important rituals of eighteenth-century sociability and refinement, especially among women.[5] More generally, the sharing of a meal is a marker of common esteem among all participants. While Bunker Hill was the focal space of the last chapter, this chapter centers on the more private spaces of sociability where the meanings of respectability and community were negotiated and performed. The memory of those enactments prompted Bay Staters to contemplate who had a place at the table, and on whose terms.

Bay Staters of color who lived through the Revolutionary period made slavery history in the most immediate way possible: through their own lives. By their productive labor and acquisition of property, and by forging social ties on their own terms, these individuals challenged the economic exploitation and social alienation of enslavement. The respectable lives of freed people including Phillis Wheatley, Chloe Spear, Primus Hall, and Elizabeth Freeman attracted the notice of white writers, who recorded posthumous memoirs and anecdotes about them in the early to mid-nineteenth century. Only by reading these sources against the grain or alongside very different source material can we catch glimpses of how these respectable Bay Staters might have challenged the racial status quo. Fully accounting for the possibilities and limitations of their historical agency requires considering not only what these freed people did in their own time but also how their lives were represented after the fact. In other words, the ways in which free blacks such as Wheatley, Spear, Hall, and Freeman made history were constrained by the ways in which others made history out of them.

REMEMBERING PHILLIS WHEATLEY

Phillis Wheatley had secured a public name and persona well before her death. While still a slave to John and Susanna Wheatley, the young woman first found her way into print in 1767, when her poem on the shipwreck of two Nantucket merchants appeared in the *Newport Mercury*. Though her proposal for a volume of poetry failed to attract Boston subscribers in 1772, she printed poems in several broadsides and newspapers before leaving Boston for England in May 1773. This second transatlantic voyage of her brief life was intended to enable the sickly young woman to recover her health, as well as to forge ties with the Countess of Huntingdon and other evangelical Britons interested in her work and her extraordinary story.[6]

The trip to England was undoubtedly a high point in Wheatley's life, both in terms of her literary career and her personal circumstances. After securing English patronage and reshaping her proposed volume to suit British tastes, she arranged for the book's publication. Wheatley might have profited from her trip in another way as well. The recent *Somerset* decision, which freed an American slave taken to England by his master, convinced many contemporaries on either side of the Atlantic that slavery was abolished in England. Wheatley might have used the assumption that stepping on English soil freed a slave as leverage to get her master to emancipate her in exchange for returning to his household.[7] In any event, not long after Phillis arrived in England, John Wheatley wrote to say that she was needed back in Boston, where her mistress was languishing from disease. Phillis cut her travels short so she could tend to Susanna, whom she saw as a mother figure. A few months after returning to Boston—probably at some point in the fall of 1773—Phillis finally secured her legal emancipation, at around the same time that *Poems on Various Subjects, Religious and Moral* came off the presses in London. Several months later, the first copies of the book arrived in the colonies.

Even with a well-received book and the indignities of slavery behind her, Wheatley found her publishing career faltering after 1773. She published four more poems in magazines and two as broadsides, but her two proposals to publish new volumes of poetry (under her married name, Phillis Peters) failed to attract sufficient subscribers.[8] The perusal of poetry, even the works of a "rara avis in terra" (as the 1779 proposal described Wheatley), was not a priority while the colonies first prosecuted and then recovered from a war. It seems clear that the war years hit Wheatley hard, though most accounts of the poet's life in this period come not from contemporary documents but from anecdotes recorded decades later, many of them handed down by relatives of John and Susanna Wheatley. John, Susanna, and their children Nathaniel and Mary (the latter a close friend and teacher of Phillis) all died between 1774 and 1783. Other friends died or fled to England during the war. Married in 1778, Phillis sought to create a family of her own, but life in freedom was not always easy. The Wheatleys' friends and relatives did not think highly of John Peters, Phillis's husband. Peters himself is an enigmatic figure. Remembered in the nineteenth century by the sobriquet "Doctor Peter," he is said to have been a grocer, a businessman, and a lawyer with aspirations bigger than his talents or means. None of his professional ventures was especially lucrative, and he had a hard time providing for his young family.[9]

For her part, Wheatley's upbringing as the favored foster child of an elite Boston family did not prepare her for the household responsibilities of a wife and mother. Abandoned by her husband and mourning the death of her

children, she died alone in December 1784. At least, so go the accounts of
Wheatley's final years that circulated in the nineteenth century. These stories
of the least-documented period in Wheatley's American life tell more about
the anxieties of a later era than the priorities and experiences of the woman
herself. From the evidence that does survive, it is clear that Wheatley did not
die in total obscurity, as some of her later memoirists would suggest. Her
death was acknowledged in Boston newspapers in a notice that singled out
her literary status rather than her race: "Last Lord's day died, Phillis Peters,
formerly Phillis Wheatly, known to the literary world by her celebrated miscellaneous Poems." The notice invited readers to her funeral. Her death was
also mourned in a fifty-three-line anonymous elegy in the *Boston Magazine*.
From the time of Wheatley's death through 1820, *Poems on Various Subjects*
went through at least nine printings in North America. Some publishers
clearly saw her race as the most salient feature of Wheatley's work. In 1801,
a Philadelphia publisher appended Wheatley's book to a translation of
Frenchman Joseph Lavallée's antislavery novel, *The Negro Equalled by Few
Europeans*, turning the poems into a kind of affirmation of Lavallée's title.
In Halifax, Nova Scotia, in 1814, another printer packaged *Poems on Various
Subjects* with the autobiography of former slave Olaudah Equiano.[10]

The circulation of her own writing constituted only one dimension of
Wheatley's posthumous life. Eighteenth- and nineteenth-century writers and
thinkers wondered over her as a prodigy, celebrity, and curiosity: an African
slave girl who wrote poems. The memory of Phillis Wheatley provided fodder
both to the transatlantic antislavery movement of the revolutionary age and
to those who sought to articulate a new science of human difference. The
best-known example of the latter was Thomas Jefferson, who famously dismissed Wheatley's poetry in his ruminations on the mental inferiority of
blacks. Many critics of slavery and the slave trade would decry Jefferson's
mockery of Wheatley's genius. Perhaps the most influential indictment of
Jefferson came from a French priest, the Abbé Henri-Baptiste Grégoire.[11]

A member of both the Société des Amis des Noirs (France's organization
devoted to abolishing the slave trade) and the Estates-General, the republican Grégoire actively supported the Haitian Revolution. In fact, some
planters accused him of inspiring the Saint-Domingue uprising in 1791.
Having already written several pamphlets on the rights of Jews and people of
color, Grégoire confirmed his commitment to equality with the publication
of *De la littérature des nègres, ou Recherches sur leurs facultés intellectuelles,
leurs qualités morales et leur littérature* in 1808. Those included with Wheatley
in the chapter on literature included Benjamin Banneker, Gustavus Vassa
(Olaudah Equiano), and Ignatius Sancho, as well as lesser-known figures
such as Antony William Amo, a native of Guinea who studied philosophy
and medicine at Wittenberg, and Thomas Fuller, an African-born Virginian

renowned for his ability to do mental calculations. Some permutation of this cast of characters, plus a few dozen others, appeared repeatedly in the literature of the anti-slave trade movement, and subsequently in the writings of antebellum abolitionists and black historians and ethnologists. These writers frequently copied from their predecessors, with Grégoire's book becoming one of the most commonly used sources for American opponents of slavery after it was translated into English as *An Enquiry Concerning the Intellectual and Moral Faculties, and Literature of Negroes*, first published in Philadelphia in 1810.[12]

Grégoire suggested that Phillis's literary success owed not only to her innate talent but also to her refined character and the generosity of the Wheatleys: "Of amiable manners, exquisite sensibility, and premature talents, she was so cherished by the family, that they not only freed her from those painful labours reserved for slaves, but also from the cares of the household." After describing her sale to the Wheatleys, her rapid acquisition of English and Latin, and her publication of *Poems on Various Subjects*, Grégoire added:

> She married a man of colour, who, in the superiority of his understanding, to that of other negroes, was also a kind of phenomenon. We are no less surprised to see her husband a grocer, become a lawyer, under the name of Doctor Peter, and plead before tribunals the cause of blacks. The reputation he enjoyed procured him a fortune. The sentimental Phillis, who…was brought up as a spoiled child, knew nothing of domestic affairs, and her husband proposed that she should learn the household art. He began with reproaches, which were followed by a harshness, the continuance of which afflicted her so much, that in 1780 she died of a broken heart.

It is not clear how the Abbé pieced together this brief biography, the first published account of Wheatley's life after freedom. He footnoted the above passage with a letter written in 1805 by Marc-Antoine Alexis Giraud. Based in Boston, Giraud was the French Republic's Commissary of Commercial Relations for most of New England. Was his account of the last years of Wheatley's life taken from oral histories then circulating in Boston? That Giraud—and by extension Grégoire—might have drawn on oral culture (as opposed to written records) is evidenced by the many dates that the sketch gets wrong. Someone with access to written documents could easily have verified that Wheatley died in 1784, not 1780.[13]

If Giraud did collect memories of Phillis Wheatley from contemporary Bostonians, relatives of John and Susanna Wheatley might have been his informants. Though written evidence dating to the early nineteenth century is thin, later collateral descendants of Phillis's mistress clearly relished their family's connection to this famed young woman. In 1866, Charles J. Stratford, then living in Wisconsin, wrote down the stories his mother had told him about a "Female African" who lived with her great-aunt, Susanna Wheatley. Stratford's mother, Lucy, was the sister of Thomas Wallcut, who penned an admiring and schoolboyish letter to Phillis Wheatley in 1774 while he was serving as a young missionary to Indians outside of Montreal. ("What I write will hardly bear reading," sixteen-year-old Wallcut admitted—rightly—to the poet, before signing himself "your Sincere & Obliged Friend.") Later, Wallcut returned to Boston to become perhaps the most eccentric and least affluent founding member of the Massachusetts Historical Society. Thomas and Lucy Wallcut's mother, Elizabeth, was, like her aunt Susanna Wheatley, devoted to Christian evangelism. Phillis Wheatley Peters probably left her manuscripts with Elizabeth when the Peters family briefly moved to Wilmington, Massachusetts in the early 1780s. Whether out of their commitment to his-torical preservation, religious causes, or antislavery, or a simple fascination with Phillis's rise-and-fall career, the network of Wheatley relations enjoyed keeping alive the memory of this adopted member of their clan.[14]

But it was in 1834, with the Boston publication of the first full-length biog-raphy of her, that Wheatley emerged as a historical character, someone whose life story was significant even apart from her poetic production or her status as either prodigy or freak. Through her *Memoir of Phillis Wheatley*, Margaretta Matilda Odell, a relative of Susanna Wheatley (probably her great-grand-niece), brought the Wheatley family's orally transmitted mem-ories of the poet to an audience beyond local circles. The text indicates that the author's informants were Susanna's female descendants, including her granddaughter and grand-nieces, as well as the author's own grandmother (who was probably Susanna's niece).[15]

Little is known about Odell, who died in 1881. She seems never to have published anything else, and she never married. Whatever aspirations Odell might have had for a career or life of her own were curtailed in 1847, when her uncle had her declared legally insane. She spent the rest of her life in the homes of various family members and guardians. Only the memoir itself reveals anything about her motivations for writing it. Near its close, Odell expressed a fear that Wheatley would be forgotten, asking, "may not this lit-tle record…perpetuate her name?" She also briefly invoked the poet's example as a counter-argument to slavery. "Friends of liberty! Friends of humanity!" she begged, "when will ye appoint a jubilee for the African, and let the oppressed go free?" It probably was the recent proliferation of aboli-tionist organizations and publications that encouraged George W. Light to print Odell's narrative in 1834. The book was reviewed, excerpted, and adver-tised in the *Liberator*. Light packaged Odell's (unsigned) memoir with a reprint of Wheatley's *Poems on Various Subjects* and prefaced the entire volume with a four-page anonymous introduction. The writer of this introduction set Wheatley's memory in a clear antislavery context, noting approvingly "that spirit of the present time which manifestly is moving abroad on the face of society, for the amelioration of the condition, and the developement [sic] of the capacity, of the African, of every class."[16]

Nevertheless, even as the memoir was marketed for an antislavery audience, the desire to abolish slavery seems not to have been Odell's primary motivation in writing it. Even as she condemned the persistence of slavery in the American South, Odell could be evasive about describing the institution in the North and assigning responsibility to those who had perpetuated it there—including, of course, her own relatives. "Had Phillis fallen into less generous and affectionate hands, she would speedily have perished under the privations and exertions of common servitude," Odell observed, the verb "fallen" obscuring that it was an economic transaction, and not a stroke of serendipity, that landed the young girl in the Wheatley home. Like other descendants of Susanna Wheatley, Odell expressed great admiration for the "excellence" of this family matriarch, who is nearly as much the heroine of the memoir as Phillis herself. By law, the Wheatleys owned Phillis, but "the chains which bound her to her master and mistress were the golden links of love, and the silken bands of gratitude." Odell speculated that her readers would wonder why "Phillis has not borne a more decided testimony to the kindness" of her mistress. She explained that Susanna was a woman of such piety and humility that she would have destroyed any poems devoted to her and that she specifically asked Phillis (who was well known for her elegies) not to write anything upon her death. That Phillis never gave Susanna all the praise she deserved proved what a worthy person Odell's great-great-aunt had been.[17]

While antislavery sentiment afforded a few lines in the memoir, and filiopiety a few more, the narrative of most interest to Odell was a cultural nationalist one. She brought a gendered slant to her description of the flourishing of arts and letters in the early republic, as the nation pulled itself out of the cultural wasteland of the colonial era. Odell deplored "the days of Phillis" as a period when "the great mass of American females could boast of few accomplishments save housewifery." Unlike their counterparts in Britain and France, where even women stood in the "wide-spreading beams" of the Enlightenment, colonial Americans "had no philosophers, no historians, no poets." That changed when the "spirit of Liberty," set in motion by God and urged on by wise and brave American statesmen, "breathed upon our sleeping nation, awakening the genius of the people to appear...in a thousand new and multiplying forms of ever-varying beauty." Thankfully, in Odell's day, a woman could pore over volumes of science and literature alongside (or at least "somewhat nearer") her husband; she could "form her own opinions, and give them forth to the world."[18]

As grandly as Odell described the rise of American cultural greatness, she situated Wheatley outside of this narrative. Since Wheatley could claim the inspiration of no female intellectuals, Odell reasoned that her genius could be credited only to the grace of God. Moreover, since Wheatley's literary success had preceded the outbreak of the Revolutionary War, it could not be considered part of the outpouring of intellectual production that followed America's Revolutionary awakening. The sad irony, then, was that even as she served as an indicator of the transformation to come, Wheatley could not experience its joys, which coincided with the period of decline in her own life as a nominally free American: "True, she had heard the alarum of Liberty, but it was in suffering and sorrow; and when the shout of triumph was raised, it fell upon a chilled heart and a closing ear." The strange career of Phillis Wheatley did not belong to the American republic.[19]

RESPECTABLE PHILLIS

In order to endow her subject with impeccable respectability, it was imperative that Odell represent Wheatley, from the very beginning of the narrative, as a person of "humble and modest demeanor." Wheatley's modesty was especially noteworthy in light of her spectacular (albeit short-lived) international career. Odell assured her readers that even as Wheatley became known as a poet and attracted a wide range of visitors "of high standing in society," "she never for a moment lost sight of that modest, unassuming demeanor, which first won the heart of her mistress in the slave-market." From that day forward, Susanna had been fiercely protective of her charge. One time she dispatched another slave, Prince, to retrieve Phillis, who had gone to visit some of her Christian admirers. From a window of her house, Susanna caught a glimpse of the returning chaise and exclaimed, "Do but look at the saucy varlet—if he has n't the impudence to sit upon the same seat with *my Phillis!*" Recognizing that Susanna extended to Phillis an affection not accorded to her household's other slaves, Odell added, "Poor Prince received a severe reprimand for forgetting the dignity thus kindly, though perhaps to him unaccountably, attached to the sable person of 'my Phillis.' "[20]

If in this passage Odell discerned the oddness of Phillis's position in the Wheatley household from Prince's perspective, in other places she noted uncritically, and even approvingly, that Wheatley was treated differently from other servants and slaves. As soon as the Wheatleys discovered Phillis's talents for learning, they removed her from the domestic responsibilities they had originally expected her to fill. Instead she became Susanna's personal project, forbidden "to associate with the other domestics of the family, who were of her own color and condition," and instead "kept constantly about the person of her mistress." Phillis's treatment was unique not only within the Wheatley home but also in Boston at large. According to Odell's narrative, when Phillis visited the home of one of Susanna's relatives, "the domestics [in that household] observed, 'it was the first time they ever carried tea to a colored woman.'" Did sharing tea with her mistress and other respectable whites make Phillis their social equal? It certainly created a tight bond between Phillis and Susanna: "Phillis ate of [Susanna's] bread, and drank of her cup, and was to her as a daughter; for she returned her affection with unbounded gratitude, and was so devoted to her interests *as to have no will in opposition to that of her benefactress.*"[21]

Did Odell realize that just a breath after referring to Phillis as Susanna's daughter she had also characterized the girl as the perfect slave? In nineteenth-century political discourse, to lack a will of one's own was to be a "cipher," a person empty of civic identity and political agency. As both a woman and a slave, Phillis Wheatley was doubly ciphered. It was not just a civil death that Odell unwittingly described in this scene, but also a social one. Phillis's tea-taking and bread-breaking with Susanna and her friends did not endow her with an independent social identity because her participation in these rituals of sociability happened only by the design and approval of her "benefactress" (Odell's euphemism for mistress or owner). By keeping Phillis away from other slaves, and by assimilating her into a kind of mother-daughter relationship, Susanna sealed Phillis's "natal alienation," in sociologist Orlando Patterson's terminology: "It was this alienation of the slave from all formal, legally enforceable ties of 'blood,' and from any attachment to groups or localities other than those chosen for him by the master, that gave the relation of slavery its peculiar value to the master." That those who publicized memories of Phillis Wheatley in nineteenth-century Boston were Susanna's blood relatives emphasizes the continuing alienation of Wheatley's memory, both from her birth ancestors and from any social connections that she formed independent of her master and mistress.[22]

Given the choice, Phillis Wheatley might still have associated with people who happened to be Susanna's friends. Phillis's connections to white evangelicals, including people of considerable influence, such as George Whitefield, Lord Dartmouth, and Selena Hastings (the Countess of Huntingdon), were clearly significant to her, spiritually, personally, and professionally. What Odell's account obscures is that Wheatley also had a social network of people of color. Her correspondence with Obour Tanner, a free black woman in Newport, and Samson Occom, the Mohegan missionary, are evidence of significant relationships she had with New Englanders of African and Native ancestry.[23] Even while she was still legally enslaved, Wheatley did have opportunities to act on her own volition. Recent scholarship has emphasized how she tried to shape her own literary career and set the terms for her own emancipation.[24] And, of course, there are the poems: for all that Wheatley remains an enigma to us, we have access to more words written in her own hand than we do for any other Revolutionary-era woman of color.

In considering Wheatley's life after death, however, it is vital to recognize that posthumous representations of her, shaped largely by Grégoire and Odell, placed her outside of a larger historical narrative of emancipation. Especially in Odell's version, Wheatley's life story ran directly counter to the emancipatory history of the American Revolution: the rise of national freedom coincided with Wheatley's descent into obscurity and poverty. In this telling, to the extent that Wheatley is part of any "community of memory," it is the community created and populated by relatives of Susanna Wheatley. Indeed, in her record of Susanna's descendants' memories, Odell emphasized that Phillis herself had a very poor memory. All she could recall of her childhood in Africa was "the simple circumstance that her mother *poured out water before the sun at his rising*–in reference, no doubt, to an ancient African custom." Remarking that most people remembered much more of their childhoods than Phillis did, Odell speculated that the "various degrees and kinds of suffering" that Phillis experienced through the slave trade "might naturally enough obliterate the recollection of earlier and happier days." Odell also noted that even though the young girl was prodigiously talented at recalling what others told her–hence her rapid acquisition of the English language–she was hopeless when it came to retaining "the creations of her own fancy." If she did not write her thoughts down right away, all would be forgotten. Whatever "peculiar structure of mind" accounted for these lapses, Odell's emphasis on them legitimated her own role as Wheatley's biographer. Wheatley literally could not hold onto her own history, so Odell had to create a history for her.[25]

Odell portrayed Phillis Wheatley as an admirable person of color at a moment when popular culture frequently presented "black respectability" as an oxymoron. In the years before Odell published her memoir, another "Phillis" had become a recurring figure in what scholars call the "Bobalition broadsides." In Boston and other New England cities from 1816 through the 1820s, printers published a series of broadsides mocking the respectable aspirations of free people of color in general, and, more specifically, freedpeople's commemorations of their emancipation from slavery. A typical sheet appeared in Boston in 1825, with the headline "Grand Celebration of the Bobalition of African Slavery!" At the top is a large woodcut depicting a group of lavishly dressed blacks (five men and one woman) drinking wine around a table. One man is so drunk he has fallen to the floor; two others have their arms around the woman, who is wearing an enormous feathered hat and what appears to be a fur collar. On the Boston Public Library's copy of this broadside, someone has hand-written a word bubble next to one of the men, who drawls to the over-dressed woman, "Oh Phillis!"[26]

Grand Celebration of the Bobalition of African Slavery, 1825? Broadside. *Courtesy of the Trustees of the Boston Public Library/Rare Books*

It is not clear whether the artists and writers who placed "Phillis" in these racist caricatures meant to evoke Phillis Wheatley specifically, or whether "Phillis" (often depicted with her laughingstock of a husband, "Pompey") was a stock figure.[27] What is unmistakable is the broadsides' derision of African Americans' attempts to develop a commemorative culture of their own. As several historians have recently noted, blacks in the nineteenth-century North sought to create community around the commemoration of historical turning points, especially the abolition of the American slave trade, which took effect on January 1, 1808. On July 14 of that year, about two hundred people of color paraded through the streets of Boston, then gathered in the African Meeting House (the home of the African Baptist Church) to hear a sermon by white minister Jedidiah Morse. Black leaders embraced such commemorative occasions as an opportunity to display their community's respectability to their white neighbors. Not all white observers regarded these African American performances favorably. By the mid-1810s, the black community's carefully orchestrated abolition celebrations were recognizable enough to become the subject of parody and satire in the Bobalition broadsides featuring Phillis, Pompey, and others.[28] The broadsides mocked what their creators saw as African American men and women's misguided efforts to appropriate the commemorative practices of patriotic whites. In an exaggerated dialect, the text below the engraving of Phillis's drunken feast from 1825 outlined the celebration's "general order," toasts, and songs, mimicking the form of the souvenir programs distributed at contemporary commemorative occasions such as the Bunker Hill semicentennial.

Another engraving reprinted on several broadsides in the 1810s and 20s depicts a crowd of white men assaulting a black couple. The man comes off as weak and emasculated as he slinks away on crutches, leaving his wife to defend the two of them. She looks ridiculous trying to fight off a hail of rocks with only a broom. A broadside with this image labels the woman as "Phillis"; this version was printed in 1816 and again in 1827, probably in Boston.[29] The text below is a letter from Phillis to a friend, in which she describes the "dreadful riot" in verse, or, as she puts it, in "de langrage of Massa Pope and Milton." The reference to these English poets, whose work Phillis Wheatley admired and in whose style she wrote, suggests that the writer intended to invoke Wheatley's memory. A long section of the poem describes the destruction of the couple's house. Phillis lists everything she owns, her card table, curtains, mahogany desk, coffee urn, and much, much more, all itemized as precisely as a probate inventory. By drawing attention to Phillis's worldly belongings, the author characterized the black woman as excessively vain and assured white readers that it was absurd for black people to own these material indicators of refinement. Many African Americans couldn't afford a "hogany Desk wid polish shine," like the one the rioters destroyed in Phillis's home. The irony is that those who did enjoy greater economic success could find themselves the targets of racial violence.[30]

Historian Joanne Pope Melish contends that the Bobalition broadsides are only superficially different from the fond remembrances of individual people of color published in the 1820s and 30s, of which Odell's memoir of Phillis Wheatley is a perfect example. The racist broadsides and the admiring memoirs together served to "remove" people of color from any meaningful or sustainable role in the culture or the body politic. In these stories of deceased black role models, Melish argues, "the sainthood of the imaginary few ... foregrounded the human frailties of the majority and served further to distort whites' view of the complex reality of black lives." This argument is provocative and important in that it encourages us to consider the cultural work performed by white authors' reminiscences of people of color they deemed "respectable" or "good." Yet for all that recent historians have had to say about the Bobalition broadsides—which provide some of the baldest evidence of northern racism in the antebellum period—stories concerning respectable blacks have received little scholarly attention. This oversight is unfortunate. White people's reminiscences of blacks they deemed "respectable" were stylized and constructed, but they weren't created out of thin air. Instead of reading these memoirs, obituaries, and anecdotes as accounts of the "imaginary few," we might interpret them as reviews of real people's performances of respectability. Respectability was associated with the refinement and discipline of the self, but it was not a status one could attain *by* oneself. The very word suggests that respectability was fundamentally performative in its demand that within settings of both public and private sociability, individuals acted in such a way that it was possible for *others* to respect them. Phillis Wheatley provided one of the most spectacular and complicated shows of her day, and one that was revived and critiqued throughout the nineteenth century. But to understand the complexities of how free people of color sought respectability and how whites perceived and remembered their performances, it helps to step away from Wheatley's limelight.[31]

THE TROPE OF THE TEA TABLE

Unlike Phillis Wheatley, Chloe Spear never wrote a word, but as was the case for her better-known foil, plenty of words would memorialize her. Her death notice in the *Columbian Centinel* was brief, albeit longer than those of other ordinary Bostonians commemorated in that column. Whereas many of the notices included only the decedent's age (and often the name of a woman's father or husband), Spear's listing noted parenthetically, "a colored woman, highly respected." Spear's minister, Thomas Baldwin of Boston's Second

Baptist Church, amplified that terse statement with a two-page obituary detailing the African-born woman's conversion and contributions to the faith. A full seventeen years after Spear's death, another of her friends, a white evangelical reformer named Mary Webb, commemorated her in more detail still, in the 108-page *Memoir of Mrs. Chloe Spear, a Native of Africa, Who Was Enslaved in Childhood, and Died in Boston* (1832).[32] This memoir was an account of a life much like the one Phillis Wheatley might have led had she not been a poet and had she not died at the tail end of the Revolutionary War. In fixating on what was exceptional about Wheatley, we lose one dimension of what made her significant to those who remembered her into the nineteenth century. Chloe Spear proved that a Massachusetts woman of color did not have to achieve international fame in order to be remembered locally. On the one hand, when compared to Wheatley, Spear lived a more representative experience of the Bay State's transformation from slavery to freedom. On the other, her story reminds us that whenever one examines an individual life at close range, the lines between ordinary and extraordinary become harder and harder to discern.

Like Wheatley, Spear was kidnapped from her West African family as a young girl. Also like Wheatley, she was described as sickly and the "smallest of the lot" of slaves transported with her. The Middle Passage took Chloe first to Philadelphia, where she was purchased by merchant-captain John Bradford, who soon brought her to his Boston home. This was probably around 1762, just a year after John and Susanna Wheatley bought a seven-year-old girl off a ship in Boston Harbor. Bradford was not nearly so benevolent a master as the Wheatleys. Chloe, like young Phillis, had a passion to learn, and she scrimped together pennies to hire a local schoolmistress to teach her to read. But when her master discovered her trying to work her way through the Psalter, he whipped the young woman, charging that "it made negroes saucy to know how to read." Bradford made no effort to teach his slave about Christianity—a failure the evangelical author of the *Memoir* found most deplorable. Nevertheless, Spear befriended a "truly pious and devoted Christian" who showed more concern for her soul, and she continued to study scripture on her own. Moved by what she found there, she joined the New North Congregational Church.[33]

Although her biographer represented Spear's profession of faith as a triumphant moment, proving that God was no "respecter of persons," Spear was still John Bradford's slave when she joined the church.[34] She had married Cesar Spear in October 1776 and given birth to several children while she and her husband were still bound to different masters. In the posthumous accounts of her life, the circumstances of Spear's emancipation are vague, reflecting nineteenth-century Bay Staters' fuzzy understanding of how slavery ended locally. According to Spear's obituary, during the Revolution her master had promised to manumit her in the near future, but before he could act on his plans, "by a law of the Commonwealth, all the slaves in the State were made free." Possibly the "law" in question was the state constitution of 1780, which some people interpreted as invalidating slavery.[35]

Spear's story encourages us to think about emancipation not as something that happens with the sweep of a legislator's pen or a master's spasm of generosity but instead as an unfolding process. Even if the law perceived Spear as a free woman from the early 1780s onward, her day-to-day life at that time might not have felt much different from the routine she had established while enslaved. For a time, she continued to live and work in the Bradford household, though now she collected wages. Later, upon leaving the Bradfords, she made a living through hard work: doing laundry for wealthy Bostonians and helping her husband operate a boardinghouse. By 1798, the Spears had acquired enough money to purchase half of a house in the North End. Over the years, Chloe furnished it with a variety of necessities and a few luxuries, including "1 Ebony Tea Table," "2 Small Looking Glasses," "5 Pictures," and a seven-dollar "Brass Fire Sett." By the time she died in 1815, her real and personal property was worth $1,428.20, at about the median for Boston estates probated that year. For a woman who had once been property herself, to own this much must have proved that the world could occasionally offer some small sort of justice.[36]

Beyond work, the other constant in Chloe Spear's life was faith. In 1788, she joined the Second Baptist Church. Spear's involvement in Boston's Baptist circles brought her into contact with those who would posthumously commemorate her in print, including Thomas Baldwin, author of her two-page obituary in the *Massachusetts Baptist Missionary Magazine*; James Loring, publisher of the *Memoir*; and Mary Webb, the *Memoir*'s most likely author. Webb was a spinster who devoted her long life to charitable and religious causes, including missionary work and the education of children of color. Like Spear, she was a respected member of the Second Baptist Church, and for at least the last few years of Spear's life, the two women lived a few blocks from each other in the North End. It is likely that Webb and Spear met both at church and in the neighborhood.[37] After her husband's death in 1806, Spear became a lay leader of sorts among Boston Baptists by holding religious meetings in her home. Many people, both black and white, ranging from beginners in the faith to her beloved minister Thomas Baldwin, enjoyed coming to hear her testimony. "There was much of life and animation in her manners," Webb recalled, "and she was peculiar for conveying her ideas in metaphors which originated in her own mind, and thus often engaged the attention, and rendered herself agreeable to persons, who were not particularly serious" about religion. Indeed, Spear proved adept at winning new converts to the faith: "So happy was her talent in conversation with persons, in the early stages of religious conviction, that in seasons of revival in the neighbouring towns, she was frequently invited to visit them, and was instrumental of good."[38]

In passages like this one, the *Memoir* presents Spear as a pivotal figure in a network of evangelicals, bound together by the Spirit, regardless of worldly circumstances. But the Baptist church, or the community of Christians more broadly, could not claim to be free of all trappings of worldliness. Webb saw no inconsistency in praising Spear's deference to her social superiors when they attended gatherings at her house: "Occasionally, pious ladies, of the first respectability, were pleased to make her an afternoon visit; when, with her accustomed modesty, she would wait on them, and then take her own tea by herself." It went without saying that these visitors "of the first respectability" were white. For Webb, Spear's respectability was in her modesty, while the white women evidenced the virtue of benevolence by condescending to call on a black sister in Christ. Webb went on to explain how these "ladies" further demonstrated their magnanimity by convincing Spear to have tea along with them.[39] There was nothing inherently wrong with blacks and whites sharing a table, but blacks had a place there only on white people's terms—even when the table in question belonged to a black woman herself.

This motif—call it the trope of the tea table—appeared in other white authors' fond remembrances of individual African Americans. In 1838, an obituary reprinted in the *Liberator* hailed New Jersey Quaker David Mapps, "of the African race," as "a highly intelligent and respectable man," adding "his home was open to all respectable persons who chose to visit him, his unassuming modesty and humility was such, and he so respected the feelings of others, that he would not sit at his own table, to eat with his white visitors, unless at their pressing solicitations." In her 1834 memoir of Phillis Wheatley, Margaretta Matilda Odell approvingly noted that "whenever [Wheatley] was invited to the houses of individuals of wealth and distinction, (which frequently happened,) she always declined the seat offered her at their board, and, requesting that a side-table might be laid for her, dined modestly apart from the rest of the company." A reviewer of Odell's memoir for a New York magazine singled out this passage, echoing Odell's assertion that Wheatley's behavior at these tea parties was "both dignified and judicious" and noting that such conduct, if practiced more widely, "would unquestionably add to the harmony of society at large." In the eyes of those who commemorated their lives, both Mapps and Wheatley deserved praise for deferring to the "feelings" of others—even when doing so cost them their own happiness. "She must have been painfully conscious of the feelings with which her unfortunate race were regarded," Odell mused of Wheatley, but she also implied that Wheatley's self-effacing behavior was the only respectable course of action for her to take.[40]

The trope of the tea table appeared in reminiscences even of certain people of color generally known for thwarting the racial hierarchy of the new republic. A case in point is the distinguished sea captain Paul Cuffee of Nantucket and New Bedford, who by the early nineteenth century was one of the wealthiest men of color in the nation, a vocal abolitionist and civil rights advocate, and a primary backer of African American emigration to Sierra Leone. Daniel Ricketson, town historian of New Bedford, related how Cuffee once stopped at a local tavern, where the proprietor offered to set up a table for him separate from other patrons. Cuffee politely declined, explaining, "much to her chagrin, that he had previously accepted an invitation to dine with William Rotch," a respected Quaker. Ricketson went on to relate how, on another occasion, Cuffee invited Rotch and a group of English Friends to dine at his home. Upon arriving, Rotch noticed that

> Paul and his wife had no chairs set for themselves, and were modestly preparing to retire or remain until their guests had dined. At this Friend Rotch rose, and, in a firm but kind manner, addressing his host and hostess, said that he could not consent to such an arrangement, and that he should not take his seat at the table unless Paul and his wife presided. With all his gentleness and humanity, no man was more unflinching where a matter of conscience was concerned than Friend Rotch, and Paul was too well acquainted with this trait in his friend's character to demur.[41]

This pair of anecdotes mapped out a precise racial etiquette that simultaneously affirmed black claims to respectability and white assertions of social authority. The tavern scene established Cuffee's respectability: he was worthy of Rotch's dinner invitation, and he treated the tavern-keeper with politeness, despite her insinuation that he ought not eat with whites. Ricketson then reinforced the point that integration was compatible with the existing social order through the scene in Cuffee's own home. Rotch, not Cuffee, is the focus of attention and the primary agent in this scene. Cuffee gestures that he is willing to abide by the customs of racial deference, but the white man refuses to consent to that code. In this moment, the biography of one of the nation's most successful men of color turns into a celebration of the "gentleness and humanity" of a well-to-do white Quaker. All dine together, and the authority of the white man remains intact.

The pervasiveness of the trope of the tea table is underscored by more overtly abolitionist appropriations of it, which played on the familiarity of the scene even as they called the justice of its racial etiquette into question. In an 1852 memoir of a black Vermonter, Baptist Elder Charles Bowles, John W. Lewis inverted the trope of the tea table so that it no longer sanctioned black acquiescence to racial codes but instead skewered white arrogance. In condemning those whites who professed to oppose slavery but balked at the idea of listening to Bowles preach, Lewis (himself a black Baptist) recalled his own experience visiting an unnamed white New Englander's home. He conversed civilly with the master of the house until tea was served, at which point the host "showed his guest out into a back kitchen to sit by himself, while the family ate in another apartment." Lewis's epithet for this host—"cod-fish aristocrat"—evoked his sense that the man had confused worldly gentility with provincial chauvinism.[42] In contrast, while Odell, Webb, and Ricketson didn't necessarily condone racial separation, they nevertheless approved of blacks who abided by it rather than making a scene. In their view, if racial etiquette were ever to change—if people of color were to secure a place at the table—it would be only because white people had invited them to take a seat.

An abolitionist writer revised the trope yet again to highlight why it was worthwhile for whites to include people of color at their tea tables. An anonymous anecdote for the *Anti-Slavery Record* described a visit young Phillis Wheatley made to the family of "Colonel Fitch," who had owned her briefly before selling her to John and Susanna Wheatley. (To the extent that this story has any basis in fact, it is worth noting that merchant Timothy Fitch owned the *Phyllis*, the ship that had transported the young girl across the Middle Passage.) The Fitch daughters were quite startled to learn from their mother that their guest would be taking tea with the family. Unable to countenance "the idea of sitting down at table with a colored person, even though she had sat at table with a countess," the girls "pouted a little, but submitted to their mother's directions." And they were glad they did, for it turned out that Wheatley had marvelous stories to tell of her recent trip to England: "They became more and more inquisitive to learn what she had seen, and found that with all their wealth and advantages, she knew more than they did. As she went on with her stories, they forgot she had been a slave; they felt no prejudice against her because she was black, and they felt ashamed they had ever made any objections to her having a seat at the tea-table."[43]

The *Anti-Slavery Record*'s anecdote, like the memoirs of Wheatley and Spear and the story about Paul Cuffee and William Rotch, modeled behavior for whites to follow in their interactions with blacks. The differences in the tea table encounters in the abolitionist story and Webb's and Odell's memoirs suggest the distinct audiences that these writers imagined for their works. Readers of Odell's memoir were invited to sympathize with Wheatley, who was excluded from the tea table despite her respectable comportment. At the same time, within the cultural logic of the nineteenth-century parlor, Wheatley's willingness to suffer her exclusion, rather than protest it, enhanced her respectability. Webb's version of a similar scene encouraged white female readers to emulate Spear's coreligionists and invite black women into the refined space of the tea table. The tea table thus became a place where benevolent white women guided their black sisters in the codes of genteel womanhood. The abolitionist version of the trope of the tea table inverted this relationship by making the black woman the one to bring refinement and culture to the table. At Mrs. Fitch's tea party, it was Wheatley, not the Fitch daughters, who had visited Westminster Abbey and St. Paul's Cathedral, seen Queen Charlotte's dresses, and observed the Countess of Huntingdon's charity to the poor.

The *Anti-Slavery Record*'s tea table story expresses the utopian vision of a certain strain of abolitionist thought. In this most unlikely of places, the parlor of a slave trader's home, a democratic ritual was enacted, wherein people of dramatically different backgrounds came together to learn that "wealth and advantages" did not necessarily confer knowledge or moral worth. After taking tea with Wheatley, the Fitch daughters "felt no prejudice against her because she was black." There is a tension between the two clauses in this sentence: the difference between Wheatley and the Fitches is reinforced ("she was black") even as it is apparently erased (the daughters "felt no prejudice"). History is erased as well. In order to accept Wheatley at their table, the daughters "forgot she had been a slave." In other words, Wheatley's stories (about royal visitors, English cathedrals, kindly countesses) supplanted Wheatley's story (about her own enslavement and emancipation). The success of this scene hinged not on Wheatley's own autonomous agency but upon her proper performance of the script that Mrs. Fitch had established, a kind of "guess who's coming to tea" for the eighteenth century. This anecdote is refreshing in its acknowledgment of white prejudice as a real obstacle to social equality. But what unifies this scene with more common versions of the trope of the tea table is that even as these texts ostensibly honor women of color, they also celebrate the white women (such as Mrs. Fitch, Susanna Wheatley, and Chloe Spear's white Christian patrons) whose benevolence has elevated black women to the status of respectability.

In the nineteenth century, black advocates of the politics of respectability argued that performances of middle-class values would eventually win white people's recognition of racial equality. But what if whites viewed the humble, modest, and deferential behavior of respectable blacks as evidence of subservience rather than uplift? What if whites continued to understand their hospitality to blacks as the outgrowth of noblesse oblige, rather than an expression of reciprocal esteem? Unlike the Fitch daughters, most white people never had their understanding of race and refinement turned upside down through an encounter at the tea table. Mary Webb, for one, clearly approved of Chloe Spear's decision to remove herself to a separate table until her white guests asked her to join them. Throughout the *Memoir*, Webb vacillated between presenting Spear as a universal example of religious sincerity and setting her off as a racial oddity. There was something discomfiting for

Webb about observing such virtue in a woman of color. As she warned her (presumed white) readers, "how dreadful then will it be...should any, who have read this little history, be found unprepared for [Christ's] coming, while this uncultivated African shall sit down in the kingdom of heaven." Putting the strangeness of the situation in more concise terms, one first-time "Christian visiter" to Spear's home quoted the Song of Solomon, marveling, "She is *black, but comely.*"[44]

"Black, but comely." "A colored woman, highly respected." Spear's respectability and religiosity did not make whites indifferent to color; rather, her color visibly clashed with what they knew of her character. The *Columbian Centinel*, which published Spear's one-line obituary in 1815, rarely used the words "respectable" or "respected" in death notices of white people but frequently used them in commemorating people of color. In a context in which relatively few black decedents were the subject of obituaries to begin with, this choice of words suggested that being both respectable and "colored" was worthy of note. Meanwhile, the respectability of white decedents literally went without saying. So the *Centinel* honored, among others, James Hawkins, "a respectable man of color"; Joseph Wicks, "a person of color an honest man and faithful domestic"; and Phillis Bradstreet, "a respectable black lady, once a Princess in Africa." The obituary of Lemuel Haynes, a Congregationalist minister ousted when his Vermont congregation decided they didn't want a black pastor any longer, made the implied tension between blackness and respectability explicit with a well-placed "but": "He was a man of color, but enjoyed the esteem of all who knew him." While the black elite's politics of respectability was supposed to appeal to the logic of "racial synecdoche"—whereby one person's behavior stood in for the whole group—these obituaries show how respectability sometimes served instead as a way for white people to set individuals such as Wheatley, Spear, Hawkins, Wicks, Bradstreet, and Haynes apart from people of color collectively.[45]

COLORED WOMEN, HIGHLY RESPECTED

Heightening the contrast between those individuals singled out as respectable and people of color in general were the counter-examples of women and (especially) men who violated white standards for black respectability. In Odell's memoir of Phillis Wheatley and Webb's of Chloe Spear, these negative examples came in the form of husbands. There are striking similarities in the memoirs' portrayals of John Peters and Cesar Spear as men of dubious respectability. Webb structured the *Memoir of Mrs. Chloe Spear* as a series of liberations: Chloe's conversion from spiritual bondage to Christian truth, her release from chattel slavery, and, finally, her "triumphant departure" to "the shores of immortality, beyond the reach of oppressors, or the fear of invaders." But before Chloe attained this "perfect liberty," her penultimate emancipation was from the trials of marriage. As Webb delicately put it, while wedded to Cesar, Chloe "did *not enjoy all the domestic happiness that was desirable.*" The *Memoir* portrays Cesar as a good-for-nothing who left most of the bread-winning to his wife.[46]

Webb claimed that the Spears acquired their house solely through Chloe's initiative and thrift. Once she had saved enough to buy it, she went to her husband:

> Being aware that the purchase must be made in her husband's name, "'cause he de *head*," she said to him, "Cesar, house to sell; I wish we buy it." He laughed at her, for thinking such a thing, but asked her, "how much e price o it?" "Seben hundred dollar," she answered. "*Seben hundred dollar!!*" exclaimed Cesar, "I no got de money, how I buy a house?" "I got money," said Chloe.

What escaped Webb's notice was that the purchase of the house was not made in the name of "de *head*" alone. Instead, the deed specified that the property belonged to "Ceasar Spear of Boston aforesaid Cooper and Cloe his Wife." It was unusual for both husband and wife to appear on a deed in this way. In a society in which racial distinctions were consolidating, gender restrictions among people of color were perhaps not so rigid as those among middle-class whites. The fact that most black women worked for pay might have given them a stronger claim to property than most white women were typically allowed.[47] If the Spears defied conventional assumptions about nineteenth-century gender divisions in this sense, they conformed to them in another: organized religion was Chloe's domain, not her husband's. Cesar's failure to convert caused his wife to worry about the state of his soul. It is possible that Cesar grumbled about Chloe's religious activities. Not until after he died did she open her house to religious meetings, for she, in Webb's words, "now [had] no one to control her."[48]

In Webb's view, Cesar's failings as a respectable husband were not limited to his inadequacies around family finances or his refusal to embrace Christianity, but extended to his failure to understand how people of color should present themselves. He sometimes asked his wife, "Chloe, why you don't wear silk gown, dress up smart, like udder colour women?" Instead of buying new dresses as Cesar suggested, Chloe saved whatever money he allowed her and anything extra she earned from her own work. Webb used this anecdote to contrast Cesar's fondness for "finery and show" with Chloe's prudence and thrift.[49] Like the trope of the tea table, this scene spelled out parameters for black respectability that were more restrictive than those applied to whites. Nineteenth-century Americans and the historians who study them have often equated respectability with fashionableness, but the connection holds only to a point. To be too concerned about fashion was to sacrifice the self-discipline that respectability demanded.[50] Whites viewed blacks, so recently released from chattel slavery, as especially vulnerable to becoming slaves to fashion. Popular culture (including the Bobalition broadsides) mocked blacks who tried to "dress up smart," depicting them wearing ludicrously excessive finery. The clear message was that African Americans' character and social station could never match their clothing, so they would look ridiculous so long as they sought to be fashionable. In one characteristic image from Philadelphia, a black woman dressed in mountains of ruffles and lace complains of the day's heat, sighing to her companion, "I aspire too much."[51]

For Webb, Chloe's virtue stemmed from not being "like udder colour women." She longed for those things obtainable through hard work and deep faith—a modest house, the hope of rewards in a future world—things that her memoirist believed were appropriate for a person of color to desire. Cesar's problem might not have been that he was unwilling to work or to believe, but that he wanted more. In legal documents, Cesar was routinely described as a cooper. That he had his own trade suggests that he was hardly entirely dependent on his wife for support, though it was notoriously difficult for free black tradesmen to find regular employment in northern cities after the Revolutionary War. The demand for women's labor was more consistent (even though it paid less), so black families often counted on women for steady income.[52] Cesar's name also appears on a list of Freemasons, members of the African Lodge established by Prince Hall. Membership in the brotherhood was a mark of respectability and leadership within black Boston. Webb's portrayal of Cesar as dissolute and irreligious is curious in light of his Masonic connections, since the African Lodge demanded that its members exhibit upright behavior and Christian faith. What made Cesar respectable to his brothers likely made him seem uppity to Webb.[53]

John Peters, Phillis Wheatley's husband, was also remembered among whites for his excessive aspirations. Representations of Peters are somewhat more ambiguous than Webb's characterization of Cesar Spear. Wheatley's biographers were conscious that making Peters out to be nothing more than a cad would reflect ill on the famed poet who had chosen this man as her husband. Henri Grégoire, who in 1808 became the first to publish an account of Wheatley and Peters's unhappy marriage, blamed the initial souring of the relationship on Phillis's refusal to "learn the household art."[54] In her version, Odell suggested that it was Peters who brought Wheatley down. In March 1778, her former master, John Wheatley, died, followed quickly to the grave by his daughter, Mary Wheatley Lathrop. These losses left Phillis friendless and nearly penniless:

At this period of destitution, Phillis received an offer of marriage from a
respectable colored man of Boston...a man of very handsome person and
manners; [who] wore a wig, carried a cane, and quite acted out 'the gentleman.'
In an evil hour he was accepted; and he proved utterly unworthy of the distinguished woman who honored him by her alliance....He is said to have been
both too proud and too indolent to apply himself to any occupation below his
fancied dignity.[55]

Peters and Wheatley actually announced their intent to marry nearly six
months before Mary Lathrop died, so Odell was wrong in implying that
Phillis had made a bad marriage decision because she was so deep in
mourning. In any case, Odell had no kind words to waste on John Peters.
When applied to him, "respectable colored man" was to be pronounced ironically. Odell emphasized Peters's outward traits: his "handsome person"; the
wig and cane that advertised his frivolity; the way he "acted out" (but in
truth was not) "the gentleman." Phillis Wheatley's (fatal?) mistake, according
to her biographer, was that, in a moment of weakness, she let Peters's
performance win her over.

But what if there was more to John Peters than Odell admitted? What of
the suggestion in Grégoire's book that he was a lawyer of sorts who argued
"the cause of blacks," or that he was a man of particular intelligence? Several
other nineteenth-century observers (including one of Susanna Wheatley's
granddaughters) made similar claims, though it is unclear whether they
were simply embellishing Grégoire's account. Wheatley's most thorough
modern biographer wonders if Peters was really so destitute as earlier writers
made him out to be.[56] Furthermore, tax assessments from late eighteenth-
century Boston variously describe him as a "physician," a "doctor," a "printer,"
and a "mender." The records also show that though he was in debtor's prison
in 1784, he was later a property owner in a part of town where few, if any,
other black men resided.[57] Wherever he was and whatever he was doing in
the late eighteenth century, nineteenth-century anecdotes and memoirs of
his wife pictured Peters as all those things a man of color wasn't supposed to
be: aspiring, profligate, controlling, refined. He and relatives of the Wheatleys
were evidently at odds over who could claim Phillis's legacies. A bitter Odell
contended that Peters had refused to inform the extended Wheatley family
about Phillis's funeral, while Peters seemed upset that a Wheatley relative
was still holding onto some of her manuscripts after her death. In the end,
the Wheatley descendants were the winners in the contest for Phillis's legacy,
for Odell's biography of the poet would form the basis for most subsequent
accounts of her life.[58]

Scholars who look back on this period have tended to present the key-
words of African American political discourse—including "respectability"—
as gendered male. They have done so with good reason. A critical term in

black politics, "manhood" challenged the emasculating indignities of slavery, especially the way it made grown men dependents in another man's household. "Manhood" and "respectability" were closely related categories within the politics of "elevation" or "uplift." In contrast, nineteenth-century whites gendered black respectability as feminine, precisely because to do so contained the social mobility associated with (masculine) respectability. Odell's and Webb's memoirs introduced the reading public to individual women of color whose lives seemed (to whites) both safe and worthwhile to commemorate. The wives in these narratives fare better than their husbands because the traits that the memoirs cast in an approving light—humility, piety, modesty, deference—were gendered feminine. In a context in which the primary activities of civic agency (voting and military service) were the province of men, a feminized black respectability did not openly challenge white supremacy in public life. The life stories of black women like Wheatley and Spear were palatable to mainstream white audiences.[59]

This appropriation of African American life stories by white authors and audiences often meant that social ties among people of color were excluded from the narratives. The *Memoir of Mrs. Chloe Spear* situated Spear in the evangelization movement led by white Baptists and obscured connections she might have had to Boston's communities of people of color. The *Memoir* mentioned in passing that Thomas Paul attended Spear's funeral and that Spear was "much in the habit of calling [him] her *son*."[60] The close relationship between Spear and Paul—the inaugural pastor of the African Baptist Church—hints at Spear's involvement in the organizational life of black Boston. Her relationships with Paul and other black Christians suggest that she held a respectable status within the black community. All of her heirs were people of color, most of whom had connections to the Second Baptist Church.[61] According to the *Memoir*, God had been "pleased to make her useful, more especially among those of her own colour," raising the possibility that she had been instrumental in bringing these or other black believers to the faith. Her bequest of $333.33 to the Second Baptist Church specified that the interest should go toward "the Relief of the sick and poor of said Church special reference being always to the members of Colour provided there shall be any who need it." Even within the integrated Second Baptist Church, Spear recognized the black members as a distinct group.[62]

We might imagine Spear's world of faith as a set of circles: sometimes concentric, as in the small group of black believers fitting itself within the larger Second Baptist Church; sometimes overlapping, as the interracial congregation of Second Baptist interacted with the members and leadership of the African Baptist Church. From the distance of some two hundred years, we don't have access to Spear's inner circle, but as outsiders we can attempt to see how the various circles fit together. This mapping of Spear's world contextualizes some of the comments and stories that the *Memoir* attributes to her. According to Webb, Spear "frequently spoke" of being kidnapped from her native Africa and taken to a strange new country. Referring to this journey of slavery and freedom, she declared, "*They* [the slave traders] *meant it for evil, but God meant it for good. To his name* be the glory." It is possible to interpret these lines as some have read Phillis Wheatley's poems on her conversion ("'Twas mercy brought me from my pagan land…"): the slave's wholehearted embrace of Anglo-American religion was a betrayal of African heritage and an apology for slavery. An alternative is to see these lines as a kind of psychological liberation. Her conversion showed Spear that the glory of God was the one thing that could render powerless the evils of both the slave ship and the master's whip. The fellowship of other Christians provided Spear with a ready space in which she could separate herself from these and other sins of the material world. Historian Susan Juster uses the anthropological term *communitas* to describe this space, where Baptist believers gathered after heeding the call "to 'come out and be ye separate,' to reject the bonds of family, neighborhood, and society."[63]

Reading Spear's spiritual testimony as a plea for *communitas* puts her performance at the tea table in a different light. Take this story which, according to Webb, Spear liked to tell:

> My mistress sometimes used to send me wid present to lady; de lady say, 'Tell Mrs. B. I *very much obliged to her;* and, (in a low and indifferent tone,) I thank you, Chloe, for bringing the parcel. So I lub my minister, and all Christian frien, dat try to do me good. I thank them: but I feel under *very great obligation* to *God*, who gib me de blessing, and make use ob his children to *bring* it to me.

This story appears in a chapter of the *Memoir* replete with examples of Spear's humility. When a man who had injured her asked her forgiveness, she readily granted it, saying "when any body bow to me, I always *drop*"— meaning, Webb explained, "that she was willing to take 'the lowest place.' " "She compared her own mind, in distinction from others, to a very small vessel"; she felt "a deep sense of her unworthiness to make mention of [Christ's] name."[64]

Webb's emphatic praise for Spear's humility suggests that the memoirist did not notice all the nuances of the story about presents and obligations. That story—a parable, really—seems not to be primarily about Spear's unworthiness, but about the greatness of God's blessings above what any human being could offer. Even though the first sentence reminded listeners that Spear had once been a slave, dispatched on errands for her mistress, the analogy that followed placed her in the position of the "lady" who felt "very much obliged." Spear could accept with thanks the gift of the gospel that her minister and friends had brought to her, but her true obligation was not to them, but to God. Similarly, her willingness to follow social convention and take tea apart from her white visitors does not necessarily mean that she saw social inequality as morally justified. Instead, it indicates her sense that what really mattered was presence at *God's* table, and that social status in the temporal world had no bearing on who was welcome in the world to come.

Spear's fusion of earthly deference with respectability and self-respect was facilitated not only by her theology but also by her gender. The overlap between feminine virtues and the traits that whites desired blacks to embody made it relatively easy for white writers to represent certain black women as respectable. Representing respectable black manhood in print required careful crafting and significant omissions. The activities associated with manly respectability among whites—taking a stand in the political sphere, seeking the main chance in economic life—often earned black men the derision of the white press. But men could be cast as worthy of remembrance when they appeared to embrace the deferential character and behavior of respectable black women. In this respect, the life and legacy of Primus Hall provides a valuable counterpoint to the stories about Chloe Spear. Though Hall served in the military during the Revolution and subsequently became a respected community leader in Boston, he was remembered in print for his association with George Washington—specifically, for sharing a bed with the revered general. Washington offering his bed to Primus Hall resonates with the trope of the tea table that appeared in other white-authored reminiscences of free people of color. In all these cases, black people in the presence of whites were to assume servile roles, taking care of their own needs to eat or sleep only when out of sight. A respectable white person could invite (or, in Washington's case, demand) a black person to share a bed or meal, but this was an act of magnanimity, not a recognition of equality.[65]

In material terms, both Chloe Spear and Primus Hall left behind estates that were impressive in size, especially for people who had devoted much of their lives to unfree or ill-paid labor. They also made their mark in print—another potent currency in the nineteenth century—although here their legacies became assimilated into a feminized narrative of black respectability. In Hall's case, print commemorations assimilated his story into the narrative of national emancipation, rather than connecting his Revolutionary service to the struggle for African American emancipation or describing his civil rights activism more explicitly.[66] The trope of the tea table made people like Spear, Hall, and Wheatley into history, but it did not always fully account for the kind of history these individuals had made. Instead, recorded memory sought to situate their aspirations and their agency in terms of the social relations comfortable and familiar to mainstream whites. We might read these memoirs as evidence of white people's efforts to exert mastery over the lives and legacies of blacks. But that mastery was uneven, and in the breach were moments of astonishment.

ASTONISHING JESUS

"A colored woman, highly respected" was not Elizabeth Freeman's epitaph, but it might as well have been. Her gravestone noted that Freeman—known in slavery as "Bett" and affectionately as "Mumbet"—"could neither read nor write, yet in her own sphere she had no superior nor equal." The epitaph emphasized those characteristics that constituted her individual respectability—a gendered, racialized respectability—in a rapidly industrializing society: "She neither wasted time, or property. She never violated a trust, nor failed to perform a duty. In every situation of domestic trial she was the most efficient helper and the tenderest friend."[67]

Legend had it that while a slave in the Ashley family of Sheffield, Berkshire County, Bett intervened when her mistress tried to strike another slave (Elizabeth's sister) with a glowing hot kitchen shovel: "Mum Bett interposed her arm, and received the blow; and she bore the honorable scar it left to the day of her death." Some years after this incident, Bett found the language to articulate her instinctive sense of the wrongness of slavery. In the waning days of the Revolution, she heard the Declaration of Independence read in the Sheffield meeting house. The very next day, she appeared before attorney Theodore Sedgwick, announcing to him, "I heard that paper read yesterday, that says, all men are born equal, and that every man has a right to freedom. I am not a dumb *critter*; won't the law give me my freedom?" In 1781, Sedgwick initiated a case on behalf of Bett and Brom, another of Ashley's slaves, in the Berkshire County Court of Common Pleas. The jury refused to recognize Brom and Bett as Ashley's property. This case is notable in Massachusetts legal history because it was the first to apply the "free and equal" clause of the recently ratified state constitution to the plight of chattel slaves. Not long after, the state's highest court decided in favor of Quok Walker, the man of color who had contested his slave status in Worcester County. The outcome of Walker's case convinced Ashley that his own appeal to the Supreme Judicial Court was unlikely to succeed, and he gave up his claim to Brom and Bett. The latter promptly took on the name Elizabeth Freeman, while the fortunes of the former have been lost to history.[68]

After her successful lawsuit, Freeman worked for many years as a domestic in her attorney's household. With their own mother long suffering from mental illness, the Sedgwick children looked to Freeman as a maternal figure. In 1831, two years after Freeman's death, Theodore Sedgwick, Jr., reminisced about her in an antislavery lecture he gave before the Stockbridge Lyceum. Two decades later, Theodore's sister Catharine Maria, the best-selling author of historical novels such as *Hope Leslie*, brought memories of Freeman to a wider audience in an essay in *Bentley's Miscellany* called "Slavery in New England." Freeman left her mark in visual and material culture as well as in print. In 1811, Susan Ridley Sedgwick, wife of Theodore, Jr., painted a miniature portrait of the sixty-five-year old domestic. Susan's daughter Maria gave the picture to the Massachusetts Historical Society in the 1880s. Another Sedgwick descendant donated Freeman's string of gold beads, which had been handed down through several generations of Sedgwick women. The donor remarked that by virtue of the association with Freeman, the bracelet Catharine Maria Sedgwick had fashioned from the beads "marks so striking an epoch in our social and political progress, that I thought it might be worthy of a place in the Cabinet of the Massachusetts Historical Society."[69]

Susan Anne Livingston Ridley Sedgwick, portrait of Elizabeth "Mumbet" Freeman (ca. 1742–1829), 1811. Watercolor on ivory. *Courtesy of the Massachusetts Historical Society*

The memories associated with Elizabeth Freeman show that it was possible for nineteenth-century white Bay Staters to incorporate the emancipation experience of people of color into the nationalist narrative of the Revolution. As told by the Sedgwick children, Freeman's story highlighted the radicalism of both the Declaration of Independence and the Massachusetts constitution, the documents that inspired and underwrote her plea for liberty. But for the Sedgwicks, as for many other chroniclers of the Bay State's history of slavery, the problem of slavery ended (at least locally) with the Revolution, and the radicalism of the Revolution ended with emancipation. After describing Freeman's lawsuit, Catharine Maria Sedgwick narrated a series of anecdotes about how Freeman staved off marauders from the Sedgwick estate during the unrest surrounding Shays's Rebellion. Her egalitarian tendencies hemmed in by her respect for property and social order, Sedgwick criticized the Shaysites for their mistaken belief "that the mountains and mole-hills of gentle descent, education, and fortune would all sink before the proclamation of a republic." In this context, Freeman earned approval because she knew her place in the republic: guarding the Sedgwick family and property, as the loyal household servant she was.[70]

The Sedgwicks' stories about Freeman revived the local history of slavery only to set it apart from the barbarity of the institution in the South. Despite recounting the story about the mistress beating her slave with a shovel, Catharine Maria claimed that New England slave owners generally treated their chattel "with almost parental kindness." The clearly defined roles of the colonial household paradoxically created social bonds across status lines. At the end of the work day, "the white and the black, like the feudal chief and his household servant, sat down to the same table, and shared the same viands." Such intimacy made discipline by force (such as Mrs. Ashley's attack on Elizabeth Freeman's sister) "a picturesque exception from the prevailing mildness of the parental government." The Sedgwicks depicted Freeman herself as another "picturesque exception" to people of color in general. Catharine's brother Theodore noted in his Stockbridge Lyceum address that following the altercation with her mistress, Freeman had stormed from the house, for "she resented the insult and outrage as a white person would have done." By this account, Freeman's sense of personal dignity and autonomy made her intelligible to white people and set her apart from the mass of blacks. Catharine deplored that much of Freeman's scrupulously saved earnings had been squandered away by her child and grandchildren, "who, like most of their race, were addicted to festive joys." For the Sedgwicks, Freeman represented something that free people of color might have been but lamentably often were not.[71]

Perhaps Elizabeth Freeman's story simply proves that a woman who challenged her subjection in one realm had to accept it in another in order to be worthy of remembrance by whites. But the complexities of Freeman's case become more evident if we juxtapose it with a story about a marginalized woman seeking inclusion in a very different historical context. Free black Northerners in the nineteenth century were well versed in the Bible, and one New Testament parable that particularly resonated with their experience as ethnic outsiders concerned Jesus's encounter with a woman from Canaan. On the road to Tyre and Sidon, the Canaanite woman found Jesus and begged him to cure her daughter. At first Jesus ignored her. Then, with his disciples insisting that he get rid of the tearful gentile, he turned to the woman and said, "I am not sent but unto the lost sheep of the house of Israel." Unmoved, the woman continued to implore him for help. Jesus persisted in turning her away: "It is not fair to take the children's bread and throw it to the dogs." The woman answered, "Yes, Lord, yet even the dogs eat the crumbs that fall from their masters' table." Finally convinced, Jesus cured the daughter, telling her mother, "O woman, great is thy faith."[72]

Matthew's text cries out for adverbs, but (at least in the English translation) they aren't there. "Even the dogs eat the crumbs that fall from their masters' table": how did she say it? And how did *he* hear it? What made him give in? Some commentators read the Canaanite woman's story as a parable about humility and deference. Once the woman explicitly acknowledges that she does not merit a place at the table, that the crumbs that fall from it are enough for her, only then does she finally get what she most desires. If this parable is a lesson about Jesus's special relationship to the Jewish people, then the woman's self-effacement seems straightforward enough. But even though African American Christians identified with Jewish historical experience in its Old Testament context, it is likely that they would have put themselves in the shoes of the gentile (the outsider) here. What if we read the woman as speaking not with meekness and submission but with boldness and dignity, and perhaps even a touch of sarcasm? What if her comment about the dogs eating the fallen crumbs is not an acceptance of the order of things but an effort to shake Jesus, to make him see how perverse that order is?

Thomas Paul, pastor of the African Baptist Church and fictive son to Chloe Spear, preached this text in 1818, before an overflowing crowd that included Prince Saunders, a New England-born Haitian government official who himself knew a few things about tea table politics.[73] In 1854, the African American feminist and abolitionist Frances Ellen Watkins turned the story into a poem, "The Syrophenician Woman." (In the Gospel of Mark, Matthew's Canaanite woman is said to be Syrophoenician.) Watkins made the woman's voice dominate the poem, but it was Jesus who got the last word: "'Woman,' said th' astonish'd Lord, / 'Be it even as thy word! / By thy faith that knows no fail, / Thou hast ask'd, and shalt prevail.'" Besides fitting the scripture into her own rhythm and rhyme, Watkins added a word to the text that clarified the reason behind Jesus's extraordinary response: he was "astonish'd." This single, violent word confirms that Watkins saw the woman as the person with the power in this exchange. The principal dynamic was not Jesus testing or trapping the woman, but her outwitting him, transforming him, *astonishing* him—the word originates in the Latin term for "thunder."[74]

Mainstream print culture's obituaries, anecdotes, and memoirs of people like Wheatley, Hall, Spear, and Freeman likely aroused curiosity and fond remembrances among their readers, but they often seem to have been carefully crafted not to be too astonishing. Print commemorations of exemplary people of color represented their behavior as sufficiently in line with existing racial etiquette so as to exact ready approval from white audiences. Even in the most genuinely marvelous case—Wheatley's—the poet's respectability (particularly her "modesty" and her close relationship to her mistress's family) tempered the astonishment of her literary gifts and her up-and-down career. Through literary conventions such as the trope of the tea table, these commemorations implied that respectable people of color accepted a state of affairs in which their share in the meal consisted only of fallen crumbs (or whatever was set aside for them on a separate table). What made these posthumous anecdotes and memoirs all the easier to reconcile with racialized standards of social propriety was the fact that all their subjects were dead and thereby unable to augment or protest the stories that other people put into print.[75]

Yet what distinguished these reminiscences from explicitly racist caricature (such as the Bobalition broadsides) was the possibility that these stories, based in the richness and complexity of ordinary people's lives, could serve as parables, or brief invitations to imagine another order of things: a world where kings lie with servants, where "colored women" are "highly respected," where Milton's English sings from the mouth of an African girl.[76] Consider this passage from Catharine Maria Sedgwick's essay on Elizabeth Freeman, in which Freeman described the aftermath of her beating: "I had a bad arm all winter, but Madam had the worst of it. I never covered the wound, and when people said to me, before Madam—, 'Why Betty! what ails your arm?' I only answered—'ask missis!'" Marveling at this exchange, Sedgwick added, "Which was the slave and which was the real mistress?" Freeman's response astonished Sedgwick, in a manner akin to the transformation the Canaanite woman's remarks worked on Jesus. Both exchanges enact a role reversal within the guise of conformity. The Canaanite woman's exaggerated humbling of herself made Jesus, the great teacher, see himself as a theological naïf; Freeman's demurral ("ask missis!") shamed her mistress by forcing her to admit her own lack of mastery over herself. Catharine Maria's brother Theodore articulated Freeman's effect on him even more emphatically: "Having known this woman as familiarly as I know either of my parents, I *cannot* believe in the moral or physical inferiority of the race to which she belonged." Personal intimacy between white and black New Englanders could breed paternalism and condescension, but there were moments, too, when the politics of respectability worked exactly as black leaders planned, elevating the race as a whole through the behavior of exemplary individuals.[77]

These stories did not always have this revelatory effect, nor did all readers and listeners interpret them in the same way. But there is something in these memories that both invites interpretation and resists the finality of it. Their subversive and transformative possibilities, couched in the ubiquitous yet often ambiguous language of respectability, made these stories appeal to abolitionist audiences. Though Mary Webb's *Memoir of Mrs. Chloe Spear* betrays no Garrisonian sympathies, the book was advertised and excerpted in the *Liberator* and sold at the shop of publisher James Loring, an abolitionist with ties to Baptist missionary circles.[78] Together with excerpts from Odell's narrative of Wheatley, the anecdotes about Hall's encounters with Washington eventually appeared in Nell's *Colored Patriots of the American Revolution*. Wheatley's story would be reprinted in many other antislavery texts, most of which closely followed (or outright plagiarized) the narrative that Odell put forth in 1834.[79]

This genre of fond, white-authored remembrances of individual people of color was a product of a particular historical moment—or more accurately, of a longing for a moment that had passed even before the stories were written down. These memoirs evidence their authors' nostalgia for the deference politics of the period immediately following the Revolution. As Nell wrote of Darby Vassall, who died in 1861 at the age of 92, "he was probably the oldest colored man in Massachusetts, and in his death has been severed the last link which associated many of his race with the wealth and dominant class in Boston." Vassall, born a slave to a wealthy family of Loyalists, was a founding member in 1796 of Boston's African Society, an organization of black men who pledged themselves to respectable and virtuous citizenship. Upon his death Vassall was interred, as he had long before requested, in the tomb of his former master's family. Chloe Spear, too, went to her rest in a plot belonging to her former master. The families of their masters and employers took responsibility for the less tangible remains of freedpeople as well. Odell put into print the stories that various Wheatley relatives had shared about the talented slave girl who had shared their family name. And Elizabeth Freeman's connections to the influential Sedgwick clan ensured that she, among the various plaintiffs in the Bay State's emancipation lawsuits, would be the one remembered into the twenty-first century. Her final resting place was in the circle of Sedgwick graves in a Stockbridge cemetery.[80]

In the 1850s, a descendant of a Massachusetts slave owner would go public with inherited memories of his family's human chattel. On March 5, 1858, at a ceremony commemorating the Boston Massacre, Samuel H. Brown "narrated to several persons the traditions extant in the family relating to Crispus Attucks." Brown's grandfather, William, had been Attucks's master, at least until September 30, 1750, when Attucks ran away. We don't know what Brown had to say in 1858, but we do know what he had to show: a goblet and a powderhorn, which according to family tradition had belonged to Attucks. Later, Brown's descendants would also present a worn teapot as another artifact of the erstwhile slave who tied their family to the origins of the American Revolution. According to Samuel Brown's reminiscences, Attucks had been a "faithful servant," apart from his "runaway excursion" in 1750. After his brief wanderings, Attucks had returned to the Browns, working as a cattle broker for the family. It was on a trading trip to Boston on March 5, 1770, that he was drawn into the King Street melee.[81]

Brown's story of a Crispus Attucks who was a humble Framingham cattle-hand did not catch on in the 1850s. Though Darby Vassall survived into the 1860s—at the 1858 Boston Massacre commemoration, abolitionist Theodore Parker introduced him as a "venerable relic" of the Revolution—the era of deference politics was over.[82] In this context, Brown's most apt memento of Attucks was not the goblet or the teapot but the powderhorn. Black politics in the 1850s could not be confined to the tea table. As people of color asserted themselves as both actors and narrators in history, they reinvigorated historical figures who were unambiguously astonishing. In a word, they replaced tea with gunpowder.

5

Fugitives and Soldiers

"What am I to be? An American no longer?" This was Massachusetts Senator Daniel Webster's horrified response on the seventh of March 1850 to the prospect of secession. If Webster found the continuing existence of American slavery distasteful, he perceived the fracturing of the American nation to be far worse. *Am I to be an American no longer?* In the 1850s, thousands of black men and women also asked themselves this question, with a mix of resignation, sorrow, hope, and jubilation, as they pondered leaving the South and even the United States to get as far away from slavery as possible. Although ever since the 1820s black abolitionists had vehemently attacked plans to resettle free people of color outside the United States, the 1850s saw a resurgence in African American support for emigration schemes. Most of slavery's fugitives would not ultimately leave the country, but those who did would be joined by thousands of black Northerners and earlier escapees who feared that the new Fugitive Slave Law put all people of color in the North at risk. Following the law's passage as part of the Compromise of 1850, dozens of blacks in Boston, including sixty members of the Twelfth Baptist "fugitive slave church," left for Canada. Over the course of the following decade, others would plot emigrations to Latin America, Britain, the Caribbean, and Africa.[1]

Am I to be an American no longer? With righteousness and rage, black Bay Staters, who had some access to the privileges of citizenship, asked this question of those who attempted to curtail their rights. In the nation at large, as James Kettner has shown, citizenship was in theory a uniform category, carrying the same set of privileges for all who claimed it. But in practice, the civic status of free blacks at the federal level was unclear before 1857. The antislavery movement, therefore, ran in tandem with a movement for African American civil rights. The 1850s witnessed some of the most ardent battles for social equality in the Bay State, including the final and victorious push in Boston's long struggle for school desegregation, as well as the effort to include blacks in state militias. For people of color across the North, several decades of modest advancement toward civic equality would be painfully offset in 1857 when the *Dred Scott* decision nullified African American claims to citizenship. Black men and women would then ask the question again, this time with utter horror (albeit in a different key than Webster's), once they heard the Supreme Court's ruling that no, black people were not to be Americans—they never had been.[2]

Am I to be an American no longer? Before the *Dred Scott* decision, but with an even greater intensity after, William Cooper Nell asked this question, lingering on the last two words. If the state of affairs in the 1850s threatened to rob people of color of their citizenship and nationality, Nell contended that their historical identity as Americans was nevertheless irrefutable. In the decade before the Civil War, as the abolitionist movement became ever more militant and African American claims to citizenship ever more urgent, Nell and other historically minded activists revived the memory of black participants in the American Revolution. "Colored Americans," Nell argued, should be treated as the good citizens they were and—as history proved—the good patriots they had always been. One of Nell's colleagues, William J. Watkins, asked an all-white committee of the Massachusetts legislature, "Why should *you* be a chosen people more than *we?*" The kind of historical chosen-ness that Webster had bestowed on Americans in his Bunker Hill addresses belonged to people of color as much as whites, Watkins contended, for "the great poiniard of British tyranny, which was plunged in the heart of *your* Fathers, and caused their noble blood to flow so freely, brought the purple flood from *our* hearts also." Watkins used this speech to implore legislators to charter a militia of black men. Representing black men as actors in the Revolutionary past was integral to Watkins's effort to secure his right to self-defense. In this view, a black man could appear in history not only as a symbol, a victim, or an auxiliary, but as an agent and a citizen prepared to strike against slavery and exclusion, someone who had made slavery history before and was prepared to do so again.[3]

1850: UNCOMPROMISING

When Webster told his fellow senators on March 7, 1850, that he stood before them "not as a Massachusetts man, nor as a Northern man, but as an American," he meant only to proclaim his commitment to the union. He sought to show how he could subsume his local and regional attachments into his love for the nation. But for those in his home state for whom "Massachusetts" was inextricable from a certain historical definition of "freedom," it was becoming nearly impossible to reconcile national loyalties with antislavery ones. In the 1840s, when Webster came to Boston to dedicate the Bunker Hill Monument, local abolitionists ridiculed him for being out of touch with the primary battle of his own day, even as he sang paeans to a past war for liberation. Following his infamous "Seventh of March" speech in support of the Compromise of 1850, abolitionists had little time or patience for mockery. Their distaste for Webster turned to outright hatred.[4]

The despised compromise did not create new anxieties so much as it exacerbated ones that were already there. But in the contest within Massachusetts over different interpretations of what the American Revolution meant—liberty or union—it raised the stakes higher than ever before. As abolitionists saw it, the Compromise of 1850 constituted a radical break from all that was noble in the Bay State's Revolutionary history. In his response to the Seventh of March speech, white abolitionist minister Theodore Parker recalled an oration Webster had delivered in Boston in the spring of 1850, in which the senator had chided his constituents that in the struggle to preserve the union, the key question was not whether South Carolina would agree to moderate her proslavery stance but "whether Massachusetts...will conquer her own prejudices." Calling Webster the worst American traitor since Benedict Arnold, Parker darkly suggested that the senator's advocacy of the Compromise of 1850 indicated that he had indeed vanquished those "prejudices"—which Parker glossed as the state's historical biases in favor of liberty, equality, and self-evident and inalienable rights. If Webster had indeed forgotten that he was a Massachusetts man, the richness of her past would prevent the Commonwealth as a whole from giving up so easily: "She will first have to forget two hundred years of history. She must efface Lexington and Bunker Hill from her memory, and tear the old rock of Plymouth out from her bosom."[5]

Abolitionists believed that the Compromise threatened to bring slavery to Plymouth, Lexington, and Bunker Hill. The major question in 1850 was whether slavery could be bounded, or whether it might push itself out toward the Pacific Ocean and up to the Canadian border, lapping at the heels of the men and women trying to escape its grasp. Congress came up with a proposal that was, in the eyes of the Garrisonians, as corrupt as the Constitution that Daniel Webster swore himself to defending. There were concessions to antislavery folk in the Compromise: the abolition of the slave trade in the nation's capital, the admission of California as a free state. But in leaving the legality of slavery up to popular vote in New Mexico and Utah territory, the plan would not contain the accursed institution. Most offensive to the historical legacy of liberty that Bay State abolitionists vested in their landscape and their persons, the compromisers agreed to a new and more expansive Fugitive Slave Act. Now, when slave catchers pursued runaways into the North, there would be no juries to determine the fate of the captives. Rather than being put before ordinary citizens, possibly with antislavery sympathies, fugitive cases would instead be decided by federal commissioners given monetary incentives to find for the putative slave owners.[6] Moreover, the Fugitive Slave Act pushed the demands on Northerners much further than the Supreme Court had defined them in 1842. In *Prigg v. Pennsylvania*, the Court had ruled that although states could not interfere with federal enforcement of the Constitution's fugitive slave clause, officers of the states were not compelled to carry it out themselves. In contrast, the new law of 1850 not only mandated northern law enforcement officers to apprehend fugitives, but it also required ordinary bystanders to participate in the captures. "All good citizens are hereby commanded to aid and assist in the prompt and efficient execution of this law": with this clause, the Fugitive Slave Law perverted what, to abolitionists, were the rights and obligations of "good citizens" in general, and "Massachusetts men" in particular.[7]

Twelve days after the new law took effect, a group of black Bostonians issued a resolution: "While our hearts gratefully acknowledge the noble stand taken by many in this city and elsewhere, volunteering their positive co-operation in aid of our remaining free in the Old Bay State, we shall nevertheless tenaciously remember, that eternal vigilance is the price of liberty, and that they who would be free, themselves must strike the blow." This resolution, recorded by the meeting's secretary, William Cooper Nell, highlights two significant features of black abolitionism in Massachusetts at this point in time. First, those who assembled in Samuel Snowden's black Methodist church on Beacon Hill that night didn't see the Fugitive Slave Act exclusively or even primarily as a threat to people far away in the plantation South. Amid "an excitement already akin to that which characterized the 'Latimer war of 1843,'" these residents of "the Old Bay State" were once again concerned about how a decision made in Washington would alter Boston's proud history of freedom. Second, while the presence of Boston's most revered white abolitionist, William Lloyd Garrison, "was hailed with enthusiastic demonstrations," this gathering was primarily about preparing black men to act on their own behalf. The line from Byron—"Hereditary bondsmen! know ye not / Who would be free themselves must strike the blow?"— was much beloved by abolitionists of all stripes, but particularly by those of color.[8]

Black Bay Staters in the 1850s, then, were fighting to protect their own freedoms on their own ground. Black abolitionists and some of their white allies gathered again about a week after the meeting at Snowden's church. From the Belknap Street Church (formerly the African Meeting House), they issued a "Declaration of Sentiments of the Colored Citizens of Boston, on the Fugitive Slave Bill!!!" It quoted Joseph Warren and Patrick Henry and invoked the names of Washington and Jefferson. The assembled citizens put themselves in the tradition of those who threw tea into Boston Harbor in 1773 and defended the redoubt at Bunker Hill in 1775. At a time when some people of color were fleeing the United States, one of the resolutions passed at the meeting implored black Bay Staters to stay: "The ties of consanguinity, bid *all* remain, who would lend a helping hand to the millions now in bonds. But, at all events, if the soil of Bunker Hill, Concord and Lexington is the last bulwark of liberty, we can nowhere fill more honorable graves."[9]

Such invocation of the American Revolution was hardly new. But after 1850, it sounded more urgent than ever before as abolitionists made use of every available Revolutionary symbol. If they had excoriated the Bunker Hill Monument when it was first dedicated, they soon appropriated it for their own purposes. Their animosity toward Webster, Everett, and other leaders of the Monument Association did not keep abolitionists from visiting what had become one of the city's premier attractions. On a swing through Boston in 1852, antislavery lecturer Sallie Holley climbed the three hundred stairs to admire the sweeping views, then noted, "it seems to me the anti-slavery reformers have the best right to visit here, as the monument was erected to commemorate the abolitionists of that day."[10] It wasn't clear to abolitionists whether Bostonians were worthy of their cherished monument. Shortly after the celebrated fugitives William and Ellen Craft were forced to flee to England following the passage of the Fugitive Slave Act, a weary abolitionist proposed that a monument to that law's most notorious northern defender might better represent the city's allegiances: "Instead of the people of Boston pointing to the Bunker Hill Monument, and boasting of the heroic deeds of their fathers, they should pull it down, and erect upon its ruins a monument to Webster, and engrave upon it in characters not to be mistaken, 'No protection here for the oppressed.'"[11]

What raised tensions highest was the prospect that the nightmarish scene an abolitionist writer had imagined in 1843—fugitive slaves being snatched from beneath the Bunker Hill Monument, as a crowd of thousands of Bay Staters stood idly by—might now actually happen.[12] Georgia Senator Robert Toombs fueled this fear by allegedly promising gleefully to "call the roll of his slaves in the shadow of the Bunker Hill Monument." While it is unclear whether Toombs ever spoke these words, abolitionists repeatedly attributed them to him as a sign of the Slave Power's resolve to spread its corruptions into the North. In 1857, in the wake of the *Dred Scott* decision, they were especially outraged that Senator James Mason of Virginia, reviled for his role in drafting the Fugitive Slave Act, spoke at the unveiling of a statue of Joseph Warren on Bunker Hill Day.[13] Throughout this period of terror, abolitionists turned the haunting image in Toombs's purported phrase—"the shadow of the Bunker Hill Monument"—to their own purposes, ruing the irony of fugitives sneaking away from slave catchers in a city watched over by a monument to freedom.[14] Their worst fears materialized in 1851, with Boston's first slave rendition under the Fugitive Slave Act of 1850. Hundreds of deputies and civilian supporters held off potential "rescuers" as young runaway Thomas

Sims was ushered to the ship that would return him to Georgia. "Under the shadow of Faneuil Hall and Bunker Hill Monument, a man has been torn from [Boston's] soil and carried into slavery," one Massachusetts newspaper mourned. Another dreaded how the rendition of Sims would tarnish the Bay State's history: "A thousand years from now … the doings of the slave hunters in Boston during the month of April, 1851, will stand forth in her history as the darkest and most disgraceful crime that has ever been perpetrated, or could be perpetrated in a government or among a people, calling themselves Christian and Republican."[15]

In 1854, that "darkest and most disgraceful crime" was committed a second time. Having escaped from Virginia, Anthony Burns had been living and working in Boston for weeks or months (depending on whose testimony one credited) when he was arrested on May 24. While not all activists agreed about what course of action to take, nearly every major figure of Boston abolitionism immediately rallied to Burns's side, from the radical white preacher Theodore Parker to lawyer and orator Wendell Phillips, from the Virginia-born black minister Leonard Grimes to community activist Lewis Hayden, himself a fugitive slave from Kentucky. Echoing their cries on behalf of George Latimer twelve years earlier, abolitionists appealed to Bostonians' historical sensibility in gathering support for Burns: "Men of Boston! Sons of Otis, and Hancock, and the 'Brace of Adamses'! … See to it that no Free Citizen of Massachusetts is dragged into Slavery, WITHOUT TRIAL BY JURY! '76!" Inspired by such calls, on the night of May 26, about 500 people stormed the courthouse where Burns was imprisoned. Not only did the crowd fail to reach him, but in the melee surrounding the attempted rescue, someone killed one of the courthouse guards. It is still unclear who was responsible for James Batchelder's death. But it is known that some of the rioters were armed, and at least two of them fired shots in the courthouse. Back in 1837, Henry B. Stanton had called the Massachusetts abolition movement "a moral contest for holy freedom" in which the "only weapons are truth and love." By 1854, for a growing number of antislavery activists, "truth and love" seemed insufficient to overwhelm the Slave Power.[16]

The rendition of Anthony Burns turned into one of nineteenth-century Boston's most dramatic moments of street theater. The police having ordered all the shops closed, tens of thousands of people crowded into the streets to watch several military companies escort Burns to the wharf. Black bunting and upside-down American flags covered the facades of downtown buildings. Someone carried a coffin labeled "Liberty." Church bells tolled. Historian Albert von Frank captures the funereal atmosphere of the event by calling the Burns procession a "cortège."[17] Abolitionists' emotions were not limited to the sorrow of mourning; they were also spilling over with rage. Her thoughts turned toward Bunker Hill, Charlotte Forten, a free black schoolgirl and diarist then living in Salem, was outraged that such a scene could take place "in sight of the battle-field, [where] thousands of brave men fought and died opposing British tyranny, which was nothing compared with the American oppression of to-day."[18]

A few days before Anthony Burns's rendition to slavery in Virginia, young Charlotte Forten had dined with the Garrison family. She deeply admired William Lloyd Garrison's principles of nonviolence and pronounced him the finest Christian she had ever met. Forten admitted that Garrison set a standard "to which I cannot hope to reach, however, for I believe in 'resistance to tyrants,' and would fight for liberty until death." If a sixteen-year-old girl could make a resolution like this, there is little question that adult men did so as well (this was, after all, a culture in which armed defense of liberty was a sign of manhood). At the black Bostonians' meeting to protest the Fugitive Slave Law in 1850, Joshua Bowen Smith had cautioned the assembly not to "preach *Peace*, for, as Patrick Henry said, '*There is no Peace.*' " Instead, Smith advised all runaways to purchase revolvers and prepare to fight, even to commit suicide if the situation became desperate. He scoffed at a fugitive friend of his who spent his days "skulking around his place of business, evidently anticipating the hour of successful seizure." Rather than live in fear, Smith ordered, the fugitive should "show himself a man,—*If Liberty is not worth fighting for it is not worth having.*" Smith, Forten, and many other Massachusetts blacks in the 1850s continued to appreciate Garrison's commitment to antislavery. But they also broke with his tactics. This shift was about more than the broadened acceptability of violence as a response to slavery. For black men particularly, it constituted a more powerful assertion of their own agency.[19]

REVIVING CRISPUS ATTUCKS

Men and women of color had always been key leaders and constituents in the antislavery cause. The typical division of American antislavery activism into two phases—the fight against northern slavery and the transatlantic slave trade from the Revolution through 1808, followed by the emergence of a new mass movement after 1830—is misleading. One of the shortcomings of this conceptualization is that it overlooks the continuous efforts of African Americans to combat slavery and inequality, from the Revolution all the way through the Civil War. In particular, this periodization obscures the ways in which black activists drew white sympathizers into the abolitionist fold.[20] What we see most dramatically after 1850 is not people of color suddenly becoming historical actors in the present—there was nothing new in that— but people of color being *represented* as actors in the American past.

Consider Paul Revere's famed engraving of the Boston Massacre. People in 1770 would have known from newspaper reports that one of the victims, Crispus Attucks, was a man of color, but Revere chose not to call attention to Attucks's presence as an individual, and especially not as an individual of color. In contrast, a print published by Boston's Henry Q. Smith in 1856 imagined this scene very differently. This artist maintained several of the key components of Revere's (actually Henry Pelham's) composition: the facades on either side of King Street converging on the towered town hall, the neat line of British troops firing their rifles toward the Americans. Picturing one redcoat fallen to the ground and one colonist with a club raised, the violence of the revised image is more balanced than Revere's scene, which had been largely responsible for turning the two-sided "affray" into a veritable "massacre." But the most obvious difference in the later representation is the front-and-center presence of a dark-skinned man, head thrust backward as he tries to repel a British bayonet with one hand and grasps a club with the other.[21]

William Cooper Nell praised this "large and handsome lithograph" for "assigning Attucks his true and leading position." It was a position that Attucks had lost after the Revolutionary War, and one that he had only slowly regained in the nineteenth century. Even before the end of the war, when the

"Boston Massacre, March 5, 1770," 1856. Copy of chromolithograph by John Bufford after William L. Champney, ca. 1936–1942. *National Archives and Records Administration, College Park, Maryland*

Boston Town Council decided to suspend annual commemorations of the
Boston Massacre, Crispus Attucks had little meaning for Americans "beyond
his status as a body in the street," as Stephen H. Browne puts it. From the late
eighteenth into the early nineteenth century, his living presence as someone
whose actions had threatened tyranny was far less important than his dead
weight as evidence of what tyranny could do to its subjects. While William
Gordon's history of the Revolution (first published in 1789) mentioned in
passing that one part of the mob on March 5, 1770, "appear[ed] to be headed
by the mulatto Attucks," his name more often appeared simply as one of five
in a list of the dead. Early nineteenth-century readers could encounter
Attucks as murder victim in the transcripts of the Massacre trials, which
were republished in 1807 and 1824. The account of the trials also gave readers
the Crispus Attucks that John Adams created: a menacing outsider, who
seemed "to have undertaken to be the hero of that night."[22]

Nell's version of Crispus Attucks does not seem to have come directly
from the trial transcripts. In 1841, Nell confessed to Wendell Phillips that he
had been "unable to find out much about the History of Attucks."[23] Although
the Boston martyr would later become an essential entry in biographical dic-
tionaries of people of color, he did not appear in the anthologies of "Negro"
genius and accomplishment that appeared before 1850.[24] Instead, Nell cited
just two sources that mentioned Attucks. One was an account of the American
Revolution by Italian historian Carlo Botta. First translated into English and
published in Philadelphia in 1820, Botta's *History of the War of Independence
of the United States of America* went through ten editions by 1848; it was a
popular and oft-quoted work praised by Thomas Jefferson and John Adams.
Botta, who spent much of his life in France, had participated in his adopted
country's Revolution but eventually favored what he saw as the American
Patriots' more considered approach to political transformation. To that end,
his history was sympathetic to the Americans, particularly Washington.[25]

Botta's account of the Boston Massacre drew on the trial transcripts to
evoke a nightmarish episode of mob violence, similar to the scene that John
Adams conjured up in his closing arguments as defense attorney:

> The cries, the howlings, the menaces, the violent din of bells, still sounding the
> alarm, increased the confusion and the horrors of these moments: at length
> the mulatto and twelve of his companions, pressing forward, environed the
> soldiers, and striking their muskets with their clubs, cried to the multitude: "*Be
> not afraid, they dare not fire; why do you hesitate, why do you not kill them, why
> not crush them at once?*"

Botta's inspiration for that last line probably came from the trial, where one
witness reported that "The People before firing said [of the British soldiers]
damn 'em they durst not fire, dont be afraid." In Botta's more poetic version,

the speaker was not the more generic "People" but "the mulatto and twelve of his companions." This subtle change gave a more definitive role to Attucks, and it also highlighted the lawlessness of the scene: under the terms of the British Riot Act, a felonious mob was defined as a group of twelve or more people disturbing the public peace. Ever the moderate, Botta went on to praise the acquittal of the British soldiers accused of killing Attucks and his comrades. In his eyes, Adams's defense and the jury's decision showed that justice and order could prevail in America, even in the midst of political division. A functioning legal system could rein in the excesses of Revolutionary fervor exemplified by Attucks and his twelve angry men.[26]

While Botta's intent was to celebrate the rule of law, William Cooper Nell read the Italian's history very differently. For Nell, the thrill of Botta's version of the Boston Massacre came from its presentation of a man of color who wasn't afraid to stand up to his oppressors and was an undisputed leader in the Patriot cause. In Nell's own historical writing, the account of the Massacre and Attucks's role in it is almost entirely direct quotation from Botta, including the rousing call, *"why not crush them at once?"* The second source Nell cited, Benjamin Bussey Thatcher's memoir of George Robert Twelves Hewes, also emphasized Attucks's leadership on the night of March 5. "According to all accounts," Thatcher explained, Attucks "figured pretty largely among" the crowd. One witness "saw him at the head of twenty or thirty sailors"; another "remembers Attucks distinctly," having watched him taunt a British guard. Thatcher, like Botta, took pains to emphasize that the soldiers were so provoked and threatened by the crowd that their eventual acquittal for the murder of Attucks and the others was surely justified. Historian Alfred Young's study of Hewes, an ordinary shoemaker swept up in the extraordinary events of the Revolution, suggests why Thatcher described the crowd action of the 1760s and 70s in careful, colorful detail even as he condoned the response of the British soldiers and the verdict in their trial. Against the rising labor movement of the mid-1830s, the Whig lawyer Thatcher saw in the humble shoemaker's life story a way both to acknowledge the "lower sort's" contributions to the Revolution and to stem working-class efforts to claim the Revolution as their own. "Thatcher's challenge," Young explains, "was to make an acceptable hero of the actor without condoning the actions." The American Revolution, once again, would be "tamed."[27]

A biographer or historian could try his best to conform his telling of events to his political agenda. He could do much less to control how those who read his account would turn it to their own purposes. Nell claimed that Botta's and Thatcher's histories "establish the fact that the colored man, ATTUCKS, was *of* and *with* the people, and was never regarded otherwise." Neither Botta, who openly deplored the excesses of the French Revolution, nor Thatcher, a quintessential New England conservative, was inclined to

vaunt or trust "the people." Thatcher accepted John Adams's description of
the crowd as "a motley mob of saucy boys, negroes and mulattoes, Irish
teagues, and outlandish Jack-tars" as "not far from a true account of a quite
considerable part of the collection." A fellow Whig might have looked to
Thatcher's books to assuage his concerns about the decay of American social
order. Instead, Nell turned to such histories in search of evidence that people
of color were integral to the project of the American Revolution and therefore had undeniable claims to American citizenship.[28]

Visual culture, as well as written history, contributed to Crispus Attucks's
transformation from a disorderly stranger in colonial Boston into a central
player in the American Revolution. Indeed, visual and literary representations of the Revolution played off each, with authors and artists freely quoting one another as they translated words into pictures and pictures into
words.[29] Artists and viewers also looked back at older images with new eyes.
For abolitionists, *The Death of General Warren*, John Trumbull's 1786 painting
of the Battle of Bunker Hill, was especially deserving of a second look.
Trumbull himself had explained that the black figure at the right margin of
his canvas was a "faithful Negro," standing behind his master. Starting
around the 1820s, stories circulated in print about a black Bunker Hill soldier—most frequently identified as Peter Salem—who had fired the shot that
killed British Major Pitcairn. At some point in the nineteenth century, people
began to conflate these two representations of blacks at Bunker Hill, the
figure in Trumbull's painting and Peter Salem, Pitcairn's alleged slayer. "In
some engravings of this battle," Nell explained, "this colored soldier occupies
a prominent position; but in more recent editions, his figure is *non est inven-
tus*. A significant, but inglorious omission." Drawing heavily on Nell's historical research, Theodore Parker wrote to George Bancroft, "In the engravings
of the battle when I was a boy, the black man, Peter Salem, appears in the act
of shooting Major Pitcairn; but now-a-days, a white man is put in his place."
The old engravings that Nell and Parker referenced were undoubtedly versions of Trumbull's painting.[30]

While modern critics tend to emphasize how Trumbull's scene marginalized black participation in the Revolution, Nell and his collaborators approved
of what they perceived as the image's commemoration of black patriotism
and Revolutionary-era ideals of equality. In making the case for integrating
Boston's public schools in 1845 (a cause close to Nell's heart), Henry Bowditch
pointed to the appearance of a man of color in "the far-famed picture of
the Battle of Bunker Hill" as evidence that "in those times there was less
prejudice than exists now, for the negro marched shoulder to shoulder with
the white man in the armies of the revolution."[31] Even as Nell and other
historically minded abolitionists appreciated Trumbull's work, when it came
to creating their own narratives and images of the Revolution, they made the

significance of people of color even more transparent. The two illustrations that Nell included in his book-length work, *The Colored Patriots of the American Revolution* (1855), both reworked Trumbull's *Death of Warren*. The frontispiece, captioned "Crispus Attucks, the First Martyr of the American Revolution," preserved the essence of Paul Revere's famed depiction of the Boston Massacre: the line of redcoats with weapons at the ready, a cloud of smoke, and a tower in the background. The foreground of this scene, however, is a dark-skinned man, stretched on the ground with his upper body supported by a white compatriot. Another white man stands above the two, trying to hold off the British fire. The triangle formed by these three figures, a dying man and two of his countrymen, mimics the shape and composition of the central scene of Trumbull's *Death of Warren*, down to the details of one supporter's outstretched arm and the fallen man's weapon and tricon hat strewn nearby. The resemblance was hardly coincidental. Although others had perished for the cause earlier, Warren's status and prominence made him a "first" in the pantheon of heroes killed. By positioning Crispus Attucks in the posture of this beloved Revolutionary martyr, Nell's illustrator reinforced the claim of Attucks's priority and significance.[32]

Crispus Attucks, the First Martyr of the American Revolution, King (now State) Street, Boston, March 5th, 1770. Page 16.

"Crispus Attucks, the First Martyr of the American Revolution." Frontispiece from William Cooper Nell, *Colored Patriots of the American Revolution*. Boston: Robert F. Wallcut, 1855. *Courtesy of Documenting the American South, the University of North Carolina at Chapel Hill Libraries*

   The other illustration in *Colored Patriots* revised the right half of Trumbull's canvas. This image dispelled any ambiguity concerning the identity of the black man in the scene. Captioned "Peter Salem, the Colored American, at Bunker Hill," this scene recapitulated Trumbull's depiction of Pitcairn falling backward into the arms of two of his men. To the right of that cluster is Peter Salem, the man said to have killed the British officer. As in Trumbull's painting, the black man here is stepping toward the right but looking back over his left shoulder. Also as in the original scene, this man holds a rifle over his chest. But unlike Trumbull's version, the gun in the later illustration clearly belongs to the man who is carrying it, not his master, for this Peter Salem *has* no master. The white man who stood in front of him in the *Death of Warren* has disappeared. In short, the citizen-soldier has replaced Trumbull's "faithful Negro."

"Peter Salem, the Colored American, at Bunker Hill." Illustration
from William Cooper Nell, *Colored Patriots of the American
Revolution*. Boston: Robert F. Wallcut, 1855. *Courtesy of
Documenting the American South, the University of North Carolina
at Chapel Hill Libraries.*

These two images capture Nell's overarching objective in his histories: to show people of color as historical agents, especially in the most commemorated and revered period of American history. His assertion of black historical agency staked Nell's ground in a long-standing debate about African Americans' fitness for freedom. This debate took place not only between abolitionists and their opponents, but also among black and white abolitionists, and even (perhaps most searchingly) among black activists and intellectuals, who also considered the question's flip side: could the United States of America ever be a fit place for people of color to live freely? In addition to contributing to these ongoing discussions within the black community about the nature and demands of agency and autonomy, Nell's historiography also participated in urgent political work at mid-century concerning the relationship of black people (primarily black men) to the state. Both of these contexts—the black intellectual and political tradition, and the particular exigencies of the 1850s—help to frame the idiosyncrasies and complexities of *The Colored Patriots of the American Revolution*.[33]

NO SEPARATE DESTINY, NO SEPARATE PAST

William Cooper Nell's life fused the two ways people "participate in history...as actors and as narrators."[34] Born in Boston in 1816, he had already had a long activist career by the time he published *Colored Patriots* in 1855. While his mother, Louisa, was a Bay Stater by birth, his father was from Charleston, South Carolina. William Guion Nell, like his son, was a reformer, involved in community politics among Boston's blacks in the 1820s. One of the elder Nell's close associates was David Walker, author of the *Appeal... to the Colored Citizens of the World* in 1829. Due in part, no doubt, to his upbringing in this activist circle on Beacon Hill, William Cooper Nell was attuned to the injustices of northern society from an early age. One of the formative experiences in his politics of equality occurred when he was thirteen years old. His performance at the African Meetinghouse school earned him a city-wide academic achievement award endowed by a bequest from Benjamin Franklin. While the white winners received medals and invitations to a banquet in their honor, all young Nell and each of the other black honorees got was a copy of *The Life of Benjamin Franklin*. From that point forward, Nell recalled, he committed himself to educational equality for children of all colors. He believed unwaveringly that education was essential to racial uplift and that the elimination of all forms of segregation was necessary to social progress. Over the course of a long activist career, the integration of Boston's public schools was only one of the many reforms he advocated.[35]

Just a few years after the Franklin award incident, Nell began working for an upstart antislavery newspaper in Boston. Initially serving as the *Liberator's* errand boy, he soon became an apprentice to Garrison in the printing trade. Over the next thirty years, even as he continued to play a vital behind-the-scenes role in the newspaper's production, Nell also contributed many of his own articles for publication in the *Liberator*. He took a hiatus from his work in Boston's abolition circle from 1847 to 1849, when he went to Rochester as publisher for Frederick Douglass's new paper, the *North Star*. For Douglass, the establishment of the *North Star* in upstate New York was an effort to distance himself from Garrison and the control he attempted to exert over black abolitionists in Boston. Although Nell long professed loyalty to Garrison, perhaps he also had misgivings about the way Boston's white abolitionists treated their black colleagues. In 1840, financial trouble had prompted the Massachusetts Anti-Slavery Society to abruptly dismiss Nell from the office job he had held there for three years. Black Bostonians were incensed at what they saw as part of a larger pattern of white abolitionists' insensitivity toward blacks' desire for positions of influence within the anti-slavery movement and their need for economic opportunities in the world at large. Eventually, Nell would side with Garrison in his acrimonious rift with Douglass in the 1850s. Nevertheless, during his tenure at the *North Star*, Nell's philosophy began to diverge from that of his first patron. Following on the larger abolition movement's turn from moral suasion to electoral politics in the 1840s, Nell ran (unsuccessfully) as a Free Soil candidate for the Massachusetts legislature in 1850. Around the same time, he edged away from Garrisonian nonresistance, and he turned his attention to African American participation in the Revolutionary War.[36]

On March 5, 1851, Nell and others presented a petition to the Massachusetts legislature requesting funds toward a monument to Crispus Attucks. The committee rejected the petition, on the grounds that the first martyr of the Revolution was really Christopher Snider, one of a group of young boys who taunted and threw stones at a customs official, Ebenezer Richardson, in February 1770. Enraged, Richardson had drawn out a gun and shot and killed Snider; the boy's massive funeral took place just days before the Boston Massacre. Nell did not deny that Snider had died first, but he called his death "the result of a very different scene from that in which Attucks fell." Perhaps he attributed to the grown man a kind of political agency lacking in a young boy.[37] Nevertheless, Nell was unsurprised by the legislature's response. "The rejection of this petition was to be expected, if we accept the axiom that a Colored man never gets Justice done him in the United States, except by mistake," he dryly observed.[38] Rather than content himself with this injustice, Nell resolved that anyone intent on denying patriots of color proper gratitude would have to willfully overlook a public and accessible record of all that "colored Americans" had done to secure their nation's freedom. So he assembled a twenty-four-page pamphlet, *Services of Colored Americans, in the*

Wars of 1776 and 1812, documenting examples of black heroism, from Crispus Attucks to Richard Seavers ("King Dick"), a community leader among black prisoners at Dartmoor during the War of 1812. Nell's research strategy in collecting these stories was multifaceted. He copied down epitaphs and obituaries. He mined histories of the Revolutionary War for passing mentions of "mulattoes" and "Negroes." He interviewed survivors whenever possible, and he spoke with the survivors' survivors when that was the best he could do. He perused government records for statutes, petitions, and legal rulings that shed light on the history of slavery and freedom. Finally, in 1855, he compiled over three hundred pages of his discoveries into a book.

The Colored Patriots of the American Revolution, with Sketches of Several Distinguished Colored Persons: To Which Is Added a Brief Survey of the Condition and Prospects of Colored Americans is, to modern tastes, an odd read. Like many writers of history in his day, Nell copied liberally from other sources. The book is rich with transcriptions from government archives, biographical sketches assembled from newspapers and gravestones, and anecdotes gathered from oral history. Arranged by state, it has the compendious quality of many a nineteenth-century biographical or local history, with no obvious interpretive thread holding the material together. (True to its author's Yankee origins, by far the longest chapter in the book, at over a hundred pages, is devoted to Massachusetts.) Nell defined his theme broadly, to include information about emancipation and abolitionism in the northern states, as well as biographical sketches of distinguished blacks who lived after the Revolution was long over. The Massachusetts chapter, for instance, eulogized two men born in the 1780s, Richard Potter, known primarily for his talents in ventriloquy and sleight-of-hand, and Isaac Woodland, a grain inspector active in Boston's antislavery movement. Potter and Woodland stood out for their respectability—the hard work, self-sufficiency, honesty, and integrity that earned them the admiration of their communities.[39]

Nell said little about his rationale for including particular documents, individuals, or anecdotes in his book, but in a letter to Wendell Phillips in July 1855, as he struggled to raise the money for publication, Nell said of his compilation, "Each name and every fact has its use." While there is no way to pinpoint an individual "use" for each of the anecdotes in the book, Nell was speaking to a heterogeneous audience, and he had multiple agendas. To address all of them, he found it necessary to move beyond the military records he had assembled for his earlier historical pamphlets. "Aside from the military facts," he explained to Phillips, "the other departments dovetailed in are what will be attractive and instructive to Colored people, and anti-slavery friends—To new converts they will be serviceable in the political campaign now sounding its Battle cry over the country."[40]

Nell's message to these antislavery warriors not only demanded an end to slavery but also extolled the virtue of equal American citizenship. Many white antislavery sympathizers had yet to be convinced that their black compatriots had the capacity to be good citizens. On the other side, amid the outrages of the 1850s, black Americans were uncertain not of their own worth as citizens, but of the value of fighting to be included in a nation that seemed so set on rejecting them. Nell approvingly quoted the black abolitionist minister J. W. C. Pennington, who contended, "*The colored population of the United States have no destiny separate from that of the nation of which they form an integral part....* If we, born in America, cannot live upon the same soil on terms of equality with the descendants of [Europeans], then the fundamental theory of the American Republic fails and falls to the ground." In his own writing, Nell turned to history to argue to a varied and skeptical audience that black people and the United States of America needed each other.[41]

One element of Nell's strategy was to craft a heroic narrative of black participation in American military history. The contributions of Crispus Attucks, Peter Salem, and dozens of other black veterans whose names fill *Colored Patriots* "disrupted the assumption that people of color are a people without a history."[42] When directed toward a white audience, examples of black heroism challenged what historian George Fredrickson has called "romantic racialism," a nineteenth-century conceptualization of human difference that associated blackness with meekness and docility. Espoused not only by apologists for slavery but also by leading white abolitionists—Harriet Beecher Stowe's "Uncle Tom" is the quintessential romanticized black martyr—this ideology attributed the supposed infrequency of slave rebellion to innate differences between people of African and European (particularly Anglo-Saxon) descent. Indeed, Stowe provided an introduction to Nell's book that both nodded to racialist assumptions and noted that *Colored Patriots* would overturn them: "The colored race have been generally considered by their enemies, and sometimes by their friends, as deficient in energy and courage...This little collection of interesting incidents, made by a colored man, will redeem the character of the race from this misconception."[43]

For Nell and other black civil rights leaders in the 1850s, claiming a history of military heroism was critical to rehabilitating black men's image from the feminization of romantic racialism. Their call for "manhood and citizenship" linked agency and manliness in a context in which the major privileges and obligations of citizenship, including military service and suffrage, were confined to men. Within the gendered logic of nineteenth-century political theory, black male citizenship would also benefit black women under the legal principle of coverture. Historian James O. Horton explains that "to demand the manhood of the race was to demand racial independence and respect," securing political recognition for women through the agency of their husbands or fathers.[44] Though Nell's appeal to militaristic and masculinist conceptions of citizenship might seem an odd move for someone who in other contexts endorsed nonresistance and women's rights (both causes championed by his mentor Garrison), it was in line with black intellectuals' priorities at mid-century, which included critiquing racial essentialism and asserting black agency.[45]

Though scholars have tended to concentrate on the military heroism of *Colored Patriots*, this compendious and somewhat eccentric book spoke to more than just that narrative. Robert J. Cottrol situates Nell's book as part of a "process of rectification" that countered white assumptions of black inferiority with specific examples of black genius and achievement. What needed rectifying in the 1850s, however, was not just white racial attitudes but also black commitment to the American national project that (Nell argued) Attucks had initiated. In *Colored Patriots*, stories from the Revolutionary era about owners freeing their slaves, legislators debating antislavery bills, and juries siding with people of color in emancipation lawsuits permitted readers to link nineteenth-century abolitionism with early American patriotism, making antislavery endemic to what it meant to be American. These accounts of whites acting out against slavery during the Revolution and early republic gave blacks reason to believe that there was something in American history worth redeeming. In other words, Nell was not only making an argument to whites about the heroism of blacks but also assuring blacks of the potential for humaneness among American whites. He made his argument to men and women of color most explicit in "Conditions and Prospects of Colored Americans," an essay appended to the historical chapters of *Colored Patriots*. In introducing a chapter on "citizenship," which detailed various cases in which blacks had either been granted or denied passports, he noted, "The following facts showing the theory and practice of this government, capricious as the latter has been, yet furnish precedents favorable to the colored man." Identifying historical precedents not only for black agency but also for the inclusion of people of color into national privileges and institutions was essential to making integration seem viable.[46]

And it was integration, more than anything else, that Nell sought. Reviewing the history of the abolition movement since 1830, he was critical of all racially exclusive antislavery and civil rights organizations, including the Massachusetts General Colored Association (formed in the 1820s by his father, William Guion Nell, and David Walker, among others), as well as the conventions of black citizens that met frequently in the northern states. Nell even went so far as to equate the participants in these "colored institutions" with the most reviled of reformers—those in the American Colonization Society:

How indignant does the colored man feel, when some colonizationist denies his equal rights in churches, public places and conveyances, by saying, "*Why don't you go among your own people, where you belong?*" And yet, in many instances, the very individuals whose sensibilities are thus wounded, are themselves active in upholding colored institutions. By such a course, they blunt the sword of their denunciations against colorphobia.[47]

All its examples of extraordinary heroism and ordinary respectability made *The Colored Patriots of the American Revolution* an extended answer to the colonizationist's question. By necessity, it was also a response to other blacks, whom Nell heard asking "why don't you *stay* among us, your own people?" For Nell, this question was nonsensical; Crispus Attucks's blood proved that he, and all other people of color, belonged among Americans.

At times Nell's critique of identity politics suggested that blacks simply needed to emulate whites in order to overcome their subjugation: "If colored genius will but imitate the successful examples among the whites, the public will surely reward the persevering effort....It is possible so to deport ourselves, that the idea of color shall be forgotten."[48] At a moment when many were coming to see themselves as a "nation within a nation," other black activists made powerful arguments for the convention movement and other race-specific organizations as constituting an alternative public sphere, a "discursive, critical arena" for self-help, mutual support, and political debate and strategizing among people of color. Even as they also embraced the politics of "uplift" (albeit for different purposes), some participants in this oppositional public sphere would have seen Nell as hopelessly naïve in his assumption that black respectability would earn the esteem of whites.[49] Nell's constant challenge in his historical work was to balance disappointment and possibility. As black thinkers and activists in the 1850s looked back over the course of American history, they found different ways to measure their hopes and dreams against a record of betrayal and injustice.[50] Interpreters of black Americans' "prospects" did not always agree about the likelihood that their desires for democratic citizenship could be fulfilled within the United States, but authors on either end of the spectrum from integration to separation had more in common than many scholars have recognized. Historian Patrick Rael advisedly questions the tendency to frame black politics in this period as a debate for or against nationalism, since nationalist assumptions saturated so much of mid-nineteenth-century political discourse, both among African Americans and within American society more generally.[51]

The pervasiveness of certain ideas about nation and citizenship is evidenced by the striking connections between *Colored Patriots* and a contemporary text that, on the surface, seems as different from Nell's as one could get: Martin Delany's *Condition, Elevation, Emigration, and Destiny of the Colored People of the United States, Politically Considered* (1852). The book proposed that African Americans leave the United States to establish communities in Central and South America; later Delany would consider emigration to Africa (though he vehemently opposed the American Colonization Society's Liberia project). While Delany has sometimes been called the father of black nationalism, his politics were more varied and ambivalent than that label implies. Emigration was a last resort for Delany. Appropriately enough, it takes a long time for *The Condition... of the Colored People* to get to his emigration scheme. Instead, the book begins with a lengthy review of the history and present situation of African-descended people in the United States.[52]

Delany made it clear that people of color ought to be legally recognized as citizens. "We are Americans," he declared, "having a birthright citizenship—natural claims upon the country...which may, by virtue of unjust laws, be obstructed, but never can be annulled." While Nell's historical writing tended to consist of long lists of facts and anecdotes, Delany was inclined to mix data with political theory. Delany offered a definition of "citizen" that supported the premise of *Colored Patriots*, even if Nell never so clearly articulated it. Call it the investment theory of citizenship: "The legitimate requirement... necessary to the justifiable claims for protection and full enjoyment of all the rights and privileges of an unqualified freeman...is, that each person so endowed, shall have made contributions and investments in the country. Where there is no investment there can be but little interest." Delany noted that the highest patriotic investment came from military service. This was why Nell's examples of black presence and especially black agency in the Revolutionary War mattered so much. In elaborating this point, Delany turned to the Boston Massacre and Bunker Hill:

> If we establish our right of equal claims to citizenship with other American people, we shall have done all that is desirable in this view of our position in the country. But if in addition to this, we shall be able to prove, that colored men, not only took part in the great scene of the first act for independence, but that they were the actors—a colored man was really the hero in the great drama, and actually the first victim in the revolutionary tragedy—then indeed, shall we have more than succeeded, and have reared a monument of fame to the history of our deeds, more lasting than the pile that stands on Bunker Hill.

To build this "monument of fame" in his own book, Delany relied almost entirely on examples quoted or paraphrased from Nell's *Services of Colored Americans*, the precursor to *Colored Patriots*. Nell's histories, Delany touted, "should be read by every American the country through."[53]

That Martin Delany and William Cooper Nell moved from a common understanding of citizenship and a common recognition of black participation in American history to such different interpretations of the national commitments of people of color underscores the complexity of black politics after 1850. Before that point, Delany and Nell were, quite literally, in the same place. Delany was coeditor of Douglass's Rochester-based *North Star* when Nell served as its publisher in the late 1840s.[54] At the time, the three reformers shared a commitment to black elevation within the United States. Two major incidents, one national and one personal, alienated Delany from American society after 1850. On a national level, the passage of the Fugitive Slave Act, which he blamed for the "national disfranchisement of colored people," convinced Delany that African Americans had no chance of being incorporated into the American body politic.[55]

Delany's disillusionment stemmed not only from politics in Washington but also from an experience he had in Boston. In November 1850, Delany and two other black men were the first students of color accepted to Harvard Medical School. A large group of the school's white students protested the presence of classmates "whose company we would not keep in the streets, and whose Society and associates we could not tolerate in our houses." By March, school administrators had asked the black students to leave. Though he complied with the request to withdraw from Harvard, Delany didn't forget the indignity. "The majority of white men cannot see why colored men cannot be satisfied with their condition in Massachusetts," he wrote to Garrison in response to the *Liberator*'s review of his book, "Blind selfishness on the one hand, and deep prejudice on the other, will not permit them to understand that we desire the *exercise* and *enjoyment* of these [citizenship] rights, as well as the *name* of their possession." If Delany could encounter such blatant discrimination in the supposed stronghold of abolitionism and liberty, what chance for citizenship did people of color have in the nation at large?[56]

Nell knew firsthand the limitations on white Bay Staters' conceptions of equality, but he did not mention Delany or his struggles at Harvard in *Colored Patriots*. He did write about the New York-born John DeGrasse, a successful physician who had studied medicine at Bowdoin College and in Europe before becoming in 1854 the first person of color admitted to the Massachusetts Medical Society. At the close of the chapter on Massachusetts in *Colored Patriots*, Nell quoted an Italian sundial: "*I mark only the hours that shine.*" "We should not dwell always upon the darker portion of the picture," he advised:

> What a satisfaction to the proscribed colored American is the fact, that, in this slavery-cursed land, there are those true hearts ready to accord the rights and privileges to others so prized by themselves; that, in the highways and byways of life, on the railroad car and in the steamboat, in the lyceum and college, in the street, the store, and the parlor, a noble band is found, united in purpose, uncompromising in principle, fearless in action, whose examples are like specks of verdure amidst universal barrenness,—as scattered lights amidst thick and prevailing darkness.[57]

If Nell seems naïve at times, it's worth remembering that he lived in a moment characterized both by total despair and marvelous dreaming (there is, after all, an element of fantasy in Delany's idea that black Americans would find republican salvation in Nicaragua). Nell could see the "thick and prevailing darkness" that clouded the American nation. But in *Colored Patriots* as a whole, and in this passage more succinctly, he crafted an alternative vision of the nation. The various "highways and byways" that Nell listed constituted a public sphere where abolitionists, black and white, encountered each other and pressed their claims to represent what was truly American. This nation existed not only across different pockets of space but also across distinct moments in time, linking, for instance, the Revolutionary-era patriotism of Crispus Attucks and John Hancock to the nineteenth-century agitation of those who mourned the rendition of Anthony Burns.[58]

Nell would ever give the edge to any evidence of progress in history. Ironically, to recognize the possibility of progress, it helped to look well back in time, to the 1770s, the most significant moment of change in American history. He warned at the end of *Colored Patriots* that fully realizing the promise of that moment would require a second revolution: "The Revolution of 1776, and the subsequent struggles in our nation's history, aided, in honorable proportion, by colored Americans, have (sad, but true, confession) yet left the necessity for a second revolution, no less sublime." With at least a toe still in Garrison's nonresistant camp, Nell didn't come right out and say "To arms, men!" In the 1850s, other black Bostonians did.[59]

TOWARD A SECOND REVOLUTION

Martin Delany wasn't the only reader who admired Nell's Revolutionary research. Reviewers praised *Colored Patriots* for the good it would do for African American uplift by bringing to light a forgotten aspect of American history. "Read this book, and learn that patriotism, courage, and talents are not confined to peculiar races, or complexion," the *New Bedford Standard* commanded. "A thrilling history it is," noted the *Hartford Republican*, "one which makes the blood boil in the reader's veins, when he reflects that the descendants of these Revolutionary heroes are insulted and abused by the dominant power." Nell's laborious research even earned his book some grudging praise from the South. "Aside from the ridiculous and absurd pretension which it sets up in behalf of the negro race, it contains some things in connection with our Revolutionary struggle, that are quite interesting," the *Virginia Liberty Sentinel* admitted, adding that the book was impressive enough that it was unlikely to have been written solely by "a gentleman of so dark a hue as the author is represented to be."[60]

William J. Watkins also appreciated Nell's work: so much so that he read *Services of Colored Americans* to a committee of the Massachusetts legislature. A former agent for the *Liberator* and a Free Soil party activist, the Baltimore-born Watkins was making good Nell's wish that his research "be serviceable in the political campaign now sounding its Battle cry." When he came before the legislators on February 24, 1853, Watkins represented sixty-five men of color seeking a charter to form an independent militia. The title of the published version of his speech was "Our Rights as Men," and "men" and "manhood" were recurring words within it. "Manhood" accounted both for the gendered claim that Watkins was making, the right to participate in the militia, as well as his claim to agency: "Regard us not as obsequious suppliants for favor, but as men, proud of, and conscious of the inherent dignity of manhood." Later, Watkins directly criticized romantic racialist ideals of black submissiveness. He accused the white legislators of only accepting people of color "if they, like Uncle Tom, submit to your indignities with Christian meekness and becoming resignation."[61]

Watkins himself refused to be an Uncle Tom. His speech to the Legislative Committee on the Militia was caustic, indignant, and stirring. Consider this passage in which Watkins chastised New England Whigs Edward Everett and Daniel Webster for advocating African colonization:

> Every avenue to honor and renown is piled up with mountains to obstruct our progress…and then, to add insult to injury, we are gravely told that God has drawn a broad line of demarcation between us; that we are inately [sic] inferior to the white man….And [they] tell us in the same breath, that we are the people to evangelize and christianize Africa….Colonization does for us in Africa, what God cannot do for us in America. *Mirabile dictu!*

Watkins's assertion of manhood and citizenship picked up where David Walker had left off a generation earlier. Imploring whites to "treat us like men," Walker had charged, "You are not astonished at my saying we hate you, for if we are men we cannot but hate you, while you are treating us like dogs." Some twenty years later, the forcefulness and anger in Watkins's speech reinforced the point that no man of dignity could silently suffer the hatred and abuse long inflicted upon people of color. The people he represented were "among the most respectable men in the community…law-abiding, tax-paying, liberty-loving, NATIVE-BORN, AMERICAN CITIZENS; men who love their country, despite its heinous iniquities…some of them are the descendants of revolution sires, and revolution mothers." The pages he read from Nell's pamphlet cemented the connection to the Revolutionary forebears and emphasized the agency of black men in history.[62]

About a week later, another man of color appeared before the Joint Committee on the Militia. Robert Morris also appealed to history: "During the entire revolutionary struggle, our fathers fought side by side with your fathers all over the country, to overthrow and relieve themselves from British oppression and secure to themselves and their posterity the blessings of a free republic." He mourned the irony that "at the termination of that prolonged and severe contest our fathers who had so bravely fought in defence of American liberty, were immediately reduced to slavery." As a trained lawyer—apparently the first black attorney to argue in an American courtroom—Morris based most of his argument on legal reasoning and logical consistency. As a result, the tone of his speech and his representation of the present condition of people of color were quite different from Watkins's. Morris concentrated on all that was open to people of color: "In the New England States, and particularly in Massachusetts, we have and enjoy nearly all the rights and immunities of citizens generally," including the elective franchise, property ownership, and equal access to public institutions. He even used the discriminatory federal militia statute as evidence of blacks' citizenship. The militia law of 1792 called for the enrollment of "each and every free able-bodied white male citizen" of appropriate age. Morris noted that the modifier "white" (not to mention "male") would not have been necessary had "citizen" excluded blacks. The cases of blacks serving in times of war—indeed, of whites *relying* on black service—only solidified the argument that the nation depended on the civic participation of people of color. In short, Morris sought to show that allowing black Massachusetts men to form a militia would hardly be revolutionary (though it would certainly be Revolutionary). It would simply be a logical extension of all the rights they already held and a reasonable response to all the contributions they had already made.[63]

Neither Watkins's nor Morris's approach worked. In what Watkins called a "legislative farce," the committee "asked leave to withdraw" from the question, thereby absolving themselves from any serious consideration of it. Black Bostonians did not relent. Just a few months after the hearings before the legislative committee, they tried another tactic. With a constitutional convention meeting through the late spring and summer to debate a new legal framework for Massachusetts, black activists saw their chance to petition for a permanent change in the state's discriminatory militia law. The petitioners had several vocal advocates on the floor of the convention, so rather than being swept under the rug again, the proposal sparked serious discussion among the delegates. Henry Wilson, Free Soil delegate from Boylston, reminded the assembly that "the colored people of this Commonwealth" descended from men who "fought, bled and died at Bunker Hill"; later he gave a nod to Crispus Attucks as a man of color martyred at the beginning of the Revolution. Supporters also looked to the Bay State's legal history. Using reasoning similar to Morris's, delegate Briggs of Pittsfield noted that there was in Massachusetts "nothing to debar the colored person from receiving all the civil and political rights that are possessed by every other citizen." "That, I believe is the fact, and it is one of which Massachusetts may well be proud," he announced, adding "we ought to know no distinction of color here."[64]

The real sticking point was the irrepressible one of the 1850s, the problem that Webster had hinted at in the opening lines of his Seventh of March speech. Could one be both a Massachusetts man and an American? At issue was the relationship between state-chartered militias and the federal government. The federal act of 1792, which outlined the circumstances in which the president could call forth state militias, clearly stated only that *white* men were required to enroll in the militia. The most recent state statute governing the militia echoed this call for "every able-bodied white male citizen" to enroll.[65] The question the delegates debated was the extent to which the federal regulation was binding over the states. Could Massachusetts change its law so that it permitted a more expansive group of militiamen to enroll? Favoring a states' rights approach, the contingent supporting the black petitioners argued that the state could charter military companies apart from those that might be called forth by the president. Opponents worried that chartering a black militia would put the state in direct conflict with federal laws, and it was this perspective that held the day. Various amendments that would have permitted blacks to enroll in militias failed, as, ultimately, did the proposed constitution itself.[66]

Why did participation in militias matter so much to these petitioners? At its deepest level, the call for equality in the militias tapped into a long-held notion of citizenship that was as much about obligations as about rights. The autonomous citizen was not only one who could exercise freedoms but was also empowered—indeed, obligated—to act in defense of those freedoms, even at the risk of his own life. Foundational as it was to American Revolutionary ideology, this idea about the nature of citizenship reached all the way back to the ancient Greek *polis*. That black activists drew on this tradition is a reminder that they were not working toward a simple idea of an unencumbered freedom but that instead they were looking for ways to make themselves agents in their own history.[67]

Militia service embedded black men in American and African American social traditions as well. Historians Jeffrey Kerr-Ritchie and Hal Goldman put the formation of independent military companies (and the attempted formation of state-chartered militias) in the 1850s in context of a longer tradition of black "military self-presentation" and militant activity throughout the nineteenth century.[68] It is also worth contextualizing the black militias within broader trends in American military history. The militia system was in decline by the 1850s, with many states having dismantled their programs of mandatory militia service. For much of the nineteenth century, and especially after the War of 1812, state militias were primarily social organizations rather than clusters of citizen-soldiers anxious to serve the common good.[69] Just as white militia companies gathered on the Fourth of July, black men attempted to assemble in public to observe days of significance to them, such as the anniversary of the abolition of the slave trade, with similar parades and shows of solidarity. These gatherings provoked relentless derision—not to mention violence—from racist whites, who found the military character of the black men's displays especially laughable.[70]

Yet black men continued to see the fraternal and political bonds formed through such assemblies as important. Through the mid-1850s, Morris repeatedly drew up petitions to the Governor's Council and the legislature. In some cases he and his allies sought charters for independent militia companies, while in others they simply requested "that the word 'white' be struck from the Militia Laws of this Commonwealth."[71] Even without a charter, black men in Boston, led by Morris, organized themselves into an independent military company, the Massasoit Guards, in 1855. Other black militias had been established earlier: the African Greys in Providence in 1821; the Hannibal Guards in Brooklyn in 1848; and a handful of others in cities in New York and Ohio, as well as New Bedford, Massachusetts, early in the 1850s. Many more would form as the decade progressed. The state of Rhode Island even chartered a militia of men of color, and Ohio granted one company use of state arms. There were enough black militias in existence by 1855 that Nell speculated that the Boston group took on the name "Massasoit Guards," as opposed to a more obvious choice, because two groups of "Attucks Guards" already existed, in Cincinnati and New York. The Massasoit Guards organized their first public parade for the first of August, a major date on abolitionist calendars, commemorating emancipation in the British West Indies. This choice of dates connected the Guards in Boston to people of African descent throughout the Atlantic world.[72]

There was another historical connection that the black militiamen claimed for themselves, albeit in a much more muted way than their affinity for fellow citizens of the "Black Atlantic."[73] There might well have been more to the choice of the militia's name than Nell acknowledged. Massasoit was the Wampanoag leader who in 1621 established a peaceful alliance with the Pilgrims. Nineteenth-century writers heralded him as the Indians' "greatest king" and the guest of honor at the first Thanksgiving. Was naming their group after this beloved (and depoliticized) Indian an appeal to white Bay Staters' memories of a past moment of interracial harmony in Massachusetts?[74] Perhaps. Nell noted that Massasoit was "one of those Indian chiefs, who, in early colonial times, proved himself signally friendly to the interests of the Old Bay State." Nell (who was not himself a member of the militia group)

speculated that the Guards took Massasoit's name out of "their pride of loyalty," yet he mused that "a better selection could have been made," if only
the name " 'Attucks' Guards,' after one of their own race," were not already
taken. Though Nell's own research had turned up suggestions that Attucks
was at least partly of Native ancestry, he opted to present the Boston
Massacre's hero as a man of African descent.[75]

Even with the name "Attucks" unavailable, Nell's research had revealed
the names of enough "colored patriots" that if the militiamen had wanted to
take a Revolutionary figure as their namesake, they would have had plenty of
choices. The selection of Massasoit had an additional benefit in that it gave
the militiamen a claim to historical priority that reached even further back
into time than the opening days of the American Revolution. Philip Deloria
has traced how whites in the early republic dressed and acted as "Indians" in
order to claim an "aboriginal closeness" with the American continent. But
the Massasoit Guards were not merely another case of "playing Indian."
Despite all the nineteenth-century efforts to perfect racial taxonomies, racial
labels failed to capture the complicated genealogies of many New Englanders
of color. We get an inkling of a lingering awareness of the Native heritage of
many people of color in a single remark that Morris made before the legislature's militia committee: "Some of the petitioners whom I have the honor to
represent, can trace back their ancestry to a time long before an Englishman
or any white foreigner stood upon American ground."[76]

Morris's comment was both historically correct and politically expedient.
At a time when large numbers of immigrants were pouring into the country,
Morris, Watkins, and other advocates of militia rights emphasized that blacks
were native-born Americans. "All we ask," Watkins told the legislators, "is,
that you treat us as well as you do the Irish, German, Hungarian." He then
went on to read Botta's account of Attucks at the Boston Massacre, a hint that
people of color had a much stronger and longer claim to Americanness than
recent European immigrants did. Morris, who was known as the "Irish lawyer"
due to his large immigrant clientele, noted approvingly that the state had
chartered a company of Irish militiamen. But, he added, "Having granted a
charter, to our Irish fellow citizens not native born, we confidently expect you
will grant a charter to us who are native born citizens." The discourse of
"nativeness" was at peak potency at the very moment that the Massasoit
Guards formed. In 1854, the Know-Nothings, officially known as the "American
Party," enjoyed a spectacular rise to power in Massachusetts, based both on
their opposition to slavery and their intensely nativist claims. Even to those
who weren't Know-Nothing partisans, the idea that citizenship was a birthright for those born within the United States had wide purchase.[77]

Securing their rights to military participation was important to antebellum
blacks' sense of justice and citizenship. For expediency's sake, their advocates

in the constitutional convention sometimes avoided these idealistic arguments. Free Soiler Henry Wilson argued that allowing blacks to join militias would be "of little practical importance to them or to the public." "I can see no reason why they should not be allowed to share a little of the fun and pleasure of a military display," agreed delegate Whitney. But both the black militiamen themselves and those who opposed supplying them with state arms believed that militias were about more than "fun and pleasure." Arming groups of black men had long seemed foolish and reckless to many white Americans, North and South. Indeed, modern scholars and nineteenth-century observers of the "Slave Power" have suggested that one of the primary purposes of the militia system was to have an organization in place to stifle slave rebellions. The black activists also harked back to early ideas about the militia's purpose and significance, specifically the ideal of the citizen-soldier. For them, to be permitted to join the militia was to be recognized as a citizen, someone who had a vested interest in the republic and therefore the capacity to maintain the tenuous balance between power and liberty in the defense of it. In an environment in which the threat to republican freedom seemed especially acute, the citizens' rights to collective self-defense were paramount.[78]

As the delegates debated opening up the militias, they were aware that black abolitionists and their white allies had already demonstrated their willingness to take direct action against slavery. In the 1830s and 40s, abolitionists had formed "vigilance committees," groups of men (often secret) prepared to use force to protect fugitives. Members of vigilance committees also sought to aid fugitives by providing food, shelter, and employment—assistance that was, after 1850, in flagrant violation of the Fugitive Slave Act's requirement that all citizens exercise vigilance on behalf of slaves' *owners*. Avid abolitionists complemented their involvement in moral suasion, party politics, or legal resistance with this kind of direct action. A case in point was the activism of attorney Robert Morris. While he was known for his efforts to pursue racial equality through the judicial system, Morris did not shy from extra-legal means either. In 1851, he was arrested for facilitating the successful rescue of fugitive Shadrach Minkins from a Boston courtroom. The Minkins rescue was organized entirely by black Bostonians, including those who resolved at the colored citizens' meeting of October 1850 to resist the Fugitive Slave Law by all means necessary. Kerr-Ritchie argues that those seeking to form militias in the 1850s were continuing this tradition of militancy with a renewed urgency: "What made the 1850s qualitatively different was the need for collective defence against an expansionist Slave Power that was inexorably moving west (Kansas, Dred Scott), north (Fugitive Slave Act) and south (Mexico)."[79]

Emboldened by representations of men of color striking for their nation's freedom in the Revolutionary era, blacks in the 1850s sought to claim for themselves the rights and the means to forge another kind of emancipatory history. They were not simply seeking freedom; they were seeking to be agents of their own liberation. The Revolutionary and Romantic glorification of autonomous agency made the legal obstacles and social prejudices that limited blacks' action all the more frustrating.[80] Nonetheless, black activists sought to lay claim to historical agency in any way they could. Shortly after the constitutional convention declined to act on the proposal to allow blacks in the militia, William Cooper Nell led a group of black men in submitting to the convention a petition protesting the outcome of the militia debate and entreating the delegates to reconsider. In closing, the petitioners asked that should their request be again denied, they be granted the courtesy "that this protest may be placed on the records of the Convention, and published with the official proceedings, that the stigma may not rest upon their [i.e., the petitioners'] memories, of having tamely acquiesced in a proscription, equally at war with the American Constitution, the Massachusetts Bill of Rights, and the claims of human nature." Through their act of petitioning, Nell and his cosigners asserted themselves as men, as citizens, and as participants in the civic dialogue surrounding the proposed constitution. Countering claims of black passivity, they wanted it a matter of historical record that they had not "tamely acquiesced" to their subordination. Yet they had to attempt to insert themselves into the record by these means because there were no black men among the delegates at the convention. Petitioning, at some level, has always been the domain of political outsiders, and in this case, the outsiders were duly silenced. The delegates turned down their request.[81]

In their efforts to secure full political rights for men of color, Nell, Delany, Morris, Watkins, and other black activists appealed to numerous ideas about how to determine who counted as a citizen. Was it a simple birthright? Was it something inherited through descent from Revolutionary patriots, or (as Delany put it) something earned through investment in the nation? Was it something that should be extended to people of color to preserve logical and legal consistency? All of these claims to citizenship drew on examples from history. But as suggested by the differing approaches that Morris and Watkins took in their speeches before the legislative committee, history presented people of color with an ambiguous legacy. Unsurprisingly, given their commitment to radical change in their own time, both men reinforced their present-day claims to black men's citizenship by calling attention to the historical agency of their Revolutionary forebears.

In bringing that history to bear on the civic status of nineteenth-century blacks, however, Morris and Watkins assessed present conditions in divergent ways. Watkins emphasized the persistence of racial injustice, which looked all the more galling in light of all that black men had done for the nation in its founding moments. On the other hand, Morris's chronicle of the rights that people of color *did* have created a narrative of black civic inclusion from the Revolution down to the present, in which the denial of certain privileges (such as militia enrollment) were aberrations that simply needed to be corrected to create a coherent narrative. In 1853, the Massachusetts legislature and constitutional convention declined to act on the specific question of equal militia rights, but they let the ambiguities of black citizenship stand. In 1857, the Supreme Court resolved the issue with a decision that fulfilled Watkins's darkest suspicions and vanquished Morris's dogged optimism.

THE FUGITIVE AS SOLDIER

Perhaps the most quoted (and most reviled) phrase of the *Dred Scott* decision is Chief Justice Roger B. Taney's pronouncement that African Americans "had no rights that the white man was bound to respect." What is less often recognized is that in its context within the longer decision, this was not (or at least, not only) a normative claim but a historical one. When the Revolution broke out, Taney explained, blacks in America "had for more than a century before been regarded as beings of an inferior order, and altogether unfit to associate with the white race, either in social or political relations." He insisted that the "fixed and universal" (white) public opinion at the time was that people of African descent were irrevocably subordinate to whites. The proof was in the mere existence of the slave trade and the universality of slavery across the American colonies, as well as the many colonial laws that kept people of color in subjection. Much to the shame of Bay Staters, among the statutes Taney cited were the Massachusetts proscriptions on interracial marriage. For him, all the restrictions on the liberties of Revolutionary-era blacks proved that the founders had not intended to include blacks among the "men created equal" in the Declaration of Independence or the "citizens" empowered by the Constitution. Depending on one's point of view, the Chief Justice's logic was either impeccable or atrocious. If the patriots *had* intended this language to include blacks, Taney contended, they would have been wildly inconsistent not to have abolished slavery at the time of the Revolution, but the patriots could not have been inconsistent, because they were "great men" and therefore incapable of such hypocrisy, so their lofty pronouncements about equality and liberty must only have encompassed whites. In short, the fact that the founding fathers were honorable men meant that they must have endorsed slavery. Further, Taney's admiration for these men convinced him that their intentions were binding over all succeeding generations.[82]

Taney's decision reinforced the status of blacks as a people without a history and as individuals who could not act in history. To him, the African
American experience was a state of unvarying subjection. At some level, it
appears that black radical thinkers like David Walker, who at times seemed
paralyzed by the continued degradation of people of color ("I am full!!! I can
hardly move my pen!!!"), shared Taney's sense of black people's abjection.
But African American historical consciousness incorporated the degradation of enslavement and discrimination into a narrative of either exodus or
(in Nell's more secular vocabulary) revolution.[83] In contrast, disregarding
how people of color discussed their own experience, Taney resolutely argued
that in the Revolutionary period, blacks "were never thought of or spoken of
except as property." A year to the day after the court is said to have issued
this decision, Nell brought forth a resounding rebuttal by showing how
Revolutionary blacks had thought and spoke and *acted* for themselves.[84] On
the fifth of March 1858, primarily through Nell's efforts, the anniversary of
the Boston Massacre became an annual observance in Boston for the first
time since the Revolutionary War. At no moment in the acceleration toward
the Civil War were the roles of black men as actors and as narrators in history
more perfectly or more powerfully intertwined than at the first such observance. The event was both a celebration of Crispus Attucks and a lamenta-
tion for Dred Scott. "Faneuil Hall Commemorative Festival, March 5th, 1858,"
announced one side of a promotional broadside, while the other proclaimed
"Protest against the Dred Scott 'Decision.' " Bridging these two headlines was
an engraving of Attucks taking a British bullet and falling backward into a
crowd of patriots. Together, Attucks's literal martyrdom and Scott's legal one
juxtaposed the black man's fulfillment of the obligations of citizenship
against the state's denial of the concomitant privileges. The Fifth of March
1858 was a poignant and pointed display of all the ways in which the present
was failing history.[85]

In his address at the Faneuil Hall event, William Lloyd Garrison railed
that "Judge Taney...stands convicted of grossly falsifying history, and for
a most wicked and inhuman purpose." Strictly speaking, Garrison was
wrong. While Taney had certainly been selective, he had not "falsified" history. The discriminatory statutes and practices he cited had really existed.
Only a few years before, Massachusetts abolitionists had themselves called
attention to the 1786 law reinforcing the colonial ban on interracial
marriage. They had done so as part of their effort to get the prohibition
lifted, and what galled them about Taney's use of history was that he
refused to recognize that they had ultimately succeeded, that there were
moments in a long history of oppression when the citizenship of people of
color was realized. For Garrison, as for Nell, the organizer of the Crispus
Attucks Day observances, history was not just what was remembered; it

was also what one did with those memories. The "wicked and inhuman purpose" to which Taney had turned history was stasis and complacency. In contrast, Nell, Garrison, and the other speakers at the 1858 event saw in history the possibility of change. "I hail the 5th of March as the baptism of the Revolution into forcible resistance; without that, it would have been simply a discussion of rights," Wendell Phillips declared. In the "second revolution" that Nell had forecast in *Colored Patriots*, the announcement of the *Dred Scott* decision on (or near) March 5, 1857, had marked a similar moment of baptism, the culmination of the abolitionist movement's transformation from moral suasion (the mere "discussion of rights") to "forcible resistance."[86]

The March Fifth commemorations that Nell organized for 1858 and then annually through 1865 constituted a kind of gallery of African American military participation. In front of the hall in 1858 were

a large number of interesting relics and mementoes of the olden time, among which may be mentioned a colored engraving representing the scene in King street at the time of the massacre; a small cup, owned by Crispus Attucks; a picture representing Washington crossing the Delaware, in which Prince Whipple (a colored soldier) is seen pulling the strokeoar; Certificate, in Gen. Washington's own hand-writing, of honorable discharge of Brister Baker, a colored soldier in the Connecticut Regiment, June, 1783; Letter of Capt. Perkins to Brigadier General Green, on arresting Lieut. Whitmarsh for abusing a colored soldier named Newport Rhode Island, in camp, dated Long Island, July 11, 1776; Power of Attorney for the recovery of prize-money earned by a colored seaman, Basil Garretson, on board the private armed schooner Mammoth, of Baltimore, said money being claimed by his *reputed* master, J. C. Deshong, of Baltimore—Jan. 3d, 1815; a banner presented by John Hancock to a colored company called "The Bucks of America"; a flag presented to an association of colored men, called "The Protectors," who guarded the property of Boston merchants during the Revolutionary war; a collection of documents illustrative of slavery in Boston between 1718 and 1760.

This strange and jumbled collection of documents and artifacts, many of which Nell must have discovered while researching *Colored Patriots*, reinforced the ubiquity of people of color in America's early history, as slaves and freedpeople, as fighters for freedom and victims of abuse, as individual actors and organized citizens. The following year, Nell added another document to his collection. A friend who was a collector of autographs and antiques turned up a copy of the *Boston Gazette and Weekly Journal*, dated November 20, 1750. In it, William Brown advertised for a runaway "mulatto fellow, about 27 years of age, named Crispus, well set, six feet two inches high, short curled hair, knees nearer together than common." Discovering that Crispus Attucks had been a fugitive slave cemented the link between the actions of this Revolutionary hero and the priorities of the 1850s, speaking as it did to black abolitionists' desire to convert fugitives into citizens.[87] At a moment when the state seemed increasingly intent on restricting the civic agency of people of color, the message of Nell and his allies in the 1850s was that not only was the black man here to stay, but he was prepared to fight.[88]

Epilogue

Fishbones

In some ways, the parade in Boston on May 28, 1863, resembled the one on June 17, 1843, that had marked the completion of the Bunker Hill Monument. The crowds were comparably large. Some observers claimed that 100,000 people had swarmed into the city for the Monument's dedication; twenty years later, the railroads had to add extra trains to accommodate all who wanted to witness the procession. The patriotic atmosphere in 1863 recalled that of 1843. Perhaps some of the same flags and banners flew from windows and rooftops; undoubtedly some of the same people lined the streets and the Common. But there was a crucial difference in the tone and atmosphere of the two occasions. In 1843, the spectators were commemorating a past war. In 1863, they were living out a present one.[1]

The most dramatic difference between the parades was the role and significance of people of color. Back in 1843, the commemorative parade's black presence had come in the form of a servant to President John Tyler. That anonymous man might have been nearly invisible to many an onlooker, though what he signified—the irony and agony of slavery in a land of freedom, the too-easy conflation of "black" and "slave"—was starkly evident to abolitionist observers. Twenty years later, black men marched as freedom fighters, transformed from subordinates to citizens. As William Cooper Nell saw it, the men of the Fifty-fourth Regiment of Massachusetts Volunteer Infantry, processing through the streets of Boston en route to South Carolina, were fulfilling the promise of the American Revolution that Crispus Attucks had inaugurated on the very same ground nearly a hundred years earlier. Accompanied by thirty-seven white officers, the 1,007 men of color who took leave of Boston on May 28, 1863, constituted the North's first all-black regiment of Union soldiers.[2] Nell's research and writing had helped to put these men in a position to make history. In the early 1860s, advocates for establishing a black regiment had continued to look to the Revolution in support of their claim that men of color would make good soldiers. Building on the work that Nell had published in the 1850s, several books and pamphlets about black participation in the Revolution had appeared during the early years of the Civil War.[3]

It is little surprise, then, that when Nell went to watch the Fifty-fourth's parade, he had history on his mind. His description of the scene, rendered confusing yet stirring by his frenzy of associations, layers observations of the present with memories of both the recent and distant past—and with hopes for the future:

> It was my signal good fortune to stand in State street, on the spot where fell CRISPUS ATTUCKS, in Boston massacre of March 5th, 1770,—himself a colored man, and first martyr of the American Revolution.... And as my imagination dwelt upon that event, and my memory was busy with the scenes of THOS. SIMS' and ANTHONY BURNS' return to slavery, both escorted over this identical spot by Boston officials and Boston military...contrasting all this, the shameful past with the glorious present,—a thousand armed colored American soldiers en route for the land of slavery, marching down State street, the band playing, and the soldiers singing "John Brown," all indicating the free, the happy future, as within a seeming hailing distance,—I could not help mentally exclaiming, "Glory enough for one day; aye, indeed, for a life-time."

Even though Nell was undoubtedly Attucks's most dogged champion in the nineteenth century, this passage reminds us that he knew Attucks only as a distant historical figure, mediated by a fragmentary historical record and the space of four generations. Prior to May 28, 1863, Nell's first-person memory of the State Street corner centered on the renditions of Sims and Burns—instances in which the agency and autonomy of black men were frustrated. As he gazed at the crowd gathered to honor the Fifty-fourth, Nell spotted both Thomas Sims, the fugitive finally turned freeman, as well as some of those Boston officials, now "perhaps repentant," who a decade before had conspired to return Sims and Burns to slavery. Nell sensed that change was in the air. The soldiers echoed that sentiment in singing "John Brown's body lies a-mouldering in the grave, but his soul goes marching on." On May 28, 1863, it seemed possible to abandon what was rotten and corrupt in the American past and bring something vital and spirited forward. For Nell, the possibility that black men would be the ones to vindicate the martyred souls of both Crispus Attucks and John Brown was indeed glorious.[4]

But before vindication, there would be more martyrdom. Seventy-seven men of the Fifty-fourth would die attempting to capture Fort Wagner, just outside the Confederate stronghold of Charleston, South Carolina, on July 18, 1863.[5] The historical analogy for the Fifty-fourth's crippling but heroic defeat was obvious to anyone steeped in Massachusetts history. In calling for a memorial to Colonel Robert Gould Shaw and his regiment in 1865, Senator Charles Sumner described the black soldiers' actions on that bloody South Carolina beach: "This was their Bunker Hill, and Shaw was the Warren who fell. Though defeated, they were yet victorious. The regiment was driven back; but the cause was advanced. The country learned to know colored troops, and they learned to know themselves. From that day of conflict, nobody doubted their capacity or courage as soldiers." As of July 18, 1863, Nell's "second revolution," the one that would secure the freedom and citizenship of people of color, had unquestionably begun.[6]

The story of the Massachusetts Fifty-fourth Regiment is both grim and glorious. Would the black men from all over the country who answered the recruiters' calls be recognized as citizen-soldiers, or were they merely pawns in "white people's quarrels"? Amid the debates on black military participation in the 1850s, some advocates of integration had expressed the dim view that the government would drop its qualms about enlisting blacks once the need for military manpower—or cannon fodder—was acute enough. If the state had "any real fighting to be done—any Bunker Hill battles to win," one abolitionist editorialist dryly noted, the politicians "would doubtless be then willing enough to have [black men] shot at or bayonetted." Even Robert Morris, the more conciliatory of the black speakers who appeared before the state's militia committee in 1853, sensed that if the United States were ever to face a serious threat from a foreign power, the word "white" in the militia regulation would instantaneously become "as unmenacing as the merest bubble upon the ocean." "Your colored fellow citizens would be appealed to," Morris predicted before the white state representatives, "and they would obey the first call to arms, and join you in maintaining the independence and honor of our common country."[7]

Ten years later, when the Union was rent not by a foreign force but by an internal struggle, the state, as Morris predicted, eventually had to appeal to black men for help. The soldiers of the Fifty-fourth turned the army's need for manpower into a source of patriotic pride, singing about how they were not the nation's scourge but its salvation:

> So rally, boys, rally, let us never mind the past,
> We had a hard road to travel but our day is coming fast,
> For God is for the right and we have no need to fear,
> The Union must be saved by the colored volunteer.

Of course, "never mind the past" has never been a particularly powerful political slogan in New England. Even if they could forget the historical record of injustice against people of color, the men of the Fifty-fourth did not need to look backward to find ample evidence of black people's "hard road to travel" in the white-dominated republic. The federal government initially attempted to pay these soldiers only 7 dollars a month, as opposed to the 13 dollars paid to the Army's white men. The members of the regiment went for a year and a half without pay rather than accept unequal compensation.

Given the tenuous economic status of many of these men before their enlistment, the protest created enormous hardships for them and their families. This episode undoubtedly deflated the men's hopes that military service would reestablish the citizenship claims that the Taney court had vanquished several years before.[8]

Back in 1857, a few months after the *Dred Scott* decision, Frederick Douglass had bitterly questioned the value of black men fighting on behalf of the American nation. Honoring the leader of a shipboard slave mutiny that occurred in 1841, Douglass declared that "Madison Washington who struck down his oppressor on the deck of the *Creole*, is more worthy to be remembered than the colored man who shot Pitcairn at Bunker Hill." Like many black leaders in the nineteenth century, Douglass vacillated between hope and despair when he considered the prospects of people of color in the United States. The year 1857 was undoubtedly a low point; the early days of 1863 marked a high. First Lincoln's Emancipation Proclamation confirmed that the war was about abolition as well as union. Next the establishment of black regiments inspired Douglass to become a military recruiter. But the unequal treatment of black enlistees so disgusted him that he quit by the end of the year.[9] Douglass's disillusionment exposes the limitations of the historical vision of many white abolitionists. Their fervent invocation of the American Revolution sometimes gave the sense that the struggle against the Slave Power was entirely scripted in advance by the war for independence from Britain. If so, the script often seemed woefully inadequate. Perhaps the first American Revolution really didn't have the momentum to sustain a second one. As the painful record of the nineteenth century showed, it certainly lacked the power to hold off the expansion of slavery.

The aftermath of the Civil War held its own share of disappointments. The patriotic fervor of the Revolutionary centennial matched and even exceeded the commemorative enthusiasm of the antebellum years, but supporters of civil rights again found themselves wondering if the promises of the Revolution had been fulfilled. Centennial events in the 1870s coincided with victories realized on paper—the Fifteenth Amendment, the Civil Rights Act—but also with efforts by Democrats and moderate Republicans to undermine those gains in practice. In 1875, Boston staged a grand centennial of the Battle of Bunker Hill, and Mayor Samuel Cobb invited William Lloyd Garrison to be a guest of the city at the festivities. That Garrison, with his history of ridiculing the hypocrisy of patriotic celebrations, was invited to the event indicated how quickly abolitionism was being appropriated into the historical mythology of "the Cradle of Liberty." Having come to support the Republicans during the war years, Garrison was no longer relegated to the sidelines of political culture but could share the best seats on the parade route with leading politicians and dignitaries. Or so Cobb thought. The seventy-four-year-old Garrison was not so convinced that much had changed. Confiding in his old friend Samuel May, he explained that he turned down the invitation

> not only because I do not wish to incur the discomfort and exposure of such a formal gathering, but really (in view of our past recreancy as a nation, for at least ninety years of the century) because I cannot awaken any enthusiasm in my breast on the subject. Chattel slavery, I thank Heaven, is abolished, but equal rights are not enjoyed or recognized, even for those who have been emancipated.

A decade after the war, discriminatory laws and racial violence still threatened to undermine the legal equality of black and white men. Meanwhile, the continued disfranchisement of women cheapened the rights that black men had secured.[10]

As ever, the histrionics of commemoration both disillusioned and fascinated Garrison. His refusal to be a guest of the city did not keep him home on June 17. Instead, he and two of his sons "secured some of the very best seats, in the very best position, on Columbus Avenue." For an old pacifist, it was hard to cheer on the military parade, which he found "most suggestive of painful reflections." Particularly distressing was the "excessive" applause afforded the military companies from South Carolina and Virginia: "To have been a rebel seemed the surest passport to special considerations and the warmest welcome." Apparently, sectional reconciliation was to take precedence over the principled notion of New England freedom. In the end, the hypocrisy and ostentation proved to be too much for Garrison. Three and a half hours into the four-hour parade, he and his sons "concluded to take the remainder for granted, and went home, not a little dizzied by the strain upon our visual organs."[11]

Garrison's weary departure from the centennial parade calls to mind how memory has so often been a sensory experience in Boston. The Bunker Hill Monument forced visitors to crane their necks and look upward, to climb the spiral staircase into the sky, to touch the permanence and majesty of the granite walls, to pace the surrounding battlefield and feel their own smallness, dwarfed by the shadow of monumental history. In other circumstances, the visceral experience of memory manifested itself as pain. In the twentieth century, Boston poet Robert Lowell proposed a metaphor for this sensation in his meditation on the memorial to the Fifty-fourth Regiment, which stands just across the street from the State House on Boston Common. Of Augustus Saint-Gaudens's bas-relief of Robert Gould Shaw and his men marching into battle, Lowell mourned, "Their monument sticks like a fishbone / in the city's throat." The poet's image evokes the history of slavery in Massachusetts as something out of place, not merely expendable but dangerous. But history, unlike that fishbone, is not a calcified thing. The sense that history need not choke us is what permitted Nell to look backward, despite all the fishbones that slavery had scattered over the American past.[12]

Just across the Common from the Shaw Memorial is the monument that Nell had only dreamed about in 1852, when he began his research on black Revolutionary patriots. Dedicated in 1888, the Crispus Attucks Monument (also known as the Boston Massacre Monument) is a jumble of forms. A pillar twenty-four feet tall heralds the names of the fallen, led by Attucks. Standing in front is a statue incorporating much of the classical and Revolutionary iconography of liberty: a woman in a flowing robe and liberty cap, holding a flagpole in one hand and a broken chain in the other, an open-winged eagle at her feet. But the most compelling piece of the monument is the statue's pedestal, where a bas-relief based on Paul Revere's engraving of the Boston Massacre is mounted just a few feet off the ground. Visitors can run their fingers over the town hall's weather vane, the guns of the British troops, the patriot figures in a flurry of fear and resolve, in the midst of which there is the stillness of death. The configuration of the victims' bodies does not follow Revere's arrangement exactly. While in the original engraving Attucks was hard to pick out from among the dead and dying bodies, here he stretches across the foreground, a fist clenched over his heart in the last living gesture of the first patriot to fall. The names of five men appear on the monument, but at the unveiling ceremony and dedication exercises at Faneuil Hall, it was clear that the monument and the day belonged to Crispus Attucks. The speakers christened the monument with his name, and they frequently invoked what by then they perceived as his message: that the Boston Massacre had shown that Americans of all races were, in fact, "one in blood."[13]

If the "one blood" message stressed patriotic unity, it did so in reference to a monument that, however cautiously, acknowledged individuality and difference. In this respect, the Crispus Attucks Monument gestured toward a commemorative agenda different from that of the solid, imposing, and uninscribed obelisk at Bunker Hill. One of the latest additions to Boston's commemorative landscape fully embraces this alternative vision. Unveiled in 2003, sculptor Meredith Bergmann's Women's Memorial brings Phillis Wheatley to the Commonwealth Avenue Mall, the grand promenade of Boston's Back Bay. In Bergmann's installation, statues of Wheatley, Abigail Adams, and Lucy Stone have literally stepped down off their pedestals (Wheatley has turned hers on its side to use as a writing desk). The statues of the women are barely larger than life. Not only do they stand or sit at the viewer's level, but they have broken out of conventional statuary poses. Visitors engage with the memorial in a manner entirely different from how they move through the complex at Bunker Hill. In a posture mimicking the only surviving image of her, the pensive Wheatley sits to one side of a large block of stone with her pen poised on her pedestal-desk. There is enough room to her right that a visitor might slip in beside her, so that for a moment at least she isn't sitting alone. From Wheatley one moves to Adams and then Stone, approaching each from the side. As a whole, the Women's Memorial invites horizontal motion, unlike the Bunker Hill Monument's upward climb.[14]

What distinguishes the Boston Women's Memorial most strikingly from the Bunker Hill Monument is its historicity and motion rather than timelessness and permanence. The pedestals are inscribed with the women's own words, which embed them in a historical specificity that the creators of the Bunker Hill Monument resisted in their refusal to engrave names or events on the obelisk. Approaching the Women's Memorial from the downtown end of Commonwealth Avenue, a visitor senses that the stillness of the stone figures is only transitory. Adams has paused just for a moment after climbing down from her perch, Stone is on the verge of signing off an editorial, Wheatley is about to float away, lost in her ode "On Imagination." All three of them will have moved, maybe even disappeared, in the time it takes to glance away and back. In the nineteenth century, the builders of the Bunker Hill Monument intended their memorial to outlast history. To name names seemed to them to denigrate the eternal truths of the Revolution by tying them to the mundane details of ordinary men's living and dying. The Women's Memorial recognizes that it is the living and the dying, the wondering and writing and acting and demanding, that create and re-create those truths, for one generation after another.

The genius of William Cooper Nell and other historically minded activists of his day was to recognize this mutually generative relationship between the past and the present. Nell argued that those Bay Staters who had lived in slavery in Massachusetts were not only inextricable from the state's history but vital to it. In making this case, Nell showed that he was himself embedded in that history, for his assumptions about who could make history descended from Revolutionary notions of political change as originating in "the people" and historical agency as being the province of autonomous actors. When arguments about eighteenth-century black agency came from those engaged in the nineteenth-century movement for emancipation and citizenship, memory transformed from a realm of nostalgia into a force for political change. As Nell recognized, the multilayered past could then animate the future.

What if Nell, from his corner on State Street, could have seen the future as clearly as he perceived the present and the past? If he could have seen the men before him go unpaid for months at a time and sacrifice themselves at Fort Wagner; if he could have seen the revolution in race relations ushered

in by the war rapidly erode by the end of the century; if he could have seen
the racial conflicts erupt in the streets and squares of Boston in the twentieth
century: if he could have looked forward so penetratingly, would May 28,
1863, still have been "glory enough"? We must be wary of mistaking Nell's
hopefulness for blinkered optimism. His joy at the parade of the Fifty-fourth
did not stem from certainty that the long struggle was over. Instead, as he
stood beneath a thousand flags and banners flying from windows and rooftops and alongside a thousand men processing through the streets in Union
blue, going forward as faithfully and as relentlessly as the sea, he must have
reveled in something much smaller and much bigger than a military victory:
the power of memory to move us, hopefully and purposefully, through a
broken and tumultuous world.

Notes

ABBREVIATIONS

AHR	*American Historical Review*
AQ	*American Quarterly*
BPL	Boston Public Library
JAH	*Journal of American History*
JER	*Journal of the Early Republic*
JNH	*Journal of Negro History*
Mass. Archives	SC1/series 45X, Massachusetts Archives Collection, Massachusetts Archives, Boston. Numbers refer to volume and page numbers.
MHS	Massachusetts Historical Society
MHSC	*Collections of the Massachusetts Historical Society*
MHSP	*Proceedings of the Massachusetts Historical Society*
NEHGS	New England Historic Genealogical Society
NEQ	*New England Quarterly*
RWPR	Revolutionary War pension record, Records of the Veteran's Administration, Record Group #15, National Archives and Records Administration Microfilm Publication M804. Numbers following this designation refer to microfilm reel and frame numbers.
Suffolk Probate	Suffolk County Probate Court, Record Book, Judicial Archives, Massachusetts Archives. Numbers refer to volume and page numbers.
WMQ	*William and Mary Quarterly,* 3rd series

PROLOGUE

1. In an Internet search, Attucks and Wheatley each turned up an order of magnitude more hits than other blacks associated with the American Revolution: 331,000 for Wheatley and 216,000 for Attucks, compared to 35,000 for Paul Cuffe/ Cuffee; 24,200 for James Forten; 22,500 for Peter Salem; 888 for Salem Poor (searches in Google.com, March 28, 2006). These numbers are only rough indicators of individual people's salience in popular memory, but as a way of aggregating the different ways individuals are commemorated—in book titles, historical Web sites, names of schools and organizations—it is telling that certain names turn up hundreds of thousands of results while others have only a tenth of that.

2. Phillis Wheatley to Obour Tanner, March 21, 1774, in *Phillis Wheatley and Her Writings*, ed. William H. Robinson (New York: Garland, 1984), 333.

3. Preface and John Wheatley's introductory letter in Phillis Wheatley, *Poems on Various Subjects, Religious and Moral* (London, 1773); [Margaretta Matilda Odell], *Memoir and Poems of Phillis Wheatley, a Native African and a Slave* (Boston, 1834). Scholarly biographies include Robinson, "On Phillis Wheatley and Her Boston," in *Phillis Wheatley and Her Writings*, 3–69; Julian D. Mason, Jr., introduction and "On the Reputation of Phillis Wheatley, Poet," in *The Poems of Phillis Wheatley*, rev. ed. (Chapel Hill: University of North Carolina Press, 1989), 1–34; Vincent Carretta, introduction to *Complete Writings*, by Phillis Wheatley (New York: Penguin, 2001), xiii–xxxvii; James A. Rawley, "The World of Phillis Wheatley," *NEQ* 50 (1977): 666–677.

4. The proposal, which first appeared in the *Boston Censor* on February 29, 1772, is reprinted in Robinson, *Phillis Wheatley and Her Writings*, 309–310.

5. Robinson, *Phillis Wheatley and Her Writings*, 455, raises the possibility that an unsigned verse in the *Boston Evening Post*, March 12, 1770, was the poem that Wheatley advertised as "On the Affray in King-Street." Antonio T. Bly, "Wheatley's 'On the Affray in King Street,'" *Explicator* 56 (1998): 177–180, argues that Wheatley wrote the *Evening Post* poem. Bly shows compelling consistencies between the latter poem and Wheatley's known works, but he does not prove that no one else could have written it. The *Evening Post* poem mentions Attucks and three other victims of the Boston Massacre: "Long as in *Freedom's* Cause the wise contend, / Dear to your unity shall Fame extend; / While to the World the letter'd *Stone* shall tell, / How *Caldwell, Attucks, Gray*, and *Mav'rick* fell."

6. A good overview of Attucks's place in history is Benjamin Quarles, *The Negro in the American Revolution* (1961; reprint Chapel Hill: University of North Carolina Press, 1996), 3–8. The most important nineteenth-century source is William Cooper Nell, *The Colored Patriots of the American Revolution* (Boston, 1855), 13–18. In the earliest accounts and commemorations of the Boston Massacre, references to the victims were terse; see Samuel B. Payne, Jr., "Was Crispus Attucks the First to Die?," *New England Journal of History* 57 (2001): 6. On Attucks's Native heritage, see J. B. Fisher, "Who Was Crispus Attucks?" *American Historical Record* 1 (1872): 531–533; Bill Belton, "The Indian Heritage of Crispus Attucks," *Negro History Bulletin* 22 (1959): 149–152. Erroneously attributing a nineteenth-century image to the Revolutionary-era artist Henry Pelham, Marcus Rediker emphasizes Attucks's Atlantic connections in "The Revenge of Crispus Attucks; or, The Atlantic Challenge to American Labor History," *Labor: Studies in Working-Class History of the Americas* 1 (2004): 35–45. The most exhaustive modern account of the event is Hiller B. Zobel, *The Boston Massacre* (New York: Norton, 1970). On Attucks and the invention of the "massacre," see Patricia Bradley, *Slavery, Propaganda, and the American Revolution* (Jackson: University Press of Mississippi, 1998), 55–62.

INTRODUCTION

1. For an assessment of the broader historiographical developments, see the latter chapters of Peter Novick, *That Noble Dream: The "Objectivity Question" and the American Historical Profession* (Cambridge: Cambridge University Press, 1988) and Walter Johnson, "On Agency," *Journal of Social History* 37 (2003): 113–124.

2. The language of "rescue" abounds in social history; for perhaps the most influential example, see E. P. Thompson, *The Making of the English Working Class* (New York: Vintage, 1966), 12-13. My ideas in this section owe much to Johnson, "On Agency," and to Joan W. Scott's critique of the way that "normative history" seeks to make the past "visible": "The Evidence of Experience," *Critical Inquiry* 17 (1991): 773-797. See also Kathleen Canning, "Feminist History after the Linguistic Turn: Historicizing Discourse and Experience," *Signs* 19 (1994): 368-404; as well as David Gary Shaw, "Happy in Our Chains? Agency and Language in the Postmodern Age," *History and Theory* 40 (2001): 1-9, and other articles in this theme issue on "Agency after Postmodernism."

3. Michel-Rolph Trouillot, *Silencing the Past: Power and the Production of History* (Boston: Beacon Press, 1995), 2-3, 22-25. Studies of memory and its politics are often organized around one or more of a set of oppositions, including public versus private memory, individual versus collective memory, or history versus memory. All of these relationships are pertinent to the material I am discussing here, but for my purposes, the most useful conceptual framework draws on Trouillot's identification of action and narration as the two principle processes through which people give meaning to the past. For brief discussions of other binaries in memory studies, see Pierre Nora, "Between History and Memory: *Les Lieux de Mémoire*," trans. Marc Roudebush, *Representations* 26 (1989): 7-24; Susannah Radstone, "Reconceiving Binaries: The Limits of Memory," *History Workshop Journal* 59 (2005): 134-150.

4. See Randolph Roth, "Is There a Democratic Alternative to Republicanism? The Rhetoric and Politics of Recent Pleas for Synthesis," in *Contesting the Master Narrative: Essays in Social History*, ed. Jeffrey Cox and Shelton Stromquist (Iowa City: University of Iowa Press, 1998), 237.

5. There is a lively historiography surrounding the continuities and discontinuities between Revolutionary ideology and opposition to chattel slavery. The most influential texts are David Brion Davis, *The Problem of Slavery in the Age of Revolution, 1770-1823* (Ithaca: Cornell University Press, 1975), and Edmund S. Morgan, *American Slavery, American Freedom: The Ordeal of Colonial Virginia* (New York: Norton, 1975). See also Bernard Bailyn, *The Ideological Origins of the American Revolution*, expanded ed. (Cambridge: Harvard University Press, 1992); F. Nwabueze Okoye, "Chattel Slavery as the Nightmare of the American Revolutionaries," *WMQ* 37 (1980): 3-28; Patricia Bradley, *Slavery, Propaganda, and the American Revolution* (Jackson: University Press of Mississippi, 1998).

6. These processes have been admirably discussed by Harlow W. Sheidley, *Sectional Nationalism: Massachusetts Conservative Leaders and the Transformation of America, 1815-1836* (Boston: Northeastern University Press, 1998), and Stephen Nissenbaum, "New England as Region and Nation," in *All Over the Map: Rethinking American Regions*, ed. Edward L. Ayers, Patricia Nelson Limerick, Nissenbaum, and Peter S. Onuf (Baltimore: Johns Hopkins University Press, 1996), 38-61. Joseph A. Conforti, *Imagining New England: Explorations of Regional Identity from the Pilgrims to the Mid-Twentieth Century* (Chapel Hill: University of North Carolina Press, 2001), chap. 3, argues that Connecticut was the idealized center of New England, since the witch craze of the 1690s and Shays's Rebellion of the 1780s scarred the reputation of Massachusetts. Certainly when it came to the question of slavery, Bay Staters represented themselves as having a stronger heritage of freedom than Americans anywhere

else. With the professionalization of history in the late nineteenth century, the tendency to see Massachusetts as the model for the region and the nation persisted. As Peter H. Wood pithily notes of several of the twentieth century's most influential historians (notably Samuel Eliot Morison and Perry Miller), "when writing of Massachusetts [they] called it New England, and when speaking of New England they called it America"; "'I Did the Best I Could for My Day': The Study of Early Black History during the Second Reconstruction, 1960 to 1976," *WMQ* 35 (1978): 187. While Jack P. Greene unseats New England from its central place in early American history in *Pursuits of Happiness: The Social Development of Early Modern British Colonies and the Formation of American Culture* (Chapel Hill: University of North Carolina Press, 1988), New England's primacy in historical scholarship and popular historical memory, *despite* its singularity in terms of economic and social development, is precisely what makes this region such a valuable site for a cultural history of memory and politics.

7. Hosea Easton, "A Treatise on the Intellectual Character, and Civil and Political Condition of the Colored People of the U. States" [1837] in *To Heal the Scourge of Prejudice: The Life and Writings of Hosea Easton*, ed. George R. Price and James Brewer Stewart (Amherst: University of Massachusetts Press, 1999), 103–104. Joanne Pope Melish, *Disowning Slavery: Gradual Emancipation and "Race" in New England, 1780-1860* (Ithaca: Cornell University Press, 1998), elaborates the emergence of racial ideology in the early republic; she also argues that slavery was far more significant to colonial New England's economy and society than historians have traditionally acknowledged. On New England's economic and political ties to slavery, see Kinley J. Brauer, *Cotton versus Conscience: Massachusetts Politics and Southwestern Expansion, 1843-1848* (Lexington: University of Kentucky Press, 1967), and William F. Hartford, *Money, Morals, and Politics: Massachusetts in the Age of the Boston Associates* (Boston: Northeastern University Press, 2001).

8. Melish, *Disowning Slavery*, 88; James T. Kloppenberg, "The Virtues of Liberalism: Christianity, Republicanism, and Ethics in Early American Political Discourse," *JAH* 74 (1987): 23–28, 30. Though my understanding of the relationship between "obligation" and "citizenship" is somewhat different from hers, I have found Linda K. Kerber's work invaluable: see *No Constitutional Right to Be Ladies: Women and the Obligations of Citizenship* (New York: Hill and Wang, 1998).

9. François Furstenberg, "Beyond Freedom and Slavery: Autonomy, Virtue, and Resistance in Early American Political Discourse," *JAH* 89 (2003): 1296, and *In the Name of the Father: Washington's Legacy, Slavery, and the Making of a Nation* (New York: Penguin Press, 2006), 149–151 and chap. 5. On black revolution as "unthinkable history," see Trouillot, *Silencing the Past*, chap. 3. Borrowing language from Giorgio Agamben, Linda K. Kerber likens slaves to stateless people, fellow occupants of a "state of exception" that defines what citizenship is not. In this respect, then, we might situate citizenship, rather than "freedom," as the polar opposite of slavery; see "The Stateless as the Citizen's Other: A View from the United States," *AHR* 112 (2007): 16–17.

10. Johnson, "On Agency," 113–115. Many of the people who figure in my study embrace liberal agency. It is important to recognize the extent to which they did so because it was part of their cultural milieu, rather than assuming that agency is a uniform or universal value. On the significance of liberal, individual agency to Americans in the early republic, see Furstenberg, *In the Name of the Father*; Robert H. Wiebe, *The Opening of American Society: From the Adoption of the Constitution to the*

Eve of Disunion (New York: Knopf, 1984); Maggie Montesinos Sale, *The Slumbering Volcano: American Slave Ship Revolts and the Production of Rebellious Masculinity* (Durham: Duke University Press, 1997). The meaning and value of historical agency was different in other contexts and changed over time, a point that Joseph C. Miller makes for Africa in "History and Africa/Africa and History," *AHR* 104 (1999): 20-21. One of the reasons that agency has held such sway in Western historiography is that it is a product of the same "revolutionary idiom" that produced modern social science. The irony is that it is the agenda of the same social sciences to occlude that history such that the "discrete individuating actor becomes *naturalized*." See Margaret R. Somers and Gloria D. Gibson, "Reclaiming the Epistemological 'Other': Narrative and the Social Constitution of Identity," in *Social Theory and the Politics of Identity*, ed. Craig Calhoun (Cambridge, Mass.: Blackwell, 1994), 47-49.

11. Orlando Patterson, *Slavery and Social Death: A Comparative Study* (Cambridge, Mass.: Harvard University Press, 1982), 5. In struggling to apply Western concepts of slavery and freedom in an African context, Igor Kopytoff and Suzanne Miers opt to see belonging (specifically, kinship) as the antithesis of slavery; see "African 'Slavery' as an Institution of Marginality," in *Slavery in Africa: Historical and Anthropological Perspectives*, ed. Miers and Kopytoff (Madison: University of Wisconsin Press, 1977), 3-24. Claude Meillassoux, *The Anthropology of Slavery: The Womb of Iron and Gold*, trans. Alide Dasnois (London: Athlone, 1991), 12-16, argues that Kopytoff and Miers's continuum between slavery and belonging overlooks a fundamental qualitative difference between slavery and other kinds of social relations; see also Frederick Cooper, "The Problem of Slavery in African Studies," *Journal of African History* 20 (1979): 103-125. For my purposes, what matters is what these scholars have in common: an effort to make sense of slavery and not-slavery in terms of social relationships (or limitations thereof), rather than the presence or absence of an abstract state of "freedom." None of this should be taken to suggest that enslaved people did not have social relationships or form meaningful communities among themselves. "Social death" should be understood as the condition of the idealized slave, not as a sociological reality.

12. Patrick Joyce's work suggests how we might see historical actors as simultaneously seeking belonging and autonomy: "Traditionally in Western thought the self is most often defined as an 'I' set against the social, either to maintain the autonomy of the self or to express a desire for integration in this social. But if we follow a post-structuralist, or anthropological, understanding of the self it will be apparent that the self and the social always constitute one another"; *Democratic Subjects: The Self and the Social in Nineteenth-Century England* (Cambridge: Cambridge University Press, 1994), 14. Joyce (148-151) also shows how it is through narrative that people cultivate the social; his work thus underscores my sense that we need to look to memory-making (through narrative and other representational and commemorative practices) to understand how collective sensibilities are formed.

13. The lack of gradual emancipation legislation in Massachusetts differentiated it from nearby Connecticut and Rhode Island. Two recent and influential monographs on emancipation in New England center on those two states: Melish, *Disowning Slavery*, and John Wood Sweet, *Bodies Politic: Negotiating Race in the American North, 1780-1830* (Baltimore: Johns Hopkins University Press, 2003).

14. Major considerations of historical memory of the Revolution, in Massachusetts and elsewhere, include Michael Kammen, *A Season of Youth: The American Revolution and the Historical Imagination* (New York: Knopf, 1978); Alfred F. Young, *The Shoemaker and the Tea Party: Memory and the American Revolution* (Boston: Beacon Press, 1999); Sarah J. Purcell, *Sealed with Blood: War, Sacrifice, and Memory in Revolutionary America* (Philadelphia: University of Pennsylvania Press, 2002). Studies of the institutions and genres of history in this period include David D. Van Tassel, *Recording America's Past: An Interpretation of the Development of Historical Studies in America, 1607-1884* (Chicago: University of Chicago Press, 1960); George H. Callcott, *History in the United States, 1800-1860: Its Practice and Purpose* (Baltimore: Johns Hopkins University Press, 1970); David J. Russo, *Keepers of Our Past: Local Historical Writing in the United States, 1820s-1930s* (New York: Greenwood Press, 1988); Louis Leonard Tucker, *The Massachusetts Historical Society: A Bicentennial History, 1791-1991* (Boston: Massachusetts Historical Society, 1991).

15. For another argument that the "new" in "New Social History" might be more apparent than real, see Ellen Fitzpatrick, *History's Memory: Writing America's Past, 1880-1980* (Cambridge, Mass: Harvard University Press, 2002).

CHAPTER 1

1. Jeremy Belknap, "Queries Respecting the Slavery and Emancipation of Negroes in Massachusetts, Proposed by the Hon. Judge Tucker of Virginia, and Answered by the Rev. Dr. Belknap," *MHSC*, 1st ser., 4 (1795): 191-192, 201.

2. Jonathan Edwards, *The Injustice and Impolicy of the Slave Trade, and of the Slavery of the Africans* (New Haven, 1791), 34; David Menschel, "Abolition without Deliverance: The Law of Connecticut Slavery, 1784-1848," *Yale Law Journal* 111 (2001): 187-191; Arthur Zilversmit, *The First Emancipation: The Abolition of Slavery in the North* (Chicago: University of Chicago Press, 1967).

3. *Tyrannical Libertymen* (Hanover, N.H., 1795), 4; Belknap, "Queries," 193.

4. Belknap, "Queries," 201-202; James Otis, *The Rights of the British Colonies Asserted and Proved* (Boston, 1764), 29-30; Nathaniel Appleton, *Considerations on Slavery, in a Letter to a Friend* (Boston, 1767), 19-20.

5. *A Forensic Dispute on the Legality of Enslaving the Africans* (Boston, 1773); Petition of "a Grate Number of Blackes of this Province," May 25, [1774], *MHSC*, 5th ser., 3 (1877): 432-433. See also "Lover of Constitutional Liberty," *The Appendix: or, Some Observations on the Expediency of the Petition of the Africans* (Boston, 1773); James Swan, *A Dissuasion to Great-Britain and the Colonies, from the Slave Trade to Africa* (Boston, 1772).

6. Belknap, "Queries," 201-202.

7. Belknap, "Queries," 203.

8. Town meeting minutes of Hardwick, May 1780, quoted in Lucius R. Paige, *History of Hardwick, Massachusetts* (Boston, 1883), 116; return of the town of Rochester, 1780, Mass. Archives, 277:44. See also returns of the towns of Braintree and Petersham, Mass. Archives, 277:63 and 277:104. On popular involvement in the framing and ratification of the constitution, see Oscar Handlin and Mary Handlin, introduction to *The Popular Sources of Political Authority: Documents on the Massachusetts Constitution of 1780*, ed. Handlin and Handlin (Cambridge, Mass.:

Harvard University Press, 1966), 19-26; Edmund S. Morgan, *Inventing the People: The Rise of Popular Sovereignty in England and America* (New York: Norton, 1988), 258-259; Gordon S. Wood, *The Creation of the American Republic, 1776-1787* (Chapel Hill: University of North Carolina Press, 1998), chap. 8.

9. Belknap, "Queries," 202-203; Emily Blanck, "Revolutionizing Slavery: The Legal Culture of Slavery in Revolutionary Massachusetts and South Carolina" (Ph.D. diss., Emory University, 2003), 223-229.

10. William O'Brien, "Did the Jennison Case Outlaw Slavery in Massachusetts?," *WMQ* 17 (1960): 219-241; John D. Cushing, "The Cushing Court and the Abolition of Slavery in Massachusetts: More Notes on the 'Quock Walker Case,'" *American Journal of Legal History* 5 (1961): 118-144; Robert M. Spector, "The Quock Walker Cases (1781-83): Slavery, Its Abolition, and Negro Citizenship in Early Massachusetts," *JNH* 53 (1968): 12-32; Arthur Zilversmit, "Quok Walker, Mumbet, and the Abolition of Slavery in Massachusetts," *WMQ* 25 (1968): 614-624.

11. Transcription of the charge in *Commonwealth v. Jennison* (1783), from a manuscript notebook in the Harvard University Law Library, in Cushing, "Cushing Court," 132-133.

12. On the provenance of the charge, see Cushing, "Cushing Court," 132 n. 20; *MHSP*, 1st ser., 14 (1875): 294. O'Brien, "Jennison Case," 239, questions the significance of Cushing's charge to the case's outcome—and even whether Cushing ever orally delivered it.

13. O'Brien, "Jennison Case," 240; Cushing, "Cushing Court," 135-137; Emily Blanck, "Seventeen Eighty-Three: The Turning Point in the Law of Slavery and Freedom in Massachusetts," *NEQ* 75 (2002): 30.

14. Belknap, "Queries," 203.

15. Zilversmit, "Quok Walker," argues that at least one slave owner gave up his own efforts to hold on to his slaves after he learned of the outcome of *Commonwealth v. Jennison*. Evidence that Boston officials considered slavery abolished in the early 1780s comes from the records of the municipal tax assessors. The 1780 book has a column listing slaves; the 1784 volume does not. See Chernoh Momodu Sesay, Jr., "Freemasons of Color: Prince Hall, Revolutionary Black Boston, and the Origins of Black Freemasonry, 1770-1807" (Ph.D. diss., Northwestern University, 2006), 76. State tax valuations tell a different story: "servants" were still listed as property on the abstracts for each town in 1784-1785. See "Aggregates of the Polls and Valuations of Real and Personal Property in the Towns of Massachusetts, 1784-1785," Tax Valuation Microfilm Reel 391, Special Collections, Massachusetts State Library, Boston. This discrepancy highlights the ambiguity of the status of bondspeople in the 1780s.

16. Spector, "Quock Walker Cases," 21-23; Ira Berlin, *Many Thousands Gone: The First Two Centuries of Slavery in North America* (Cambridge, Mass.: Harvard University Press, 1998), 369-375.

17. Belknap, "Queries," 204; Jane Belknap Marcou, *Life of Jeremy Belknap* (New York, 1847), 165; Jonathan Jackson to William Shepard, March 19, 1790, and Jackson to John Sprague, March 19, 1790, letterbook, *Lee Family Papers, 1535-1957*, microfilm ed. (Boston: MHS, 1982), reel 18, MHS.

18. Belknap, "Queries," 198.

19. Mark G. Schmeller, "Imagining Public Opinion in Antebellum America: Fear, Credit, Law, and Honor" (Ph.D. diss., University of Chicago, 2001), 1-19, 33-87,

quotation on 87. On the novelty of the term "public opinion" in the 1790s, see Schmeller, "The Political Economy of Opinion: Public Credit and Concepts of Public Opinion in the Age of Federalism," *JER* 29 (2009): 36–37; also Jeffrey L. McNairn, *The Capacity to Judge: Public Opinion and Deliberative Democracy in Upper Canada, 1791-1854* (Toronto: University of Toronto Press, 2000), 5–9; J. A. W. Gunn, "Public Opinion," in *Political Innovation and Conceptual Change*, ed. Terence Ball, James Farr, and Russell L. Hanson (New York: Cambridge University Press, 1989), 247–265; Hans Speier, "The Rise of Public Opinion," in *Propaganda and Communication in World History*, vol. 2, ed. Harold D. Laswell, Daniel Lerner, and Speier (Honolulu: University Press of Hawaii, 1980), 147–167.

20. James Winthrop to Jeremy Belknap, March 4, 1795, in "Letters and Documents Relating to Slavery in Massachusetts," *MHSC*, 5th ser., 3 (1877): 391. Extant letters to Belknap in response to Tucker's queries are published in this volume. No letter from Prince Hall survives, but Belknap acknowledges him as an informant in "Queries Respecting Slavery," 199.

21. Linda Prince, "White Community, Black Compromise: Blacks and the Experience of Interraciality in Boston from Slavery to Freedom, 1693-1815" (Ph.D. diss., Harvard University, 2002), 183–187; George Benson Kirsch, "Jeremy Belknap: A Biography" (Ph.D. diss., Columbia University, 1972), 308–312; "Belknap-Hazard Correspondence, Part II," *MHSC*, 5th ser., 3 (1877): 19–27, 55; Richard S. Newman, *The Transformation of American Abolitionism: Fighting Slavery in the Early Republic* (Chapel Hill: University of North Carolina Press, 2002), 32.

22. Matthew Mason, *Slavery and Politics in the Early American Republic* (Chapel Hill: University of North Carolina Press, 2006), 28; Newman, *Transformation of American Abolitionism*, 32-27; Belknap to Hazard, May 7, 1790, in "Belknap-Hazard Correspondence, Part II," 220–221.

23. Belknap to Hazard, May 7, 1790, in "Belknap-Hazard Correspondence, Part II," 221; Jeremy Belknap, *History of New-Hampshire*, vol. 3 (Boston, 1792), 256; Louis Leonard Tucker, *Clio's Consort: Jeremy Belknap and the Founding of the Massachusetts Historical Society* (Boston: Massachusetts Historical Society, 1990), xii.

24. On Belknap: Kirsch, "Jeremy Belknap"; Tucker, *Clio's Consort*; Russell M. Lawson, *The American Plutarch: Jeremy Belknap and the Historian's Dialogue with the Past* (Westport, Conn.: Praeger, 1998); Louis Leonard Tucker, "Massachusetts," in *Historical Consciousness in the Early Republic: The Origins of State Historical Societies, Museums, and Collections, 1791-1861*, ed. H. G. Jones (Chapel Hill: North Caroliniana Society and North Carolina Collection, 1995), 1–28.

25. "Constitution of the Historical Society," *MHSC*, 1st ser., 1 (1792): 1; Gordon S. Wood, *The American Revolution: A History* (New York: Modern Library, 2003), 96–99; Tucker, *Clio's Consort*, 31-32, 40-43; Jill Lepore, *A Is for American: Letters and Other Characters in the Newly United States* (New York: Knopf, 2002), 5-7, 15-41.

26. David D. Van Tassel, *Recording America's Past: An Interpretation of the Development of Historical Studies in America, 1607-1884* (Chicago: University of Chicago Press, 1960), 51–53; Tucker's letter is reprinted in Belknap, "Queries," 191.

27. Charles T. Cullen, *St. George Tucker and Law in Virginia, 1772-1804* (New York: Garland, 1987); Phillip Hamilton, *The Making and Unmaking of a Revolutionary Family: The Tuckers of Virginia, 1752-1830* (Charlottesville: University of Virginia Press, 2003).

28. St. George Tucker, *A Dissertation on Slavery: With a Proposal for the Gradual Abolition of It, in the State of Virginia* (1796; reprint, Westport, Conn.: Negro Universities Press, 1970), 5, 9, 11.

29. Tucker, *Dissertation*, 11–13. "The winter here was always unfavourable to the African constitution," Belknap wrote in "Queries," 199. For a brief introduction to Euro-American ideas about climate and "race," see Winthrop D. Jordan, *White over Black: American Attitudes Toward the Negro, 1550-1812* (Chapel Hill: University of North Carolina Press, 1968), 259–265.

30. Tucker, *Dissertation*, 64–66.

31. Tucker, *Dissertation*, 78, 89–92.

32. Tucker, *Dissertation*, 67, 18–19.

33. Tucker, *Dissertation*, 65; return of the town of Spencer, 1778, Mass. Archives 160:7; return of the town of Westminster, 1778, Mass. Archives 160:17; return of the town of Sutton, 1778, in *The Popular Sources of Political Authority*, ed. Handlin and Handlin, 231. The constitution of 1780 did have a property qualification for voters. However, it is unclear how often this provision was enforced. See Alexander Keyssar, *The Right to Vote: The Contested History of Democracy in the United States* (New York: Basic Books, 2000), 18–19; J. R. Pole, "Suffrage and Representation in Massachusetts: A Statistical Note," *WMQ* 14 (1957): 560–574.

34. Louis Ruchames, "Race, Marriage, and Abolition in Massachusetts," *JNH* 40 (1955): 250; Hal Goldman, "Black Citizenship and Military Self-Presentation in Antebellum Massachusetts," *Historical Journal of Massachusetts* 25 (1997): 157–169; Hosea Easton, *A Treatise on the Intellectual Character, and the Civil and Political Condition of the Colored People* (Boston, 1837), reprint in *To Heal the Scourge of Prejudice: The Life and Writings of Hosea Easton*, ed. George R. Price and James Brewer Stewart (Amherst: University of Massachusetts Press, 1999), 103; Price and Stewart, introduction to *To Heal the Scourge of Prejudice*, 3–10.

35. Belknap, "Queries," 191; David C. Hendrickson, *Peace Pact: The Lost World of the American Founding* (Lawrence: University Press of Kansas, 2003), 106–107, 182–183; Mason, *Slavery and Politics*, 40–41 and chap. 2. John Craig Hammond shows how the regional divide that mattered most before 1815 was between East and West in *Slavery, Freedom, and Expansion in the Early American West* (Charlottesville: University of Virginia Press, 2007).

36. Berlin, *Many Thousands Gone*, 369; Phillip Hamilton, "Revolutionary Principles and Family Loyalties: Slavery's Transformation in the St. George Tucker Household of Early National Virginia," *WMQ* 55 (1998): 541–545; Eva Sheppard Wolf, *Race and Slavery in the New Nation: Emancipation in Virginia from the Revolution to Nat Turner's Rebellion* (Baton Rouge: Louisiana State University Press, 2006), 104–105; Sylvestris [St. George Tucker], *Reflections on the Cession of Louisiana to the United States* (Washington, D.C., 1803), 25–26.

37. Hamilton, "Revolutionary Principles," 553–556.

38. Journal of the House of Representatives of Massachusetts, vol. 40 (1819–1820), 450–451, Special Collections, Massachusetts State Library, Boston (hereafter, House Journal).

39. "Approval of the Constitution, and Admission of Missouri into the Union," November 23, 1820, American State Papers: Miscellaneous 2:625; *Annals of Congress*, 16th Cong., 2nd sess., 635–640; Mason, *Slavery and Politics*, 179–180; Robert Pierce

Forbes, *The Missouri Compromise and Its Aftermath: Slavery and the Meaning of America* (Chapel Hill: University of North Carolina Press, 2007), 110-118; James H. Kettner, *The Development of American Citizenship, 1608-1870* (Chapel Hill: University of North Carolina Press, 1978), 312-315.

40. *Laws of the Commonwealth of Massachusetts*, vol. 1 (Boston, 1801), 413; "Notice to Blacks," *Massachusetts Mercury*, September 16, 1800, 3; *Pittsfield Sun*, July 4, 1821.

41. House Journal, vol. 42 (1821-1822), 62, 121. The statement of facts appeared in the *Pittsfield Sun*, July 4, 1821.

42. House Report No. 46, *Free Negroes and Mulattoes* (Boston, 1822), 1-2. Hereafter, I refer to the report as *Free Negroes*. Only Lyman's name appears on the report; I have found little about the other two committee members.

43. *Essex Patriot*, June 30, 1821.

44. *Free Negroes*, 1, 3.

45. Though Lyman's report did not quote Belknap's "publick opinion" explanation directly, Belknap's response to Tucker's queries was among the report's major sources.

46. Belknap, "Queries Respecting Slavery," 198; *Free Negroes*, 7-8.

47. *Free Negroes*, 7-9.

48. *Free Negroes*, 10-13.

49. Lyman, *Free Negroes*, 15. Though he came from a Federalist family, Lyman was not always affiliated with the party, which folded around the time his political career began. In the 1820s and 30s, Lyman's loyalties shifted from a wing of the Democrats to the Whig party. Whatever his partisan affiliation, Lyman remained true to his roots in the mercantile elite by embracing law and order over radical change. Charles Francis Adams, "Memoir of Theodore Lyman," *MHSP*, 2nd ser., 20 (1906): 148-149; Theodore Lyman III, *Memoir of Theodore Lyman, Jr.* (Cambridge, Mass., 1881), 22-23; Ronald P. Formisano, *The Transformation of Political Culture: Massachusetts Parties, 1790s-1840s* (New York: Oxford University Press, 1983), 248, 328.

50. I would argue that there is a "processual and mutually constitutive" relationship between narrative and action, as there is between narrative and ontology; see Margaret R. Somers and Gloria D. Gibson, "Reclaiming the Epistemological 'Other': Narrative and the Social Constitution of Identity," in *Social Theory and the Politics of Identity*, ed. Craig Calhoun (Cambridge, Mass.: Blackwell, 1994), 61-62.

51. Joanne Pope Melish, *Disowning Slavery: Gradual Emancipation and "Race" in New England, 1780-1860* (Ithaca, N.Y.: Cornell University Press, 1998).

52. Julian Barnes, *Flaubert's Parrot* (New York: Vintage, 1990), 90. One might argue that Lyman tailored his historical narrative to suit a preexisting antislavery or pro-civil rights ideology. The tone of his 1821 "statement of facts" suggests otherwise. While there are few clues to Lyman's attitude toward slavery circa 1820, his son's claim in 1881 that Lyman "was as strong an antislavery man as Mr. Garrison himself" is grossly misleading. In 1835, as mayor of Boston, Lyman presided over an antiabolitionist meeting in Faneuil Hall. Later that year, his handling of the mob attack on William Lloyd Garrison earned him the ire of many abolitionists, though some contended that Lyman's decision to jail Garrison saved his life. Lyman, *Memoir*, 23-27; Theodore Lyman III, *Papers Relating to the Garrison Mob* (Cambridge, Mass., 1870); Henry Mayer, *All on Fire: William Lloyd Garrison and the Abolition of Slavery* (New York: St. Martin's Press, 1998), 197-208.

53. Alfred F. Young, *The Shoemaker and the Tea Party: Memory and the American Revolution* (Boston: Beacon Press, 1999), 133-137; *Liberator*, February 26, 1831, 33; March 4, 1831, 37; March 12, 1831, 41. On historical activity in the early nineteenth century, see George H. Callcott, *History in the United States, 1800-1860: Its Practice and Purpose* (Baltimore: Johns Hopkins University Press, 1970), 25-53; Van Tassel, *Recording America's Past*, 103.

54. David J. Russo, *Keepers of Our Past: Local Historical Writing in the United States, 1820s-1930s* (New York: Greenwood Press, 1988), 21; quotation from an advertisement for Joshua Coffin's history of Newbury, *Liberator*, June 23, 1843, 99.

55. Bradford Kingman, *History of North Bridgewater* (Boston, 1866), 317; John Daggett, *Sketch of the History of Attleborough* (Dedham, Mass., 1834), 135; John S. Barry, *Historical Sketch of the Town of Hanover* (Boston, 1853), 175; George Faber Clark, *History of the Town of Norton* (Boston, 1859), 508-509.

56. Harlow W. Sheidley, *Sectional Nationalism: Massachusetts Conservative Leaders and the Transformation of America, 1815-1836* (Boston: Northeastern University Press, 1998), 31.

57. Mason, *Slavery and Politics*, chap. 2; Kevin M. Gannon, "Calculating the Value of Union: States' Rights, Nullification, and Secession in the North, 1800-1848" (Ph.D. diss., University of South Carolina, 2002), chap. 4.

58. Bruce Laurie, *Beyond Garrison: Antislavery and Social Reform* (New York: Cambridge University Press, 2005), 103-104; *Massachusetts Abolitionist*, February 7, 1839, 1.

59. E.g., David Willard, *Willard's History of Greenfield* (Greenfield, Mass., 1838), 141 (quotation); Edwin M. Stone, *History of Beverly, Civil and Ecclesiastical* (Boston, 1843), 185.

60. Charles J. Fox, *History of the Old Township of Dunstable* (Nashua, N.H., 1846), 168.

61. E.g., Francis Jackson, *History of the Early Settlement of Newton* (Boston, 1854), 95-98.

62. Oliver N. Bacon, *History of Natick* (Boston, 1856), 125; E. Vale Smith, *History of Newburyport* (Newburyport, Mass., 1854), 56; Jackson, *History of Newton*, 95.

63. Clark, *History of Norton*, 511; *Liberator*, March 26, 1858, 51.

64. Thomas Gage, *History of Rowley* (Boston, 1840), 462.

65. Joseph B. Felt, *History of Ipswich, Essex, and Hamilton* (Cambridge, Mass., 1834), 120; Joshua Coffin, *Sketch of the History of Newbury, Newburyport, and West Newbury* (Boston, 1845), 256-257.

66. Adams's letter was originally published in *Niles' Weekly Register*, March 7, 1818; Benjamin Hobart, *History of the Town of Abington* (Boston, 1866), 251; Joseph B. Felt, *The Annals of Salem* (Salem, Mass., 1827), 417.

67. Robert Rantoul, Sr., "Negro Slavery in Massachusetts: Portions of a Paper Read Before the Beverly Lyceum, April, 1833," *Historical Collections of the Essex Institute* 24 (1887): 81-82; Robert DeGroff Bulkley, Jr., "Robert Rantoul, Jr., 1805-1852: Politics and Reform in Antebellum Massachusetts" (Ph.D. diss., Princeton University, 1971), 2-5.

68. F. C. Gray, "Remarks on the Early Laws of Massachusetts Bay," *MHSC* 3rd ser., 8 (1843): 231. Drafted in 1641, the "Body of Liberties" formed the basis of the Massachusetts *Book of the General Lawes and Libertyes* of 1648, which one scholar

calls "the 'first flower' of American jurisprudence." Rantoul incorrectly backdated it to 1644. See Daniel R. Coquillette, "Radical Lawmakers in Colonial Massachusetts: The 'Countenance of Authoritie' and the *Lawes and Libertyes*," *NEQ* 67 (1994): 179–211 (quotation on 182); Gray, "Remarks," 191–237; William M. Wiecek, "The Origins of the Law of Slavery in British North America," *Cardozo Law Review* 17 (1996): 1742–1745. For examples of divergent nineteenth-century readings of the Body of Liberties and related seventeenth-century legal codes, see Thomas R. R. Cobb, *Historical Sketch of Slavery from the Earliest Periods* (Philadelphia and Savannah, 1858), cxlvii–cxlviii; James Draper, *History of Spencer, Massachusetts*, 2nd ed. (Worcester, Mass., 1860), 130; Henry B. Stanton, *Remarks of Henry B. Stanton, in the Representatives' Hall, on the 23d and 24th of February, 1837*, 2nd ed. (Boston, 1837), 79; George H. Moore, *Notes on the History of Slavery in Massachusetts* (1866, reprint New York: Negro Universities Press, 1968), 11–19. For similar evidence from modern scholars, contrast A. Leon Higginbotham, Jr., *In the Matter of Color: Race and the American Legal Process, the Colonial Period* (New York: Oxford University Press, 1978), 62, and Spector, "Quock Walker Cases," 19.

69. *Freedom's Amulet* (Lynn, Mass.), December 6, 1848. The quotation comes from Francis Jeffrey, editor of the *Edinburgh Review*; Alonzo Lewis, the *Amulet*'s editor, inserted it in front of one of his own antislavery poems, as a retort to "superficial people" who "think that writing poetry is not the way to effect the Abolition of Slavery."

70. *Liberator*, June 9, 1832, 91; see also February 15, 1839, 25. Schmeller, "Imagining Public Opinion," 53, argues that "by the early nineteenth century, 'civilization' and 'public opinion' had become interchangeable terms." On moral suasion, see Aileen S. Kraditor, *Means and Ends in American Abolitionism: Garrison and His Critics on Strategy and Tactics, 1834–1850* (New York: Pantheon, 1969).

71. Emory Washburn, "Extinction of Slavery in Massachusetts," *MHSP* 1st ser., 3 (1857): 189, 193, 196, 203.

72. John L. Brooke, "Reason and Passion in the Public Sphere: Habermas and the Cultural Historians," *Journal of Interdisciplinary History* 29 (1998): 44, 48.

73. Somers and Gibson, "Reclaiming the Epistemological 'Other,' " 47–49, discuss this "revolutionary idiom" as part of their effort to frame the "conceptual narrativity" of "agency"; I would suggest that a similar historicizing move could be made for "public opinion."

74. T. H. Breen, "Making History: The Force of Public Opinion and the Last Years of Slavery in Massachusetts," in *Through a Glass Darkly: Reflections on Personal Identity in Early America*, ed. Ronald Hoffman, Mechal Sobel, and Fredrika J. Teute (Chapel Hill: University of North Carolina Press, 1997), 72–73.

75. I have focused here on histories of Massachusetts slavery that appeared before the Civil War. The most thoroughgoing later book on the subject is George Henry Moore's *Notes on the History of Slavery in Massachusetts*, first published in 1866. Moore presented an exhaustive legislative and legal history that is still a reference for scholars today. Intent on deflating Bay Staters' historical egos, Moore concluded with the ironic observation that since Massachusetts never passed an emancipation law, the "actual" (that is, legal) prohibition of slavery in the Commonwealth depended on the votes of southern states in favor of the Thirteenth Amendment. Moore, *Notes*, 241–242; see also John David Smith, "George H. Moore: 'Tormentor of Massachusetts,' " in *The*

Moment of Decision: Biographical Essays on American Character and Regional Identity, ed. Randall M. Miller and John R. McKivigan (Westport, Conn.: Greenwood Press, 1994), 211-226.

CHAPTER 2

1. Abigail Adams to John Adams, June 18-20, 1775, in *Adams Family Papers: An Electronic Archive*, http://www.masshist.org/digitaladams/aea/cfm/doc.cfm?id=L177 50618aa; Sarah J. Purcell, *Sealed with Blood: War, Sacrifice, and Memory in Revolutionary America* (Philadelphia: University of Pennsylvania Press, 2002), 11; Richard M. Ketchum, *Decisive Day: The Battle for Bunker Hill* (Garden City, N.Y.: Doubleday, 1974); George Quintal, Jr., "Patriots of Color, 'A Peculiar Beauty and Merit': African Americans and Native Americans at Battle Road and Bunker Hill" (National Park Service report, February 2002).

2. Edward Hallett Carr, *What Is History?* (New York: Vintage-Random House, 1961), 9, 11; Quintal, "Patriots of Color," 237-239; City of Boston, *Report of the Joint Committee on Bunker Hill Tablets* (Boston, 1889); Edwin R. Hodgman, *History of the Town of Westford...1659-1883* (Lowell, Mass., 1883), 112-113.

3. For example, *Bickerstaff's New-England Almanack, for the Year of Our Redemption, 1776* (Newburyport, Mass., 1775); *The New-York and Country Almanack for the Year of Our Lord 1776* (New York, 1775).

4. Richard Frothingham, Jr., *History of the Siege of Boston, and of the Battles of Lexington, Concord, and Bunker Hill*, 2nd ed. (Boston, 1851), 170-172; Ketchum, *Decisive Day*, 56-58, 150-151; Purcell, *Sealed with Blood*, 11-48.

5. George Livermore, *An Historical Research Respecting the Opinions of the Founders of the Republic on Negroes as Slaves, as Citizens, and as Soldiers* (1862; reprint, New York: Arno Press, 1969), 91; *Boston Gazette and Country Journal*, March 12, 1770. Revere's image was actually a copy of a lesser-known print by Henry Pelham, with only a few alterations in the details. However, Pelham's print did not go on sale until a week after Revere's. Wendy J. Shadwell, *American Printmaking: The First 150 Years* (Washington, D.C.: Smithsonian Institution Press for the Museum of Graphic Art, 1969), 27-28; John Agresto, "Art and Historical Truth: The Boston Massacre," *Journal of Communication* 29 (1979): 170-174.

6. Bernard Bailyn, *The Ideological Origins of the American Revolution*, expanded ed. (Cambridge, Mass.: Harvard University Press, 1992), 7; Stephen Elliot James, "The Other Fourth of July: The Meanings of Black Identity at American Celebrations of Independence, 1770-1863" (Ph.D. diss., Harvard University, 1997), chap. 1. All the Boston Massacre addresses are collected in *Principles and Acts of the Revolution in America*, ed. Hezekiah Niles (Baltimore, 1822), 1-59. In 1776, during the Siege of Boston, the address was given in Watertown.

7. Joseph Warren, "Oration," in *Principles and Acts*, 17-18; "General Warren an Abolitionist," *Liberator*, September 21, 1838, 150. Warren also gave a Boston Massacre commemorative address in 1772 that introduced another line favored by abolitionists: "my sons, scorn to be slaves!"; *Liberator*, January 8, 1858, 5.

8. On the original gravestone, see Livermore, *Historical Research*, 92. The epitaph was the same poem that Antonio Bly, "Wheatley's 'On the Affray in King Street,'" *Explicator* 56 (1998): 177-180, attributes to Phillis Wheatley. On victims other than

Attucks, see Benjamin Church, "Oration Delivered at Boston, March 5, 1773," in *Principles and Acts*, 12; Samuel B. Payne, Jr., "Was Crispus Attucks the First to Die?," *New England Journal of History* 57 (2001): 1-10.

9. Scholars don't agree on what it means that Attucks is not racially marked in the Pelham-Revere print—or even on which body in the image is his. Barbara E. Lacey suggests that the lack of differentiation among the faces in the crowd suggests that "the sacrifice of Attuck's [sic] life... is viewed as equal to that of the others who died," while Tavia Amolo Ochieng' Nyong'o critiques this claim, contending that "the idea that humanity can only be honored through an abstemious erasure of difference forms an odd continuity between the visual strategy of Revere and Lacey's contemporary apologetic." See Lacey, "Visual Images of Blacks in Early American Prints," *WMQ* 53 (1996): 163; Nyong'o, "Uncommon Memory: The Performance of Amalgamation in Early Black Political Culture" (Ph.D. diss., Yale University, 2004), 58. Marcus Rediker argues that Revere deliberately excluded Attucks because he had "the wrong color, the wrong ethnicity, and the wrong occupations to be included in the national story"; "The Revenge of Crispus Attucks; or, The Atlantic Challenge to American Labor History," *Labor* 1 (2004): 38; a similar interpretation appears in Karsten Fitz, "Commemorating Crispus Attucks: Visual Memory and the Representations of the Boston Massacre, 1770-1857," *Amerikastudien/American Studies* 50 (2005): 468-470. Patricia Bradley contends that the Revolutionaries could only honor Attucks by granting him "honorary whitehood"; *Slavery, Propaganda, and the American Revolution* (Jackson: University Press of Mississippi, 1998), 59-61. The hand-colored versions of the print complicate these arguments somewhat. In some colored versions of the print, one of the victims appears to have a darker face and darker hair than the others. What makes it more obvious that this figure is Crispus Attucks are the two bullet holes in his chest, which spurt blood into a pool around his head. It was widely reported that Attucks had been shot on both sides of his chest. Indeed, red is the most striking hue in the colored versions of the image: on the right side of the scene are the red-coated British soldiers, while on the left the victims gush from their wounds. The primary value of coloring the engraving might have been to emphasize the brutality of the British, as it was hard to see pools of blood in a black-and-white engraving. Not all the colored versions of the print have the same color scheme, and it is not clear if some of the coloring might have been done much later. Colored versions of the print are accessible in Houghton Library, Harvard University and the New-York Historical Society; for variant versions of the print, see Clarence S. Brigham, *Paul Revere's Engravings* (New York: Atheneum, 1969), 52-78.

10. *Legal Papers of John Adams*, ed. L. Kinvin Wroth and Hiller B. Zobel, vol. 3 (Cambridge: Harvard University Press, 1965). The exception was defense witness Andrew, Oliver Wendell's slave, who referred to Attucks as a "stout man" until one of the lawyers asked him to clarify: the "stout man" was "the Molatto who was shot" (204).

11. Testimony of John Hill, in appendix to *A Short Narrative of the Horrid Massacre in Boston, Perpetrated in the Evening of the Fifth Day of March, 1770* (Boston, 1770), 5; *Adams Legal Papers*, 130-131, 195; Hiller B. Zobel, *The Boston Massacre* (New York: Norton, 1970), 257-258. On numbers of slaves, see Betty Hobbs Pruitt, *The Massachusetts Tax Valuation List of 1771* (Boston: G. K. Hall, 1978).

12. *Adams Legal Papers*, 205, 92; *Massachusetts Spy*, March 7, 1771. The trope of collusion between "Tories and Negroes" also appears in John Trumbull, *M'Fingal: A Modern Epic Poem* (Philadelphia, 1775), 23-25, and Philip Freneau, *A Voyage to Boston: A Poem* (New York, 1775), 18.

13. *Adams Legal Papers*, 268-269, 266. Captain Preston and six of the eight soldiers were acquitted on all counts; two soldiers were convicted of the lesser charge of manslaughter. Historians have debated whether the confrontation on March 5 resulted from spontaneous, directionless troublemakers (as Adams suggested) or organized political activity; see Peter Brodkin, "The Boston Massacre: Design or Accident," *Journal of the Rutgers University Libraries* 40 (1978): 78-92.

14. I agree to a point with Stephen H. Browne's assessment of the commemorative address: "Rhetorically speaking, *there was no Crispus Attucks in late eighteenth-century America* because, from the celebrant's point of view, there was no need for him beyond his status as a body in the street, a unit of proof in the colonial case against British depredations. Racially he was invisible, and as a claimant to the rights of citizenship and nationhood he existed not at all"; "Remembering Crispus Attucks: Race, Rhetoric, and the Politics of Commemoration," *Quarterly Journal of Speech* 85 (1999): 169. See also Nyong'o, "Uncommon Memory," 39. In my view, reading the orations alongside the trial documents makes it clear that the addresses rendered Attucks's race, as well as his potential threat to the social order, invisible precisely *because* they were so visible when he was alive and active.

15. Alfred F. Young, *The Shoemaker and the Tea Party: Memory and the American Revolution* (Boston: Beacon Press, 1999), 92. "Taming" is Young's term.

16. Len Travers, *Celebrating the Fourth: Independence Day and the Rites of Nationalism in the Early Republic* (Amherst: University of Massachusetts Press, 1997), 31-33. On the lack of interest in Attucks and the Boston Massacre (despite a few sporadic mentions of the event) after 1783, see James, "The Other Fourth of July," 17, and Mitch Kachun, "From Forgotten Founder to Indispensable Icon: Crispus Attucks, Black Citizenship, and Collective Memory, 1770-1865," *JER* 29 (2009): 252-259.

17. David Waldstreicher, "Rites of Rebellion, Rites of Assent: Celebrations, Print Culture, and the Origins of American Nationalism," *JAH* 82 (1995): 38. On the Massacre as an event of primarily local interest, see Robert W. Smith, "What Came After?: News Diffusion and Significance of the Boston Massacre, 1770-1775," *Journalism History* 3, no. 3 (1976): 71-75, 85.

18. Simon P. Newman, *Parades and the Politics of the Street: Festive Culture in the Early American Republic* (Philadelphia: University of Pennsylvania Press, 1997), 87, 103.

19. John Trumbull, *Autobiography, Reminiscences and Letters of John Trumbull* (New Haven, 1841), 93; Frothingham, *Siege of Boston*, 170. On the wide availability of Trumbull's image in printed form, see Purcell, *Sealed with Blood*, 119-120.

20. Jules David Prown, "John Trumbull as History Painter," in *John Trumbull: The Hand and Spirit of a Painter*, ed. Helen A. Cooper (New Haven: Yale University Art Gallery, 1982), 32; Patricia M. Burnham, "John Trumbull, Historian: The Case of the Battle of Bunker's Hill," in *Redefining American History Painting*, ed. Burnham and Lucretia Hoover Giese (New York: Cambridge University Press, 1995), 44-50.

21. An undated key to the painting identifies many of the faces in it. Seven were "real likenesses," while ten other faces were "intended as mere memorandums of

Men who were either distinguished or killed, or wounded in the Action; and of whom no actual Portrait could be obtained." Neither of the painting's black men is included on this key. John Trumbull papers, box 4, folder 58 (microfilm 3:209), Manuscripts and Archives, Yale University Library.

22. Benjamin Silliman Note Book (1858), 65–68, typescript in Trumbull papers, box 10, folder 128 (microfilm 7:78–81). The Note Book occasionally misidentifies Major Small as a colonel.

23. "Explanations of the Two Prints Representing the Battle of Bunker's Hill, and the Attack of Quebec," Trumbull papers, box 4, folder 58 (microfilm 3:194). A note on this document says it was written by Trumbull in 1798. On black soldiers at Bunker Hill, see Quintal, "Patriots of Color."

24. Silliman Note Book, 67, Trumbull papers (microfilm 7:80); Burnham, "John Trumbull," 47–48; see also catalog notes in *John Trumbull*, ed. Cooper, 50. It is unclear when viewers began to conflate the stories about Peter Salem and Salem Poor with Trumbull's painting. The catalog of a bicentennial exhibition of blacks in the Revolution identifies the figure as Peter Salem in a narrative that is more celebratory than analytical; see Sidney Kaplan, *The Black Presence in the Era of the American Revolution, 1770–1800* (Washington, D.C.: National Portrait Gallery, 1973), 18. A postage stamp honoring John Trumbull, issued in 1968, pictured the black and white man from the right side of *The Death of Warren*. Philatelists identify the figures as Thomas Grosvenor and Peter Salem. The postal service honored Salem Poor in 1975; his stamp does not appear to be based on a contemporary image. See the Ebony Society of Philatelic Events and Reflections, "African Americans on U.S. Stamps Part I," http://esperstamps.org/history1.htm.

25. Samuel Swett, *History of Bunker Hill Battle, with a Plan, Second Edition, Much Enlarged with New Information Derived from the Surviving Soldiers Present at the Celebration on the 17th of June Last* (Boston, 1826), 43; *Liberator*, August 13, 1831, 131, citing the *Worcester Yeoman*. Quintal confirms that Peter Salem and Salem Poor were two different people; "Patriots of Color," 170–180, 190–193.

26. George Edward Ellis, *Sketches of Bunker Hill Battle and Monument: With Illustrative Documents*(Charlestown, Mass., 1843), 62; William Emmons, *An Address Commemorative of the Battle of Bunker Hill, June 17, 1775* (Boston, 1834), 15; Frothingham, *Siege of Boston*, iii, 195. A somewhat later, but immensely popular, history that also makes the "negro soldier" claim is Benson J. Lossing, *The Pictorial Field-Book of the Revolution*; vol. 1 (New York, 1851), 546.

27. Extract from the notebook of Jeremy Belknap, August 24, 1787, in *MHSP*, 1st ser., 14 (1876): 93; Franklin A. Dorman, *Twenty Families of Color in Massachusetts, 1742–1998* (Boston; NEHGS, 1998), 272–274.

28. See Young, *Shoemaker and the Tea Party*, 87–91. Accounts of black soldiers' heroism may have been transmitted orally before they were recorded in writing. In 1862, George Livermore presented a paper concerning black participation in the Revolution. He included an extract of a recent letter from Aaron White of Connecticut. "About the year 1807," White wrote, "I heard a soldier of the Revolution, who was present at the Bunker-Hill battle, relate to my father the story of the death of Major Pitcairn." In this version, "a negro soldier stepped forward, and, aiming his musket directly at the major's bosom, blew him through." White sought to establish the credibility of himself, his father, and the soldier in several different ways: "My informant declared that

he was so near, that he distinctly saw the act. The story made quite an impression on my mind. I have frequently heard my father relate the story, and have no doubt of its truth. My father, on the day of the battle, was a mere child, and witnessed the battle and the burning of Charlestown from Roxbury Hill, sitting on the shoulders of the Rev. Mr. Jackson, who said to him as he replaced him on the ground, 'Now, boy, do you remember this.' Consequently, after such an injunction, he would necessarily pay particular attention to anecdotes concerning the first and only battle he ever witnessed." It is hard to evaluate this tale recorded in 1863 about a conversation in 1807 about a battle in 1775, but White's letter is nevertheless a fascinating example of how oral culture sustains and facilitates memory and a tantalizing hint that the story of a black man shooting Pitcairn has a longer and more complicated history than the documentary record can provide. Livermore, *Historical Research*, 93-94.

29. *Proposals by John Trumbull, for Publishing by Subscription, Two Prints, from Original Pictures Painted by Himself* (New York, 1790), 2, Trumbull papers, box 4, folder 58 (microfilm 3:130). Important interpretations of *The Death of Warren* include Prown, "John Trumbull as History Painter," 22-41, and Irma B. Jaffe, *John Trumbull: Patriot-Artist of the American Revolution* (Boston: New York Graphic Society, 1975), 84-90. For a broader context, see Hugh Honour, *The Image of the Black in Western Art*, vol. 4, pt. 1 (Houston: Menil Foundation, 1989), 41-46. Two other interpreters emphasize the marginalization of the black figure in Trumbull's canvas: Albert Boime, *The Art of Exclusion: Representing Blacks in the Nineteenth Century* (Washington: Smithsonian Institution Press, 1990), 21, and Matthew Baigell, "On the Margins of American History," in *Picturing History: American Painting, 1770-1930*, ed. William Ayres (New York: Rizzoli and Fraunces Tavern Museum, 1993), 204. Both Boime and Baigell identify the black man in the painting as Peter Salem and suggest that Trumbull was intentionally marginalizing his contributions to the battle.

30. Pierre Nora, "Between History and Memory: *Les Lieux de Mémoire*," trans. Marc Roudebush, *Representations* 26 (1989): 8.

31. David Ramsay, *The History of the American Revolution*, vol. 1 (Philadelphia, 1789), 200-206.

32. Trumbull, "Explanations of the Two Prints"; Burnham, "John Trumbull," 49. My approach here is informed by Louis P. Masur, "Reading *Watson and the Shark*," *NEQ* 67 (1994): 427-454.

33. John Trumbull, study for *The Death of General Warren at the Battle of Bunker's Hill*, September 1785, Yale University Art Gallery, New Haven, Conn.; Trumbull, study for *The Death of General Warren*, 1785, Historical Society of Pennsylvania (HSP), Philadelphia. The HSP study includes three versions of the retreating pair, a detailed one on which my comments here are based and two pencil sketches. In one of these sketches, there is some shading on the face of the figure at rear (who appears to be holding a gun), but it is hard to tell whether this coloring was intended to represent darker skin or a shadow.

34. Masur, "Reading *Watson*," 437.

35. At the request of Madame de Brehan, who was much enamored with the representation of Grosvenor and his servant, Trumbull prepared a separate painting just of these figures. See catalog notes in *John Trumbull*, ed. Cooper, 50.

36. Benjamin Quarles, *The Negro in the American Revolution* (1961; reprint Chapel Hill: University of North Carolina Press, 1996), 68-70; John Wood Sweet, *Bodies Politic:*

Negotiating Race in the American North, 1730–1830 (Baltimore: Johns Hopkins University Press, 2003), 202–204, 215–217.

37. Petition of Jonathan Brewer and others, December 5, 1775, Mass. Archives, 180:241; Quintal, "Patriots of Color," 170–173. According to the Boston National Historical Park's Salem Poor Site Bulletin, "Of the 2,400–4,000 colonists who participated in the battle, there is no other man singled out in this manner"; http://www.nps.gov/bost/bulletins/Salemp%7E1.pdf.

38. Quintal, "Patriots of Color," 170–173; Edward C. Papenfuse and Gregory A. Stiverson, "General Smallwood's Recruits: The Peacetime Career of the Revolutionary War Private," *WMQ* 30 (1973): 117–132. Compare the limited economic opportunities for free black men in the postwar period: James Oliver Horton and Lois E. Horton, *In Hope of Liberty: Culture, Community and Protest among Northern Free Blacks, 1700–1860* (New York: Oxford University Press, 1997), chap. 5.

39. Petition of John Cuffe, Adventure Childs, and others, February 10, 1780, Mass. Archives, 186:134.

40. On "family slavery," see William D. Piersen, *Black Yankees: The Development of an Afro-American Subculture in Eighteenth-Century New England* (Amherst: University of Massachusetts Press, 1988), 25–36, as well as a critique, Robert K. Fitts, *Inventing New England's Slave Paradise: Master/Slave Relations in Eighteenth-Century Narragansett, Rhode Island* (New York: Garland, 1998), 62–64.

41. Depositions of Edom London, May 16 and June 6, 1806, *Town of Winchendon v. Town of Hatfield*, Worcester County Court of Common Pleas (CCP), Judicial Archives, Massachusetts Archives. A manuscript copy of this deposition in the Supreme Judicial Court file papers for this case says that Bond lived in Leicester, not Lincoln.

42. Depositions of Edom London, May 16, and June 6, 1806, and deposition of Daniel Goodridge, June 5, 1806, *Winchendon v. Hatfield*, Worcester CCP. London enlisted on May 10, 1775, and served for two months and twenty-six days. For details of his service (including under surnames Lonan, Lonnon, and Lonun), see *Massachusetts Soldiers and Sailors of the Revolutionary War*, vol. 9 (Boston: Wright and Potter, 1902), 916, 931–932; Henry S. Nourse, *History of the Town of Harvard, Massachusetts* (Harvard, Mass., 1894), 321.

43. Winchendon Overseers of the Poor records (copy), file papers, 1806, *Winchendon v. Hatfield*, Massachusetts Supreme Judicial Court, Judicial Archives, Massachusetts Archives.

44. Kunal M. Parker, "Making Blacks Foreigners: The Legal Construction of Former Slaves in Post-Revolutionary Massachusetts," *Utah Law Review* 75 (2001): 84–88. For more detail, see Parker, "State, Citizenship, and Territory: The Legal Construction of Immigrants in Antebellum Massachusetts," *Law and History Review* 19 (2001): 583–644; Parker, "From Poor Law to Immigration Law: Changing Visions of Territorial Community in Antebellum Massachusetts," *Historical Geography* 28 (2000): 65–69; Douglas Lamar Jones, "The Transformation of the Law of Poverty in Eighteenth-Century Massachusetts," in *Law in Colonial Massachusetts, 1630–1800* (Boston: Colonial Society of Massachusetts, 1984), 153–190.

45. "An Act Relating to Molatto and Negro Slaves" (first passed in 1703) in *Laws of the Commonwealth of Massachusetts*, vol. 2 (Boston, 1801), 990–991; George H. Moore, *Notes on the History of Slavery in Massachusetts* (1866; reprint New York: Negro Universities Press, 1968), 53–54.

46. *Winchendon v. Hatfield*, 4 Mass. 128.

47. Abijah P. Martin, *History of the Town of Winchendon* (Winchendon, Mass., 1868), 279; John Resch, *Suffering Soldiers: Revolutionary War Veterans, Moral Sentiment, and Political Culture in the Early Republic* (Amherst: University of Massachusetts Press, 1999), 65-92.

48. Mass. Archives, 186:134; petition of Primus Grant and others, January 16, 1798, SC1/series 230, House Unpassed Leg., 1798, no. 4798, Massachusetts Archives (my emphasis). On eighteenth-century usages of the word "race," see Nicholas Hudson, "From 'Nation' to 'Race': The Origin of Racial Classification in Eighteenth-Century Thought," *Eighteenth-Century Studies* 29 (1996): 247-264.

49. On interest in African colonization, see Elizabeth Rauh Bethel, *The Roots of African-American Identity: Memory and History in Free Antebellum Communities* (New York: St. Martin's Press, 1997), 97-105.

50. Gary B. Nash, "Forging Freedom: The Emancipation Experience in the Northern Seaport Cities, 1775-1820," in *Slavery and Freedom in the Age of the American Revolution*, ed. Ira Berlin and Ronald Hoffman (Urbana: University of Illinois Press, 1986), 3-48.

51. John S. Barry, *Historical Sketch of the Town of Hanover, Mass.* (Boston, 1853), 176; George Wingate Chase, *History of Haverhill, Massachusetts* (Haverhill, Mass., 1861), 498; Daniel T. V. Huntoon, *History of the Town of Canton, Norfolk County, Massachusetts* (Cambridge, Mass., 1893), 504; Samuel A. Green, *Historical Sketch of Groton, Massachusetts* (Groton, Mass., 1894), 155; Third Census of the United States (1810), manuscript schedules on microfilm, Massachusetts Archives.

52. Hiram Barrus, *History of the Town of Goshen, Hampshire* (Boston, 1881), 116; William Barry, *History of Framingham, Massachusetts, Including the Plantation* (Boston, 1847), 65; Emory Washburn, *Historical Sketches of the Town of Leicester* (Boston, 1860), 266-269; Quintal, "Patriots of Color," 190-193. See also Elbridge Henry Goss, *History of Melrose, County of Middlesex, Massachusetts* (Melrose, Mass., 1902), 458; *MHSP*, 2nd ser., 1 (1885): 339. On Peter Salem Road, see "An Early Negro Soldier," *The Magazine of History, with Notes and Queries* 9 (June 1909): 355-356.

53. Maurice B. Dorgan, *History of Lawrence, Massachusetts* (Cambridge, Mass., for the author, 1924), 9-10; *Vital Records of Andover, Massachusetts to the Year 1849*, vol. 2 (Topsfield, Mass.: Topsfield Historical Society, 1912), 359; Laurel Thatcher Ulrich, *The Age of Homespun: Objects and Stories in the Creation of an American Myth* (New York: Knopf, 2001), 354-366. Juliet Haines Mofford of the Andover Historical Society shared her materials on Nancy and Salem Poor. For familial and community relations among New England "blacks" and "Indians," see Sweet, *Bodies Politic*, 174-179, and Ann Marie Plane and Gregory Button, "The Massachusetts Indian Enfranchisement Act: Ethnic Contest in Historical Context, 1849-1869," *Ethnohistory* 40 (1993): 587-618.

54. Thomas L. Doughton, "Unseen Neighbors: Native Americans of Central Massachusetts, a People Who Had 'Vanished,'" in *After King Philip's War: Presence and Persistence in Indian New England*, ed. Colin G. Calloway (Hanover, N.H.: University Press of New England, 1997), 207-230.

55. Parker, "Making Blacks Foreigners," 82.

56. *Boston Semi-Weekly Atlas*, March 26, 1842. Quotation: statement of Primus Hall, June 13, 1836, Hall RWPR, 1164:894. Throughout his Revolutionary service,

Hall was known as Primus Trask. In tax records from late eighteenth-century Boston, however, he is described as Prince Hall's son; Chernoh Momodu Sesay, Jr., "Freemasons of Color: Prince Hall, Revolutionary Black Boston, and the Origins of Black Freemasonry, 1770-1807" (Ph.D. diss., Northwestern University, 2006), 21, 105.

57. Timothy Pickering to Rebecca Pickering, March 23, 1781 (quotation); June ? 1781; July 5, 1781; July 6, 1781; July 8, 1781; March 10, 1782; and Rebecca to Timothy, June 29, 1781; July ?, 1781 (quotation); July 8, 1781; "Sunday evening" [undated], July 12, 1781; July 21, 1781; August 27? 1781; *Timothy Pickering Papers, 1758-1829*, microfilm ed. (Boston: MHS, 1966), MHS. On Pickering's bizarre military and political career, see Gerard H. Clarfield, "Pickering, Timothy," *American National Biography Online* (February 2000), accessed July 11, 2006.

58. Margot Minardi, "Hall, Primus," *African American National Biography* (New York: Oxford University Press, 2008); James Oliver Horton, "Generations of Protest: Black Families and Social Reform in Ante-Bellum Boston," *NEQ* 49 (1976): 244-245; Petition of Primus Hall and others, August 6, 1838, City of Boston Archives, City Council Series 1.4, Item 1838-0069-H4, http://www.cityofboston.gov/archivesandrecords/lessonplans/primus.asp.

59. See Joanne Pope Melish, *Disowning Slavery: "Race" and Gradual Emancipation in New England, 1780-1860* (Ithaca, N.Y.: Cornell University Press, 1998) and "The 'Condition' Debate and Racial Discourse in the Antebellum North," *JER* 19 (1999): 651-672; Sweet, *Bodies Politic*, esp. chap. 7-8.

60. The author of the piece, Reverend Henry F. Harrington, revered Washington and opposed slavery, but it is unclear how Hall became the pivotal figure in his anecdote. On Harrington's political views, see his speech *The Moral Influence of the American Government* (Albany, 1846).

61. Henry F. Harrington, "Anecdotes of Washington," *Godey's Magazine and Lady's Book* 29 (June 1849): 427-428.

62. Harrington, "Anecdotes of Washington," 427-428. A variation of this bed-sharing trope appeared in a memoir of Lemuel Haynes; see Richard D. Brown, "'Not Only Extreme Poverty, but the Worst Kind of Orphanage': Lemuel Haynes and the Boundaries of Racial Tolerance on the Yankee Frontier," *NEQ* 61 (1988): 512-513.

63. William C. Nell, *The Colored Patriots of the American Revolution* (1855; New York: Arno Press-New York Times, 1968), 29-32; Lydia Maria Child, *The Freedmen's Book* (Boston: Ticknor and Fields, 1866), 31.

64. Petition of Primus Hall, 1836, Hall RWPR, 1164:0896; *Journal of the House of Representatives of the United States* (December 31, 1836), 153; affidavit of Primus Hall, October 13, 1835, Hall RWPR, 1164:0824. On the power of Washington's memory, see François Furstenberg, *In the Name of the Father: Washington's Legacy, Slavery, and the Making of a Nation* (New York: Penguin Press, 2006).

65. James Edwards to Reuben Baldwin, October 29, 1835, and July 9, 1836, Hall RWPR, 1164:0841, 0853.

66. The legal distinction was unclear. The regulations governing military pensions in 1832 specified that "all persons enlisted, drafted, or who volunteered and who were bound to military service, but not those who were occasionally employed with the army upon civil contracts," were entitled to a federal pension. Officers' servants were not necessarily "upon civil contracts"; they could come from the line of soldiers. Testified one officer, "it was an established privilege and custom for the

Surgeon and Mates, as well as for the Commissioned Officers of the Army, to have a Waiter from the Line of the Army, which said Waiter was *fed clothed and paid* as the other soldiers." One black veteran was remembered as having worn a "Soldiers Uniform" while serving as an officer's waiter. Regulations under the Act of June 7, 1832, (form reproduced in many RWPRs, see for instance 1015:0657); statement of John Watrous, Cuff Wells RWPR, 2528:0704; statement of Olive Haroman, August 15, 1838, Prince Sayward RWPR, 2129:0408.

67. Statement of Ebenezer Hart, October 8, 1835, Hall RWPR, 1164:0883, emphasis added; statement of John Brown, August 12, 1836, Hall RWPR, 1164:0858; statement of Thomas Thorp, May 14, 1836, Hall RWPR, 1164:0846. See also statement of William Flint, May 17, 1846, Hall RWPR, 1164:0842. A list of Revolutionary War soldiers from Danvers confirms that John Brown served in Captain Flint's company; it also includes "Priam Traske" as having enlisted on August 25, 1777, in Captain Flint's company of Colonel Johnson's regiment, with a discharge date of December 14, 1777; *Report of the Committee to Revise the Soldiers' Record* (Danvers, Mass., 1895), 115, 133.

68. Committee on Revolutionary Pensions, U.S. House of Representatives, report on petition of Primus Hall, Hall RWPR, 1164:0891.

69. *Boston Transcript*, quoted in *Liberator*, April 8, 1842. On Hall's quest for a pension, see Margot Minardi, "Freedom in the Archives: The Pension Case of Primus Hall," in *Dublin Seminar for New England Folklife Annual Proceedings 2003* (Boston: Boston University, 2005), 128-140.

CHAPTER 3

1. *Liberator*, July 21, 1843, 114. The editor noted that this story "from the pen of a colored man" was copied from "the United States Clarion. "

2. Daniel Webster, "The Completion of the Bunker Hill Monument" [1843], in *The Works of Daniel Webster*, vol. 1 (Boston, 1851), 89.

3. So claimed Webster, "Completion of the Bunker Hill Monument," 86.

4. On memory as sensory experience, see W. Caleb McDaniel, "The Fourth and the First: Abolitionist Holidays, Respectability, and Radical Interracial Reform," *AQ* 57 (2005): 134-136; Keith Tony Beutler, "The Memory Revolution in American and Memory of the American Revolution, 1790-1840" (Ph. D. diss., Washington University, 2005); Russ Castronovo, *Fathering the Nation: American Genealogies of Slavery and Freedom* (Berkeley: University of California Press, 1995), 131-139.

5. *Liberator*, September 21, 1838, 150; David Brion Davis, *The Problem of Slavery in the Age of Revolution, 1770-1823* (Ithaca, N. Y. : Cornell University Press, 1975), 213; James Brewer Stewart, "Boston, Abolition, and the Atlantic World, 1820-1861," in *Courage and Conscience: Black and White Abolitionists in Boston*, ed. Donald M. Jacobs (Bloomington: Indiana University Press for the Boston Athenaeum, 1993), 110; Henry Mayer, *All on Fire: William Lloyd Garrison and the Abolition of Slavery* (New York: St. Martin's Press, 1998), 324-329; Kevin M. Gannon, "Calculating the Value of Union: States' Rights, Nullification, and Secession in the North, 1800-1848" (Ph. D. diss., University of South Carolina, 2002), chap. 6.

6. Sarah J. Purcell, *Sealed with Blood: War, Sacrifice, and Memory in Revolutionary America* (Philadelphia: University of Pennsylvania Press, 2002), 194-209 (quotation on 195); Purcell, "Commemoration, Public Art, and the Changing Meaning of the

Bunker Hill Monument," *Public Historian* 25 (2003): 55-71; Beutler, "Memory Revolution," 65-67; Michael Kammen, *A Season of Youth: The American Revolution and the Historical Imagination* (New York: Knopf, 1978), 43-49.

7. For a later expression of this sentiment, see an unsigned subscription paper, July 29, 1850, John Collins Warren papers, MHS (folder labeled "June 1775, Joseph Warren & Bunker Hill").

8. Purcell, *Sealed with Blood*, 199-201; Horatio Greenough, *The Travels, Observations, and Experience of a Yankee Stonecutter* (New York, 1852), 37, quoted in Purcell, 201.

9. George Washington Warren, *The History of the Bunker Hill Monument Association* (Boston, 1877), 376-384; inscriptions by Francis C. Gray and letter from Gray to Edward Everett, March 2, 1849, printed in ibid., 377-378.

10. Warren, *Bunker Hill Monument Association*, 384-385 and overleaf, 416-419; circular letter of September 20, 1824, in ibid., 115.

11. Warren, *Bunker Hill Monument Association*, 385.

12. Harlow W. Sheidley, *Sectional Nationalism: Massachusetts Conservative Leaders and the Transformation of America, 1815-1836* (Boston: Northeastern University Press, 1998), ix-xii, 30-32; Kirk Savage, *Standing Soldiers, Kneeling Slaves: Race, War, and Monument in Nineteenth-Century America* (Princeton, N. J. : Princeton University Press, 1997), 4; Castronovo, *Fathering the Nation*, 147.

13. Alfred F. Young, *The Shoemaker and the Tea Party: Memory and the American Revolution* (Boston: Beacon Press, 1999), 133; Seth Luther, *An Address to the Working Men of New England...*, 2nd ed. (New York, 1833), quoted in ibid., 148. On workers and Revolutionary memory, see Alan Dawley, *Class and Community: The Industrial Revolution in Lynn*, 25th anniversary ed. (Cambridge, Mass. : Harvard University Press, 2000), 82; Sean Wilentz, *Chants Democratic: New York City and the Rise of the American Working Class, 1788-1850* (New York: Oxford University Press, 1984), 63-77.

14. Young, *Shoemaker and the Tea Party*, 166-179; Sheidley, *Sectional Nationalism*, 86-147; Bunker Hill Monument Association, *Corrected Order of Procession, for the Seventeenth of June, 1825* (Boston, 1825).

15. Samuel Swett, *History of Bunker Hill Battle, with a Plan, Second Edition, Much Enlarged with New Information Derived from the Surviving Soldiers Present at the Celebration on the 17th of June Last* (Boston, 1826); proceedings of the April 1842 meeting of the Massachusetts Historical Society, *MHSP*, 1st ser., 2 (1880): 232n (quotation attributed to George E. Ellis).

16. Sheidley, *Sectional Nationalism*, 140-141, 191; John Seelye, *Memory's Nation: The Place of Plymouth Rock* (Chapel Hill: University of North Carolina Press, 1998), 75-85.

17. Young, *Shoemaker and the Tea Party*, 138.

18. Webster, "Completion of the Bunker Hill Monument," 92-97; Harry L. Watson, *Liberty and Power: The Politics of Jacksonian America*, rev. ed. (New York: Hill and Wang, 2006), 43-46.

19. Webster, "The Bunker Hill Monument" [1825], in *Works of Daniel Webster*, vol. 1, 61-62, 66, 59.

20. Benedict Anderson, *Imagined Communities: Reflections on the Origin and Spread of Nationalism* (London: Verso, 1991), 12; Webster, "Completion of the Bunker

Hill Monument," 89, 86. On birthright citizenship, see James H. Kettner, *The Development of American Citizenship, 1608-1870* (Chapel Hill: University of North Carolina Press, 1978); Rogers M. Smith, *Civic Ideals: Conflicting Visions of Citizenship in U. S. History* (New Haven, Conn. : Yale University Press, 1997), 33-39.

21. Webster, "Completion of the Bunker Hill Monument," 89; Purcell, "Changing Meaning of the Bunker Hill Monument," 65-66.

22. Donald M. Jacobs, "David Walker and William Lloyd Garrison: Racial Cooperation and the Shaping of Boston Abolitionism," in *Courage and Conscience*, 8-17; William E. Gienapp, "Abolitionism and the Nature of Antebellum Reform," in ibid., 21-46; James Brewer Stewart, *Holy Warriors: The Abolitionists and American Slavery*, rev. ed. (New York: Hill and Wang, 1997), chap. 3-5; Aileen S. Kraditor, *Means and Ends in American Abolitionism: Garrison and His Critics on Strategy and Tactics, 1834-1850* (New York: Pantheon, 1969); Matthew Mason, *Slavery and Politics in the Early American Republic* (Chapel Hill: University of North Carolina Press, 2006), chap. 6; Richard S. Newman, *The Transformation of American Abolitionism: Fighting Slavery in the Early Republic* (Chapel Hill: University of North Carolina Press, 2002).

23. On the Liberty Party in Massachusetts, see Bruce Laurie, *Beyond Garrison: Antislavery and Social Reform* (Cambridge: Cambridge University Press, 2005); Reinhard O. Johnson, "The Liberty Party in Massachusetts, 1840-1848: Antislavery Third Party Politics in the Bay State," *Civil War History* 28 (1982): 237-265.

24. Runaway advertisement from the *American Beacon*, reprinted in *Latimer Journal and North Star*, November 16, 1842; Asa J. Davis, "The Two Autobiographical Fragments of George W. Latimer (1820-1896): A Preliminary Assessment," *Journal of the Afro-American Historical and Genealogical Society* 1 (1980): 3-18. My interpretation of Latimer's case and its context is drawn from Robert M. Cover, *Justice Accused: Antislavery and the Judicial Process* (New Haven, Conn. : Yale University Press, 1975), 169-171; Mayer, *All on Fire*, 316-320; Thomas D. Morris, *Free Men All: The Personal Liberty Laws of the North, 1780-1861* (Baltimore: Johns Hopkins University Press, 1974), 109-117; William W. Wiecek, "Latimer: Lawyers, Abolitionists, and the Problem of Unjust Laws," in *Antislavery Reconsidered: New Perspectives on the Abolitionists*, ed. Lewis Perry and Michael Fellman (Baton Rouge: Louisiana State University Press, 1979), 219-237; Paul Finkelman, *An Imperfect Union: Slavery, Federalism, and Comity* (Chapel Hill: University of North Carolina Press, 1981), chap. 4.

25. Paul Finkelman, "*Prigg v. Pennsylvania*: Understanding Justice Story's Proslavery Nationalism," *Journal of Supreme Court History* 2 (1997): 55.

26. *Latimer Journal*, November 11, 1842. Gannon interprets the Latimer case in the context of abolitionist secessionism in "Calculating the Value of Union," 262-267.

27. *Latimer Journal*, November 11, 1842.

28. *Latimer Journal*, November 14, 1842; Wiecek, "Latimer," 228-229.

29. "Rescue the Slave!" in *The Anti-Slavery Harp; A Collection of Songs for Anti-Slavery Meetings*, comp. William Wells Brown (Boston, 1848), 28-29. Brown explains that this song was composed while Latimer was in jail in 1842.

30. *Latimer Journal*, November 16, 1842.

31. Jane H. Pease and William H. Pease, *They Who Would Be Free: Blacks' Search for Freedom, 1830-1861* (New York: Atheneum, 1974), 216.

32. In an early issue, the editors of the *Latimer Journal* (November 14, 1842) declared, "Our war is to the hilt with SLAVERY IN MASSACHUSETTS. "

33. Mayer, *All on Fire*, 319-320; Laurie, *Beyond Garrison*, 78-80.

34. *Latimer Journal*, November 23, 1842 (insert); "Original Signatures of those who undertook to canvass Boston for the Great Latimer Petition," n. d., *Papers Related to the George Latimer Case, 1842-1888*, microfilm ed. (Boston: MHS, 1993), reel 1, MHS.

35. Morris, *Free Men All*, 114-115; Massachusetts House of Representatives, House Doc. No. 41, "Fugitives from Slavery" (1843); *Latimer Journal*, May 10, 1843.

36. *Twelfth Annual Report, Presented to the Massachusetts Anti-Slavery Society, by Its Board of Managers, January 24, 1844* (Boston, 1844), 33; Anne Warren Weston to Caroline and Deborah Weston, May 28-30,1843, Ms. A. 9. 2. 18, 49, BPL; "Address to John Tyler," in *Liberator*, June 2, 1843, 87. On the authorship of this address, see *Liberator*, June 16, 1843, 94.

37. "Address to the Slaves of the United States," in *Liberator*, June 2, 1843, 87.

38. *Liberator*, June 16, 1843, 95; Anne Warren Weston to unidentified correspondent, June 1843?, Ms. A. 9. 2. 6, 42, BPL; O. A. Bowe, editor of the *Herkimer Journal* (New York) in *Liberator*, June 16, 1843, 94; Morris, *Free Men All*, 109; William Lloyd Garrison to George W. Benson, June 20, 1843, Ms. A. 1. 1. 3, 109, BPL; Mayer, *All on Fire*, 320-321; Norma Lois Peterson, *The Presidencies of William Henry Harrison and John Tyler* (Lawrence: University Press of Kansas, 1989), 176-187; Kinley J. Brauer, *Cotton versus Conscience: Massachusetts Whig Politics and Southwestern Expansion, 1843-1848* (Lexington: University of Kentucky Press, 1967), 50-58.

39. *Liberator*, June 23, 1843, 99.

40. Warren, *Bunker Hill Monument Association*, 318-320; *Boston Daily Advertiser*, June 16-17, 1843; scrapbook of newspaper clippings on the Bunker Hill Monument, MHS; George Bancroft to Martin Van Buren, June 22, 1843, in *MHSP*, 1st ser., 42 (1909): 409; Richard Henry Dana, Jr., *The Journal of Richard Henry Dana, Jr.*, vol. I, ed. Robert F. Lucid (Cambridge: Harvard University Press, 1968), 166 (quotation); John Collins Warren, diary, June 18, 1843, John Collins Warren papers, MHS; Edmund Quincy (1808-1877), diary, June 16-17, 1843, *Quincy, Wendell, Holmes, and Upham Family Papers, 1633-1910*, microfilm ed. (Boston: MHS, 1977), reel 9, MHS; Samuel May, diary and interleaved almanac, June 17, 1843, *Samuel May Papers, 1825-1903*, microfilm ed. (Boston: MHS, n. d.), reel 5, MHS.

41. Dana, *Journal*, 165-166; *Boston Daily Advertiser*, June 17, 1843; Warren, *Bunker Hill Monument Association*, 318; *Liberator*, July 7, 1843, 108; July 21, 1843, 114.

42. *Liberator*, June 23, 1843, 99.

43. Evelina A. S. Smith to Caroline Weston, June 25, 1843, Ms. A. 9. 2. 18, 62, BPL; *Liberator*, June 16, 1843, 95; Robert H. Abzug, *Cosmos Crumbling: American Reform and the Religious Imagination* (New York: Oxford University Press, 1994), chap. 6.

44. Anne Warren Weston to Caroline and Deborah Weston, June 19, 1843; this letter is taped onto another letter from Anne to her sisters, November 10, 1843, Ms. A. 9. 2. 19, 75, BPL.

45. William Lloyd Garrison to George W. Benson, June 20, 1843, Ms. A. 1. 1. 3, 109, BPL; *Liberator*, June 30, 1843, 103.

46. The key historian here was Samuel Swett: see his *History of the Bunker Hill Battle*, 43, and *Notes to His Sketch of Bunker Hill* (Boston, 1825), 25-26. In Swett's

version, "Salem a black soldier, and a number of others" shot Pitcairn just as he was shouting "the day is ours!"; in his *Notes*, Swett added that "many northern blacks were excellent soldiers" and gave an account of Cuffee Whittemore, another veteran of Bunker Hill. Alexander H. Everett, *An Address Delivered at Charlestown, Mass., on the 17th of June, 1836* (Boston, 1836), 58, repeats Swett's version of the death of Pitcairn, as does *Liberator*, August 13, 1831, 131, among other sources.

47. *Liberator*, January 1, 1831, 1.

48. See, for instance, *Liberator*, August 18, 1843, 129; December 29, 1843, 207; February 2, 1844, 17.

49. Bill of sale for "a Negro boy" from Joshua Green to James Warren, in *MHSP*, 1st ser., 13 (1876): 101. There are many examples of abolitionists praising Warren, but see especially "General Warren an Abolitionist," *Liberator*, September 21, 1838, 150.

50. *Liberator*, July 7, 1843, 107.

51. On Walker and his context, see Patrick Rael, *Black Identity and Black Protest in the Antebellum North* (Chapel Hill: University of North Carolina Press, 2002); Eddie S. Glaude, Jr., *Exodus!: Religion, Race, and Nation in Early Nineteenth-Century Black America* (Chicago: University of Chicago Press, 2000); Mia Bay, *The White Image in the Black Mind: African-American Ideas about White People, 1830-1925* (New York: Oxford University Press, 2000), chap. 2; Peter P. Hinks, *To Awaken My Afflicted Brethren: David Walker and the Problem of Antebellum Slave Resistance* (University Park: Pennsylvania State University Press, 1997), chap. 6; Bruce Dain, *A Hideous Monster of the Mind: American Race Theory in the Early Republic* (Cambridge: Harvard University Press, 2002), esp. 139-148.

52. Hinks, *To Awaken My Afflicted Brethren*, 257.

53. David Walker, *Walker's Appeal, in Four Articles; Together with a Preamble, to the Coloured Citizens of the World, but in Particular, and Very Expressly, to Those of the United States of America* (Boston, 1830), 32–33; Thomas Jefferson, *Notes on the State of Virginia*, ed. Frank Shuffelton (New York: Penguin, 1999), 169. On black revolution as "unthinkable history," see Michel-Rolph Trouillot, *Silencing the Past: Power and the Production of History* (Boston: Beacon Press, 1995), chap. 3. On Walker's theology, see Glaude, *Exodus!* 40-43; Hinks, *To Awaken my Afflicted Brethren*, 227-233.

54. Walker, *Appeal*, 62, 73; Webster, "Bunker Hill Monument," 59. On Webster and colonization, see Newman, *Transformation of American Abolitionism*, 110-111; Eric Burin, *Slavery and the Peculiar Solution: A History of the American Colonization Society* (Gainesville: University Press of Florida, 2005), 1, 28.

55. Maria W. Stewart, *Maria W. Stewart, America's First Black Woman Political Writer: Essays and Speeches*, ed. Marilyn Richardson (Bloomington: Indiana University Press, 1987).

56. Wendell Phillips Garrison and Francis Jackson Garrison, *William Lloyd Garrison, 1805-1879: The Story of His Life Told by His Children*, vol. 3 (Boston: Houghton Mifflin, 1894), 320. On Garrison's Christian perfectionism and the religious context of his abolitionism, see Stewart, *Holy Warriors*, 46-47, 88-91; Aileen S. Kraditor, *Means and Ends*, 102-106; Abzug, *Cosmos Crumbling*, chap. 6.

57. Pease and Pease, *They Who Would Be Free*, 3-4.

58. "Address to the Slaves of the United States," in *Liberator*, June 2, 1843, 87.

59. Henry Highland Garnet, "An Address to the Slaves of the United States of America," in Stanley Harrold, *The Rise of Aggressive Abolitionism: Addresses to the*

Slaves (Lexington: University Press of Kentucky, 2004), 179–188. See Harrold's introduction for more on Garnet and Garrison; also Glaude, *Exodus!*, chap. 8.

60. *North Star*, May 5, 1848.

CHAPTER 4

1. Anne Bentley of MHS showed me the Wheatley table and records relating to
its acquisition. MHS identifies it as a card table, tea table, or desk. The shape of the
table is consistent with a card table, though the tea-drinking and card-playing often
took place at the same table, especially in less luxurious settings; Gerald W. R. Ward,
"'Avarice and Conviviality': Card Playing in Federal America," in *The Work of Many
Hands: Card Tables in Federal America, 1790-1820*, ed. Benjamin A. Hewitt, Patricia E.
Kane, and Ward (New Haven, Conn.: Yale University Art Gallery, 1982), 17–19.

2. Publisher George W. Light packaged the memoir with a reprint of Wheatley's
Poems on Various Subjects under the full title *Memoir and Poems of Phillis Wheatley, a
Native African and a Slave. Dedicated to the Friends of the Africans* (Boston, 1834), with
no author listed. Hereafter I refer to the memoir in this edition as Odell, *Phillis
Wheatley*. Some sources attribute the memoir to Benjamin Bussey Thatcher, author
of a biography of a shoemaker who participated in the Boston Tea Party. Thatcher
denied that he had anything to do with the book, other than "giving it an editor's
supervision, and nothing more," and the text itself identifies the author as a woman
related to Susanna Wheatley. Charles Deane discusses the memoir's authorship in
MHSP, 1st ser., 7 (1863): 269-270 n.; on Thatcher, see Alfred F. Young, *The Shoemaker
and the Tea Party: Memory and the American Revolution* (Boston: Beacon Press, 1999),
173–174.

3. On "deference politics," see James Brewer Stewart, "The Emergence of Racial
Modernity and the Rise of the White North, 1790-1840," *JER* 18 (1998): 186–191. On
black Federalism, see John Saillant, *Black Puritan, Black Republican: The Life and
Thought of Lemuel Haynes, 1753-1833* (New York: Oxford University Press, 2003),
118–129; Linda Prince, "White Community, Black Compromise: Blacks and the
Experience of Interraciality in Boston from Slavery to Freedom, 1693-1815" (Ph.D.
diss., Harvard University, 2002), 205–208.

4. "Politics of respectability": Evelyn Brooks Higginbotham, *Righteous Discontent:
The Women's Movement in the Black Baptist Church, 1880-1920* (Cambridge, Mass.:
Harvard University Press, 1993), 185–211; Patrick Rael, *Black Identity and Black Protest
in the Antebellum North* (Chapel Hill: University of North Carolina Press, 2002), chap. 4;
Eddie S. Glaude, Jr., *Exodus!: Religion, Race, and Nation in Early Nineteenth-Century
Black America* (Chicago: University of Chicago Press, 2000), 118–125.

5. David S. Shields, *Civil Tongues and Polite Letters in British America* (Chapel
Hill: University of North Carolina Press, 1997), 99–126; Sarah Neale Fayen, "Tilt-Top
Tables and Eighteenth-Century Consumerism," *American Furniture 2003* (Milwaukee:
Chipstone Foundation, 2003), 97–99.

6. William H. Robinson, "On Phillis Wheatley and Her Boston," in *Phillis
Wheatley and Her Writings* (New York: Garland, 1983), 3–69; Julian D. Mason, Jr.,
introduction and "On the Reputation of Phillis Wheatley, Poet," in *The Poems of Phillis
Wheatley*, rev. ed. (Chapel Hill: University of North Carolina Press, 1989), 1–34;
Vincent Carretta, introduction to *Complete Writings*, by Phillis Wheatley (New York:

Penguin, 2001), xiii-xxxvii; James A. Rawley, "The World of Phillis Wheatley," *NEQ* 50 (1977): 666-677; Frank Shuffelton, "On Her Own Footing: Phillis Wheatley in Freedom," in *Genius in Bondage: Literature of the Early Black Atlantic*, ed. Vincent Carretta and Philip Gould (Lexington: University Press of Kentucky, 1999), 175-189.

7. Vincent Carretta, "Phillis Wheatley, the Mansfield Decision of 1772, and the Choice of Identity," in *Early America Re-Explored: New Readings in Colonial, Early National, and Antebellum Culture*, ed. Klaus H. Schmidt and Fritz Fleischmann (New York: Peter Lang, 2000), 202-219.

8. See Wheatley, *Complete Writings*, 86-103, 167-170. While I refer to the poet as "Phillis Wheatley" for consistency, this convention owes something to the coloniza-tion of her memory by her former master's family. Odell claimed that even after marriage Phillis used the name "Wheatley" rather than "Peters." However, at least some of the poet's surviving letters and proposals show that she signed herself "Phillis Peters." Odell, *Phillis Wheatley*, 21-22; Wheatley, *Complete Writings*, 162; Robinson, "Wheatley and Her Boston," 61.

9. Robinson, "Wheatley and Her Boston," 47, 50-53.

10. *Columbian Centinel*, December 8, 1784, with a similar announcement in the *Independent Chronicle*, December 9, 1784; "Horatio," "Elegy on the Death of a Late Celebrated Poetess," *Boston Magazine* 1 (1784): 619-620; Joseph Lavallée, *The Negro Equalled by Few Europeans, Translated from the French; To Which Are Added Poems on Various Subjects, Moral and Entertaining by Phillis Wheatley* (Philadelphia, 1801). In addition to this volume and one or two printings of the Halifax edition, the poems were printed three times in Philadelphia (1786, 1787, and 1789); once each in Albany (1793), Walpole, New Hampshire (1802), and Hartford (1804); and once in "New England" (1816). There was also a printing in London under an altered title, *Poems on Comic, Serious, and Moral Subjects* (1787). For a discussion of some of these editions, see Jennifer Rene Young, "Marketing a Sable Muse: The Cultural Circulation of Phillis Wheatley, 1767-1865" (Ph.D. diss., Howard University, 2004), 72-95.

11. Thomas Jefferson, *Notes on the State of Virginia*, ed. Frank Shuffelton (New York: Penguin, 1999), 147; *Critical Essays on Phillis Wheatley*, ed. William H. Robinson (Boston: G. K. Hall, 1982), 42-52.

12. Henri Grégoire, *An Enquiry Concerning the Intellectual and Moral Faculties, and Literature of Negroes*, trans. David Bailie Warden, ed. Graham Russell Hodges (Armonk, N.Y.: M. E. Sharpe, 1997). Warden, the text's original translator, was American consul in Paris. Anthologies that borrowed from Grégoire's included Edward Dorr Griffin, *A Plea for Africa* (New York, 1817); Abigail Field Mott, *Biographical Sketches and Interesting Anecdotes of Persons of Color* (New York, 1826 and several subsequent editions).

13. Grégoire, *Enquiry*, 102-103, 109 n. 67. On Giraud in Boston: *Independent Chronicle*, May 5, 1803. The sketch gets nearly every date wrong. *Poems on Various Subjects* was published in 1773, not 1772. In a letter to a friend Wheatley suggested she was emancipated in late 1773, not 1775 as Grégoire stated. Boston records have her marrying John Peters in 1778, not 1777.

14. Charles J. Stratford, "Philis Wheatley," Charles J. Stratford Reminiscences, 7, MHS; L. H. Pammel, *Reminiscences of Early La Crosse, Wisconsin* (n.p.: Liesenfeld Press, 1928), 92; "Memoir of Thomas Wallcut," *MHSP*, 1st ser., 2 (1841): 193-208; Thomas Wallcut to Phillis Wheatley, November 17, 1774, *Thomas Wallcut Papers*,

1671-1866, microfilm ed. (Boston: MHS, 1991), reel 2, MHS; Robinson, "Wheatley and Her Boston," 57, 65.

15. Odell, *Phillis Wheatley*, 22–23, 28–29. I have attempted to piece together genealogical relationships based on Thomas Wallcut's genealogical notes in *Wallcut Papers*, reel 1, MHS; Stratford Reminiscences; Robinson, *Phillis Wheatley and Her Writings*, 450 n. 19. Will of Margaret [Margaretta] M. Odell (1881), Suffolk Probate, 532:63–64.

16. Guardianship papers concerning Margaretta Odell (1847-1860), Suffolk Probate, 407:78, 177, 197; 409:16, 125, 147; Odell, *Phillis Wheatley*, vii, 25; *Liberator*, March 22, 1834, 47; March 29, 1834, 52; October 27, 1837, 176; December 4, 1863, 194.

17. Odell, *Phillis Wheatley*, 12, 19, 25.

18. Odell, *Phillis Wheatley*, 24–25.

19. Odell, *Phillis Wheatley*, 27.

20. Odell, *Phillis Wheatley*, 9, 11, 13.

21. Odell, *Phillis Wheatley*, 10, 28, 11-12 (emphasis mine). What I describe below as the "trope of the tea table" assumed that blacks came to the table to serve, not to be served. A Massachusetts legislator tried to use black servants' discomfiture with serving other blacks as an argument against integration of public facilities. Representative Fowle described the furor that resulted when "he had once a colored gentleman to tea at his house, and at the same time a colored servant." Upon seeing Fowle's visitor, the maid "left the room in great wrath, declaring that she came there to wait on gentlefolks, and not upon a nigger." This story disclaimed white responsibility for the racialization of respectability by representing blacks as disgusted by the prospect of people of color being considered "gentlefolks." See *Liberator*, February 17, 1843.

22. Orlando Patterson, *Slavery and Social Death: A Comparative Study* (Cambridge, Mass.: Harvard University Press, 1982), 7. On ciphers and civil death, see Nancy Isenberg, *Sex and Citizenship in Antebellum America* (Chapel Hill: University of North Carolina Press, 1998), xv, 22–24, 105-107. The processes I describe here do not preclude the preservation of Wheatley's memory in other sites or among other communities, even if Odell's narrative proved hegemonic.

23. For Wheatley's correspondence, see *Complete Writings*, 139-162.

24. Shuffelton, "On Her Own Footing"; Carretta, "Wheatley, Mansfield, and the Choice of Identity"; Kirstin Wilcox, "The Body into Print: Marketing Phillis Wheatley," *American Literature* 71 (1999): 1-29; Carla Willard, "Wheatley's Turns of Praise: Heroic Entrapment and the Paradox of Revolution," *American Literature* 67 (1995): 233-256; Dwight A. McBride, *Impossible Witnesses: Truth, Abolitionism, and Slave Testimony* (New York: New York University Press, 2001), 103-119; Eric Slauter, "Neoclassical Culture in a Society with Slaves: Race and Rights in the Age of Wheatley," *Early American Studies* 2 (2004): 111-117.

25. Odell, *Phillis Wheatley*, 10-11, 15-16.

26. *Grand Celebration of the Bobalition of African Slavery!* (Boston, 1825), Boston Public Library; John Wood Sweet, *Bodies Politic: Negotiating Race in the American North, 1730-1830* (Baltimore: Johns Hopkins University Press, 2003), 378-392; Joanne Pope Melish, *Disowning Slavery: Gradual Emancipation and "Race" in New England, 1780-1860* (Ithaca, N.Y.: Cornell University Press, 1998), 165-183; Rael, *Black Identity and Black Protest*, 72-75.

27. Sweet, *Bodies Politic*, 379.

28. *Columbian Centinel*, July 6, 1808; entry for July 24, 1808, William Bentley, *The Diary of William Bentley, D.D.*, vol. 3 (Gloucester, Mass.: Peter Smith, 1962), 372–373; Jedidiah Morse, *Discourse Delivered at the African Meeting-House* (Boston, 1808). Later sources (for instance *Liberator*, November 19, 1858) claim that these July 14 celebrations commemorated the abolition of slavery in Massachusetts. On African American festive culture in this period: Shane White, "'It Was a Proud Day': African Americans, Festivals, and Parades in the North, 1741-1834," *JAH* 81 (1994): 13–50; Elizabeth Rauh Bethel, *The Roots of African American Identity: Memory and History in Free Antebellum Communities* (New York: St. Martin's Press, 1997), 85–92; Rael, *Black Identity and Black Protest*, chap. 2; Glaude, *Exodus!*, chap. 5; Stephen Elliot James, "The Other Fourth of July: The Meanings of Black Identity at American Celebrations of Independence, 1770-1863" (Ph.D. diss., Harvard University, 1997); David Waldstreicher, *In the Midst of Perpetual Fetes: The Making of American Nationalism, 1776-1820* (Chapel Hill: University of North Carolina Press, 1997), chap. 6; Mitch Kachun, *Festivals of Freedom: Memory and Meaning in African American Emancipation Celebrations, 1808-1915* (Amherst: University of Massachusetts Press, 2003).

29. Phillip Lapsansky, "Phillis Wheatley, Derision, and Celebration," *Annual Report of the Library Company of Philadelphia* (2001): 47–51. A version of the "Negro Hill" broadside featuring the broom-wielding Phillis was apparently reprinted eleven years later under the dateline "Bosson, Ulie 47th, 180027"; see "Dreadful Riot at Negro Hill!" (1827), Library of Congress, Broadside Collection, portfolio 54, no. 10 c-Rare Bk Coll., available online at http://www.loc.gov/rr/print/.

30. Emma Jones Lapsansky, "'Since They Got Those Separate Churches': Afro-Americans and Racism in Jacksonian Philadelphia," *AQ* 32 (1980): 54–78.

31. Melish, *Disowning Slavery*, 183–184. On respectability as public display, see Victoria W. Wolcott, *Remaking Respectability: African American Women in Interwar Detroit* (Chapel Hill: University of North Carolina Press, 2001), 5–6. Melish's interpretation of stories about "good" people of color relies primarily on sources about children. Memoirs of "respectable" adults (an adjective not usually applied to children) are different in showing black men and women to be autonomous actors in civil society, something which the dependent status of children did not permit them to be.

32. *Columbian Centinel*, January 7, 1815; [Thomas Baldwin], "Biography of Mrs. Chloe Spear," *Massachusetts Baptist Missionary Magazine* 4 (March 1815): 157-158; "A Lady of Boston" [Mary Webb], *Memoir of Mrs. Chloe Spear* (Boston, 1832). The New York Public Library is the original source attributing the *Memoir*'s authorship to Webb. For preliminary information on the case for Mary Webb as author of the *Memoir*, see Margot Minardi, "Spear, Chloe," *African American National Biography* (New York: Oxford University Press, 2008).

33. Webb, *Chloe Spear*, 16-17, 22-26, 34-37, 41-42. On Bradford (whom Webb identifies as "Capt. B."), see Baldwin, "Chloe Spear," 157; [Samuel Bradford, Jr.], *Some Incidents in the Life of Samuel Bradford Sr.* (Philadelphia, 1880), 10-12; Samuel Bradford, trading records, 1760-1779, Samuel Bradford papers, MHS.

34. Acts 10:34, a favorite verse of abolitionists and evangelicals.

35. Baldwin, "Chloe Spear"; "Cloe," "Cesar Spear," and "Nathan Spear," Thwing Collection (CD-ROM by the NEHGS); Beth Anne Bower, "African American Family

History Resources at NEHGS," NEHGS, http://www.newenglandancestors.org/research/services/articles_african_family_historyresources.asp.

36. Webb, *Chloe Spear*, 48, 52-58; Suffolk County Register of Deeds, 190:153; inventory of Chloe Spear, Suffolk Probate, 113:16. I surveyed fifty Suffolk County estates probated in 1815; if anything, this comparison underestimates Spear's relative wealth, since wealthier decedents were more likely to have their estates inventoried. See Carol Buchalter Stapp, *Afro-Americans in Antebellum Boston: An Analysis of Probate Records* (New York: Garland, 1993), 38-39.

37. On Webb: Boston School Committee minutes (June 17, 1820), 2:47, BPL; Helen Emery Falls, "Baptist Women in Missions Support in the Nineteenth Century," *Baptist History and Heritage* 12 (1977): 26-36; Albert L. Vail, *Mary Webb and the Mother Society* (Philadelphia: American Baptist Publication Society, 1914); T. F. Caldicott, *A Concise History of the Baldwin Place Baptist Church* (Boston, 1854), 32, 76 (Second Baptist became the Baldwin Place Baptist Church in 1839). Ann Boylan puts Webb's work in a larger context of women's benevolence work in *The Origins of Women's Activism: New York and Boston, 1797-1840* (Chapel Hill: University of North Carolina Press, 2002). On Spear's and Webb's church membership, see membership list in Second Baptist Church, Boston, Mass., minute book, 1788-1809, Special Collections, Franklin Trask Library, Andover Newton Theological School.

38. Will of Cesar Spear (1806), Suffolk Probate, 104:301; Webb, *Chloe Spear*, 71-72, 77-78; Edward G. Porter, *Rambles in Old Boston, New England* (Boston, 1887), 188-189.

39. Webb, *Chloe Spear*, 72.

40. *Liberator*, March 23, 1838, 47; Odell, *Phillis Wheatley*, 22; "African Anecdotes," *The Knickerbocker, or New York Monthly Magazine* 4 (August 1834): 88.

41. Daniel Ricketson, *History of New Bedford* (New Bedford, Mass., 1858), 254-255. The resemblances between this scene and the story of George Washington and Primus Hall, discussed in chapter two, are striking.

42. John W. Lewis, *The Life, Labors, and Travels of Elder Charles Bowles, of the Free Will Baptist Denomination* (Watertown, Vt., 1852), 116.

43. "Phillis Wheatley," *Anti-Slavery Record* 2 (1836): 7-8. If the sole initial "F." that stands as the anecdote's signature stands for "Fitch," then this story could be another example of slaveholders' descendants appropriating the memory of their families' former slaves. On Timothy Fitch, see "The Medford Slave Trade Letters, 1759-1765," Medford Historical Society, http://www.medfordhistorical.org/slavetradeletters.php.

44. Webb, *Chloe Spear*, 45, 72, 92. Though I am concentrating here on respectability as a performance enacted for a white audience, I do not mean to suggest that its sole function was to change white perceptions. Respectability also delineated class and status differences among people of color. See Higginbotham, *Righteous Discontent*, 204-211, and James Oliver Horton's comment in the Southern Historical Association's Roundtable on Racial Modernity, *JER* 18 (1998): 221.

45. *Columbian Centinel*, January 4, 1800; August 18, 1819; January 11, 1815; October 30, 1833. "Racial synecdoche": Rael, *Black Identity*, 161. On Haynes, see Richard D. Brown, "'Not Only Extreme Poverty, but the Worst Kind of Orphanage': Lemuel Haynes and the Boundaries of Racial Tolerance on the Yankee Frontier," *NEQ* 61 (1988): 502-518; Saillant, *Black Puritan, Black Republican*. Janice Hume, *Obituaries in American Culture* (Jackson: University Press of Mississippi, 2000), 135-136, notes

that less-powerful people, including people of color, tended to be included in obituaries only when they "in no way threatened the social order."

46. Webb, *Chloe Spear*, 52–55, 62, 99, 108.

47. James Oliver Horton makes note of this passage in Webb's memoir to argue that the black woman "was limited not by her husband's demands, but by the law which limited all women in American society." However, Chloe's name on the deed attests that in at least some contexts, the law did acknowledge married women's property ownership. Webb, *Chloe Spear*, 56–57; Suffolk Deeds, 190:153; Horton, "Freedom's Yoke: Gender Conventions among Antebellum Free Blacks," *Feminist Studies* 12 (1986): 61–62.

48. Webb, *Chloe Spear*, 70–71.

49. Webb, *Chloe Spear*, 55, 70.

50. See Daniel A. Cohen's differentiation of "respectability" and "gentility" in "The Respectability of Rebecca Reed: Genteel Womanhood and Sectarian Conflict in Antebellum America," *JER* 16 (1996): 423–425.

51. The lithograph is from Edward Clay's "Life in Philadelphia" series; see Gary B. Nash, *Forging Freedom: The Formation of Philadelphia's Black Community, 1720-1840* (Cambridge, Mass.: Harvard University Press, 1988), 254–259.

52. Will of Cezar Spear, Suffolk Probate, 104:301; Suffolk Deeds, 190:153; "Cloe," "Cesar Spear," and "Nathan Spear," Thwing Collection; James Oliver Horton and Lois E. Horton, *In Hope of Liberty: Culture, Community, and Protest among Northern Free Blacks, 1700-1860* (New York: Oxford University Press, 1997), 114–117; Gary B. Nash, "Forging Freedom: The Emancipation Experience in the Northern Seaport Cities, 1775-1820," in *Slavery and Freedom in the Age of the American Revolution*, ed. Ira Berlin and Ronald Hoffman (Urbana: University of Illinois Press, 1986), 8–19.

53. Chernoh Momodu Sesay, Jr., has studied the records of the African Lodge, excavating the names of Cesar Spear and many other black Freemasons; "Freemasons of Color: Prince Hall, Revolutionary Black Boston, and the Origins of Black Freemasonry, 1770-1807" (Ph.D. diss., Northwestern University, 2006), 160, 227.

54. Grégoire, *Enquiry*, 103. One can only speculate whether the abbé's well-documented misogyny influenced his portrayal of Wheatley as wife. Alyssa Goldstein Sepinwall, *The Abbé Grégoire and the French Revolution: The Making of Modern Universalism* (Berkeley: University of California Press, 2005), 97–102.

55. Odell, *Phillis Wheatley*, 20.

56. Robinson, "Wheatley and Her Boston," 53–54.

57. Sesay, "Freemasons of Color," 97–98, 154 interprets Peters's appearances in the Boston Taking Books; his appendix 7 transcribes these records. Peters was not a Freemason.

58. Odell, *Phillis Wheatley*, 24, 29; *Independent Chronicle*, February 10, 1785. Odell's memoir "excited considerable attention at the time it was issued, and three editions of it were readily sold"; *Liberator*, December 4, 1863. It was reissued in 1863. Substantial portions of the memoir appeared as the biographical sketch of Wheatley in William G. Allen, *Wheatley, Banneker, and Horton* (Boston, 1849).

59. On the linkage of manhood and respectability in black political discourse, see Rael, *Black Identity and Black Protest*, 147; Stewart, "Emergence of Racial Modernity," 190 and "Modernizing 'Difference': The Political Meanings of Color in the Free States, 1776-1840," *JER* 19 (1999): 691–712. Assertions of black manhood were, in part,

responses to racial ideologies that described Africans as inherently gentle, feminized beings as opposed to rugged, virile whites (particularly "Anglo-Saxons"). See George M. Fredrickson, *The Black Image in the White Mind: The Debate on Afro-American Character and Destiny, 1817-1914* (1971; Hanover, N.H.: Wesleyan University Press, 1987), especially chap. 4; Mia Bay, *The White Image in the Black Mind: African-American Ideas about White People, 1830-1925* (New York: Oxford University Press, 2000), chap. 2.

60. Webb, *Chloe Spear*, 90.

61. Will of Chloe Spear (1815) Suffolk Probate, 113:9-10. To determine church membership, I cross-listed the names in the will with Baldwin, "Chloe Spear," 158; Record of marriages in Boston by Thomas Baldwin, pastor of the Second Baptist Church Boston, 1790-1825, Mss A 1586, R. Stanton Avery Special Collections, NEHGS; membership list, Second Baptist Church minute book; James de T. Abajian, comp., *Blacks in Selected Newspapers, Censuses, and Other Sources: An Index to Names and Subjects* (Boston: G. K. Hall, 1977).

62. Webb, *Chloe Spear*, 76; will of Chloe Spear, Suffolk Probate, 113:9-10.

63. Webb, *Chloe Spear*, 51; Wheatley, "On Being Brought from Africa to America," *Complete Writings*, 13; Susan Juster, *Disorderly Women: Sexual Politics and Evangelicalism in Revolutionary New England* (Ithaca, N.Y.: Cornell University Press, 1994), 4. For a nuanced reading of Wheatley's poem, see David Grimsted, "Anglo-American Racism and Phillis Wheatley's 'Sable Veil,' 'Length'ned Chain,' and 'Knitted Heart,'" in *Women in the Age of the American Revolution*, ed. Ronald Hoffman and Peter J. Albert (Charlottesville: University Press of Virginia, 1989), 355-357.

64. Webb, *Chloe Spear*, 74-80.

65. The deferential behavior of Primus Hall in the army camp contrasts with depictions of white men in the Revolution's rank and file. George Robert Twelves Hewes, who, like Hall, was a shoemaker turned soldier, recalled bowing and scraping before John Hancock (the richest man in Boston) one New Year's Day in the early 1760s, but at the height of the Revolutionary War, Hewes abandoned service on the gunship *Hancock* because its lieutenant insisted that the sailors remove their hats to him. The juxtaposition of these two events—both of which appeared in an 1835 memoir—prompts Hewes's modern-day biographer to ask "What had happened in the intervening years? What had turned the young shoemaker tongue-tied in the face of his betters into the defiant person who would not take his hat off for any man?" Reading Hewes's biography alongside the printed anecdotes about Primus Hall, the questions become, Why did the black soldier seem to accept the standards of deference that were so repulsive to the white? Why didn't the Revolution change racial etiquette as well as class mores? See Young, *Shoemaker and the Tea Party*, 3-5.

66. On the surface, this process seems different from what happened to Phillis Wheatley's memory. In retellings based on Odell, Wheatley's story declines as the nation's rises; there is no way to assimilate the former into the latter. Hall's experience as a waiter to a Continental Army officer fits into the national story, but he is not remembered (in the mainstream press at least) for anything *but* his patriotic devotion. The crucial similarity is that African Americans' experience of emancipation from chattel slavery and their struggles for equal citizenship are not represented as integral to the national narrative of freedom. This separation of African American "emancipationist" memory from mainstream national memory was also a predominant theme in

sectional reconciliation after the Civil War. I have found David Blight's discussion of these processes illuminating; see *Race and Reunion: The Civil War in American Memory* (Cambridge: Harvard University Press, 2001), 2-7.

67. Catharine Maria Sedgwick, "Slavery in New England," *Bentley's Miscellany* 34 (1853): 424.

68. Sedgwick, "Slavery in New England," 421, 424; Theodore Sedgwick, *The Practicability of the Abolition of Slavery: A Lecture, Delivered at the Lyceum in Stockbridge, Massachusetts, February, 1831* (New York, 1831); Arthur Zilversmit, "Quok Walker, Mumbet, and the Abolition of Slavery in Massachusetts," *WMQ* 25 (1968): 614-624. Theodore Sedgwick's lecture was extracted in *The Anti-Slavery Record* 2 (1836): 4-5.

69. Lucinda L. Damon-Bach and Victoria Clements, introduction to *Catharine Maria Sedgwick: Critical Perspectives*, ed. Damon-Bach and Clements (Boston: Northeastern University Press, 2003), xxii-xxiii; Karen Woods Weierman, "'A Slave Story I Began and Abandoned': Sedgwick's Antislavery Manuscript," in ibid., 122-126; *MHSP*, 2nd ser., 1 (1885): 3, 41-42.

70. Sedgwick, "Slavery in New England," 422.

71. Sedgwick, "Slavery in New England," 417, 424; Sedgwick, *Practicability of Abolition*, 15.

72. Matthew 15:21-28 (King James version).

73. Entry for 25 May 1818, *Diary of William Bentley*, vol. 4, 522-523. An abolitionist anecdote about Prince Saunders used the trope of the tea table to contrast racial prejudice in the American North with social equality in England. This story described how a white American expatriate in London shied away from offering Saunders a cup of coffee, while the Prince Regent invited him to breakfast. See *Liberator*, August 13, 1831; June 21, 1839.

74. Frances Ellen Watkins, "The Syrophenician Woman," *Poems on Miscellaneous Subjects* (Boston, 1854), 5-6; Merriam-Webster's Online Dictionary, accessed October 26, 2006, s.v. "astonish"; Gerd Theissen, *The Gospels in Context: Social and Political History in the Synoptic Tradition*, trans. Linda M. Maloney (Minneapolis: Fortress Press, 1991), 60-80; Joel Marcus, *Mark 1-8: A New Translation with Introduction and Commentary* (New York: Doubleday, 2000), 461-471; Stephenson Humphries-Brooks, "The Canaanite Women in Matthew," in *A Feminist Companion to Matthew*, ed. Amy-Jill Levine (Sheffield, England: Sheffield Academic Press, 2001), 142-145.

75. Lois Brown makes a similar point with respect to Chloe Spear and others in "Memorial Narratives of African Women in Antebellum New England," *Legacy* 20 (2003): 38-61.

76. Sallie McFague TeSelle calls a parable "a story of ordinary people and events which is the context for envisaging and understanding the strange and the extraordinary"; such stories have the potential of moving readers "from 'what is' to 'what might be'"; *Speaking in Parables: A Study in Metaphor and Theology* (Philadelphia: Fortress Press, 1975), 2, 33.

77. Sedgwick, "Slavery in New England," 418; Sedgwick, *Practicability of Abolition*, 19.

78. Charles Henry Pope, *Loring Genealogy* (Cambridge, Mass.: Murray and Emery, 1917), 102-103; Daniel Sharp, *Report of the Union Committee of the Sunday Schools of the Three Baptist Societies in Boston* (Boston, 1817), 17-21.

79. William Cooper Nell, *The Colored Patriots of the American Revolution* (Boston, 1855), 29-32, 64-73.

80. *Liberator*, November 22, 1861; Webb, *Chloe Spear*, 90-91; African Society, *Laws of the African Society, Instituted at Boston, Anno Domini 1796* (Boston, 1802), 3.

81. William Cooper Nell, *Boston Massacre, March 5th, 1770: The Day Which History Selects as the Dawn of the American Revolution, Commemorative Festival* (Boston, 1858); *Liberator*, August 5, 1859, March 16, 1860; Nancy Carlisle, *Cherished Possessions: A New England Legacy* (Boston: Society for the Preservation of New England Antiquities, 2003), 23-25. Ellen McCallister Clark of The Society of the Cincinnati provided me with a copy of Nell's pamphlet.

82. *Liberator*, March 12, 1858; Stewart, "Emergence of Racial Modernity."

CHAPTER 5

1. Daniel Webster, "The Constitution and the Union," in *The Works of Daniel Webster*, vol. 5 (Boston, 1851), 325; Robert V. Remini, *Daniel Webster: The Man and His Time* (New York: Norton, 1997), 670-678. On blacks fleeing the Bay State, see Cambridge Liberian Emigrant Association, broadside (1858), AB85 C1443L 858a, Houghton Library, Harvard University; papers relating to the Twelfth Baptist Church, in folder 12, box 39, Arlington Street Church, Boston, Mass., Records, 1730-1979, bMS 4, Andover-Harvard Theological Library, Harvard Divinity School, Harvard University; Roy E. Finkenbine, "Boston's Black Churches: Institutional Centers of the Antislavery Movement," in *Courage and Conscience: Black and White Abolitionists in Boston*, ed. Donald M. Jacobs (Bloomington: Indiana University Press, 1993), 182 (quotation); Lois E. Horton, "Kidnapping and Resistance: Antislavery Direct Action in the 1850s," in *Passages to Freedom: The Underground Railroad in History and Memory*, ed. David W. Blight (Washington, D.C.: Smithsonian Books, 2004), 161-162. On emigration in the 1850s, see R. J. M. Blackett, *Building an Antislavery Wall: Black Americans in the Atlantic Abolitionist Movement, 1830-1860* (Baton Rouge: Louisiana State University Press, 1983), chap. 5; P. J. Staudenraus, *The African Colonization Movement, 1816-1865* (1961; reprint, New York: Octagon Books, 1980), 143-146; Floyd J. Miller, *The Search for a Black Nationality: Black Emigration and Colonization, 1787-1863* (Urbana: University of Illinois Press, 1975).

2. James H. Kettner, *The Development of American Citizenship, 1608-1870* (Chapel Hill: University of North Carolina Press, 1978), 322-323. On school desegregation, see Donald M. Jacobs, "The Nineteenth Century Struggle Over Segregated Education in the Boston Schools," *Journal of Negro Education* 39 (1970): 76-85; George A. Levesque, *Black Boston: African American Life and Culture in Urban America, 1750-1860* (New York: Garland, 1994), chap. 5-6.

3. William Cooper Nell, *The Colored Patriots of the American Revolution* (Boston, 1855); William J. Watkins, *Our Rights as Men: An Address Delivered in Boston, Before the Legislative Committee on the Militia, February 24, 1853* (Boston, 1853), 11-12.

4. Webster, "The Constitution and the Union," 325. On abolitionists' feelings toward Webster, see Theodore Parker, *Historic Americans*, ed. Samuel A. Eliot (Boston: American Unitarian Association, 1908), 266-383. In response to the Compromise of 1850, black Bostonians organized an "Anti-Webster Meeting of the Colored Citizens of Boston and Vicinity"; see *Liberator*, April 5, 1850, 55. The Seventh of March speech

was widely reviled throughout New England—including by members of Webster's own Whig party; see William F. Hartford, *Money, Morals, and Politics: Massachusetts in the Age of the Boston Associates* (Boston: Northeastern University Press, 2001), 151-153.

5. Theodore Parker, "Speech at the New England Anti-Slavery Convention in Boston, May 29, 1850," in *The Collected Works of Theodore Parker*, vol. 5, ed. Frances Power Cobbe (London, 1863), 119. On Parker's use of history, see Ethan J. Kytle, "'To Be Free Themselves Must Strike the First Blow': The Romantic Liberalism of Antislavery Intellectuals in the United States, 1845-1865" (Ph.D. diss., University of North Carolina at Chapel Hill, 2004), 168-175. On 1850 as a turning point within abolitionism, see Jane H. Pease and William H. Pease, *They Who Would Be Free: Blacks' Search for Freedom, 1830-1861* (New York: Atheneum, 1974), chap. 10; R. J. M. Blackett, "'Freemen to the Rescue!': Resistance to the Fugitive Slave Law of 1850," in *Passages to Freedom*, ed. Blight, 133-148; Horton, "Kidnapping and Resistance," 149-174; James Brewer Stewart, *Holy Warriors: The Abolitionists and American Slavery*, rev. ed. (New York: Hill and Wang, 1997), chap. 7.

6. Commissioners were compensated 10 dollars when they found for the owners and 5 dollars when they ruled for the fugitives.

7. For a fuller discussion of the Fugitive Slave Act within the context of the Compromise of 1850, see Thomas D. Morris, *Free Men All: The Personal Liberty Laws of the North, 1780-1861* (Baltimore: Johns Hopkins University Press, 1974), chap. 8. The text of the Act is available online through Yale Law School's Avalon Project: http://www.yale.edu/lawweb/avalon/fugitive.htm.

8. *Liberator*, October 4, 1850, 158; George Gordon, Lord Byron, *Childe Harold's Pilgrimage* (1812), canto 2, stanza 76l; Kytle, "To Be Free," 2-7.

9. *Liberator*, October 11, 1850, 162. Hilary J. Moss develops the significance of Revolutionary memory to black activists in the 1850s in "The Tarring and Feathering of Thomas Paul Smith: Common Schools, Revolutionary Memory, and the Crisis of Black Citizenship in Antebellum Boston," *NEQ* 80 (2007): 218-241.

10. Sallie Holley to Caroline F. Putnam, August 26, 1852, in *A Life for Liberty: Anti-Slavery and Other Letters of Sallie Holley*, ed. John White Chadwick (New York: G. P. Putnam's Sons, 1899), 292. Other abolitionist visitors to the Monument included Charlotte Forten, William Cooper Nell, and John Mercer Langston. See Charlotte L. Forten Grimké, *The Journal of Charlotte L. Forten*, ed. Ray Allen Billington (New York: Dryden Press, 1953), 248; Nell to Amy Kirby Post, July 3, 1850, in *William Cooper Nell, Nineteenth-Century African American Abolitionist, Historian, Integrationist: Selected Writings, 1832-1874*, ed. Dorothy Porter Wesley and Constance Porter Uzelac (Baltimore: Black Classic Press, 2002), 206 [hereafter, Nell, *Selected Writings*]; *Christian Recorder*, December 10, 1864.

11. *North Star*, January 16, 1851. On the Crafts, see Blackett, "Freemen to the Rescue!" 140-141.

12. *Liberator*, July 21, 1843, 114.

13. *Liberator*, August 28, 1857, 139; *Inauguration of the Statue of Warren by the Bunker Hill Monument Association* (Boston, 1858), 66-70. It was not only abolitionists who attributed the incendiary phrase to Toombs; a Confederate veteran claimed that his speech had done "more to fire the hearts of the North than almost anything said or done prior to the war"; see Lot D. Young, *Reminiscences of a Soldier of the Orphan Brigade*

(Paris, Ky., n.d.), 19 [available online through Documenting the American South: http://docsouth.unc.edu/young/young.html]. Toombs himself denied speaking this line; *New York Times*, December 16, 1885, 1.

14. For one example, see Frederick Douglass's speech in Chatham, Canada West: *Frederick Douglass' Paper*, August 18, 1854.

15. *Boston Investigator* and *Norfolk Democrat*, quoted in *Liberator*, May 2, 1851, 70; Stanley W. Campbell, *The Slave Catchers: Enforcement of the Fugitive Slave Law, 1850-1860* (Chapel Hill: University of North Carolina Press, 1970), 117-121 and chap. 3-4; Albert J. von Frank, *The Trials of Anthony Burns: Freedom and Slavery in Emerson's Boston* (Cambridge, Mass.: Harvard University Press, 1998), 57, 149.

16. Placard transcribed in John Weiss, *Life and Correspondence of Theodore Parker*, vol. 2 (New York: D. Appleton, 1864), 133; Henry B. Stanton, *Remarks of Henry B. Stanton, in the Representatives' Hall, on the 23d and 24th of February, 1837, Before the Committee of the House of Representatives of Massachusetts, to Whom Was Referred Sundry Memorials on the Subject of Slavery*, 2nd ed. (Boston, 1837), 81. The best account of the Burns episode is von Frank, *The Trials of Anthony Burns*.

17. Von Frank, *The Trials of Anthony Burns*, 203-219. On demonstrations of public mourning across the state, see *Liberator*, June 9, 1854, 91.

18. Grimké, *The Journal of Charlotte L. Forten*, 37.

19. Grimké, *The Journal of Charlotte L. Forten*, 36; *Liberator*, October 11, 1850, 162; Donald M. Jacobs, "William Lloyd Garrison's *Liberator* and Boston's Blacks, 1830-1865," *NEQ* 44 (1971): 259-277.

20. A valuable reconsideration of the conventional narrative and periodization is Richard S. Newman, *The Transformation of American Abolitionism: Fighting Slavery in the Early Republic* (Chapel Hill: University of North Carolina Press, 2002). See also Blackett, *Building an Antislavery Wall*, 47-51; Paul Goodman, *Of One Blood: Abolitionism and the Origins of Racial Equality* (Berkeley: University of California Press, 1998), 23-37.

21. Little is known about the creation of this image, which was attributed to William L. Champney, made into a print by lithographer John Bufford, and published by Boston's Henry Q. Smith. "Boston Massacre, March 5, 1770," Crispus Attucks Portrait Collection, Photographs and Prints Division, Schomburg Center for Research in Black Culture, New York Public Library. The print is dated to 1856 in *A Catalogue of the Paintings, Engravings, Busts, and Miscellaneous Articles Belonging to the Cabinet of the Massachusetts Historical Society* (Boston, 1885), 85.

22. *Liberator*, August 28, 1857, 139; Stephen H. Browne, "Remembering Crispus Attucks: Race, Rhetoric, and the Politics of Commemoration," *Quarterly Journal of Speech* 85 (1999): 172; William Gordon, *The History of the Rise, Progress, and Establishment, of the Independence of the United States of America*, vol. 1 (New York, 1789), 202; *The Trial of the British Soldiers, of the 29th Regiment of Foot, for the Murder of Crispus Attucks, Samuel Gray, Samuel Maverick, James Caldwell, and Patrick Carr* (Boston, 1807), 99. Sources that simply listed the names of the victims include the multiple editions of Noah Webster, *An American Selection of Lessons in Reading and Speaking* (Boston, 1792), 145; Jonathan Russell, *The Whole Truth: To the Freemen of New-England* (Boston, 1808), 7. Mitch Kachun further catalogues Attucks's presence (or more often, absence) in historical memory between 1783 and 1850 in "From

Forgotten Founder to Indispensable Icon: Crispus Attucks, Black Citizenship, and Collective Memory, 1770-1865," *JER* 29 (2009): 252-267.

23. William Cooper Nell to Wendell Phillips, April 15, 1841, Wendell Phillips papers, b MS Am 1953, Houghton Library.

24 See Abigail Mott, *Biographical Sketches and Interesting Anecdotes of Persons of Color* (New York, 1826); Henri Grégoire, *An Enquiry Concerning the Intellectual and Moral Faculties, and Literature of Negroes* (Brooklyn, N.Y., 1810); Edward Dorr Griffin, *A Plea for Africa* (New York, 1817); *Intelligent Negroes* (Edinburgh, 1845); Robert Benjamin Lewis, *Light and Truth, from Ancient and Sacred History* (Portland, Me., 1836) and *Light and Truth; Collected from the Bible and Ancient and Modern History, Containing the Universal History of the Colored and the Indian Race* (Boston, 1844); James W. C. Pennington, *A Text Book of the Origin and History, &c. &c. of the Colored People* (Hartford, 1841); Wilson Armisted, *A Tribute for the Negro* (Manchester, Eng., 1848). Interestingly, Attucks does feature in a number of works by Samuel Goodrich, author of numerous history books for schoolchildren, including the famous "Peter Parley" series. These texts represent Attucks as the leader of a rambunctious mob. See Kachun, "Forgotten Founder to Indispensable Icon," 261-262.

25. Though Botta combed American, British, and French primary and secondary sources in assembling his account, his penchant for making up speeches for his historical actors earned him some criticism, though it may also have boosted his colorful history's readership. Jordan D. Fiore, "Carlo Botta: An Italian Historian of the American Revolution," *Italica* 28 (1951): 155-171; Stefania Buccini, *The Americas in Italian Literature and Culture, 1700-1825*, trans. Rosanna Giammanco (University Park: Pennsylvania State University Press, 1997), 170-189.

26. Charles [Carlo] Botta, *History of the War of Independence of the United States of America*, vol. 1, trans. George Alexander Otis (Philadelphia, 1820), 172-174; *Legal Papers of John Adams*, ed. L. Kinvin Wroth and Hiller B. Zobel, vol. 3 (Cambridge, Mass.: Harvard University Press, 1965), 51, 70 n. 15 (on the Riot Act). That there had been twelve men (also identified more specifically as sailors) involved in the King Street melee was mentioned repeatedly in the trials.

27. William Cooper Nell, *Services of Colored Americans, in the Wars of 1776 and 1812* (Boston, 1851), 5-6; Nell, *Colored Patriots*, 14-15; "A Bostonian" [B. B. Thatcher], *Traits of the Tea Party: Being a Memoir of George R. T. Hewes* (New York, 1835), 102-108; Alfred F. Young, *The Shoemaker and the Tea Party: Memory and the American Revolution* (Boston, Beacon Press, 1999), 143-154, 173-179 (quotation on 175).

28. Nell, *Colored Patriots*, 14-15; Thatcher, *Traits of the Tea Party*, 106.

29. So, for instance, a simple gesture mentioned in Botta's account and then quoted by Nell—Attucks grabbing a British soldier's bayonet with his left hand shortly before his death—appeared as the central scene in the print published by Smith in 1856. This detail appears to be an adaptation of a description given by John Adams; see *Adams Legal Papers*, 269.

30. Nell, *Colored Patriots*, 21; Theodore Parker to George Bancroft, March 16, 1858, in Weiss, *Life and Correspondence of Theodore Parker*, vol. 2, 234-235. I have not located any images of the Battle of Bunker Hill pre-dating Nell's *Colored Patriots* that picture a black man shooting Pitcairn, other than prints based on Trumbull's painting. See Military Collection (American Revolution), folder 1, box 1, Photographs and Prints Division, Schomburg Center. In a typical abolitionist reading of *The Death of*

General Warren, antislavery minister R. C. Waterson in 1863 "claimed that Trumbull added dignity to his canvass by portraying colored men rendering patriotic service"; *Liberator*, March 20, 1863, 47. In 1859, historical illustrator Alonzo Chappel painted the Battle of Bunker Hill as a more jumbled scene, with ordinary soldiers, rather than Warren, at the center of the canvas. A black soldier with a rifle squats just above the fallen general. "Where Trumbull portrayed Peter Salem carrying his master's gun," argue Alfred F. Young and Terry J. Fife, "Chappel portrayed him as a soldier on his own." My reading of this scene is more ambiguous. While the black man is unmistakably present, he is an observer, not an actor in the scene: all the fighting is happening over his head, in the upper two-thirds of the canvas. The presence of the black soldier could indicate Chappel's awareness of the 1850s revival of Peter Salem, though Nell earlier criticized Chappel for leaving Crispus Attucks out of an illustration of the Boston Massacre. "The Paintings of Alonzo Chappel," vol. 2, scrapbook in the Art and Architecture Division, NYPL; Young and Fife with Mary E. Janzen, *We the People: Voices and Images of the New Nation* (Philadelphia: Temple University Press, 1993), 91; Barbara J. Mitnick, "The History Paintings," in *The Portraits and History Paintings of Alonzo Chappel*, by Mitnick and David Meschutt (Chadds Ford, Pa.: Brandywine River Museum, 1992), 38–64; *Liberator*, August 28, 1857, 139; Karsten Fitz, "Commemorating Crispus Attucks: Visual Memory and the Representations of the Boston Massacre, 1770–1857," *Amerikastudien/American Studies* 50 (2005): 476–479.

31. *Liberator*, June 27, 1845, 102. In a similar example from the 1840s (which also did not identify Salem by name), a black historian from Maine wrote, "on Bunker Hill…the colored soldiers fought bravely—standing shoulder to shoulder in regiments with the whites.… [See the old map of Bunker Hill battle, a slave standing behind his master and shooting down an officer of the British army, and ready for another fire.]" See Lewis, *Light and Truth* (1844), 206. In 1856, after two young women of color were denied admission to Charlestown High School, abolitionists cited Peter Salem by name in decrying that such injustice should occur "under the shade of Bunker Hill," where, they presumably meant to imply, a black man had proved himself a local hero. See *Liberator*, May 9, 1856, 74.

32. Marcus Wood, *Blind Memory: Visual Representations of Slavery in England and America, 1780–1865* (New York: Routledge, 2000), 255–256, compares the frontispiece illustration of Attucks's death to Benjamin West's *Death of General Wolf* (1771). Trumbull was a follower of West, and *The Death of Wolf* presents the iconic image of the dying martyr in late eighteenth-century history painting. See Jules David Prown, "John Trumbull as History Painter," in *John Trumbull: The Hand and Spirit of a Painter*, ed. Helen A. Cooper (New Haven, Conn.: Yale University Art Gallery, 1982), 28–30. While mid-nineteenth-century abolitionists did discuss versions of *The Death of Warren*, I have not encountered evidence that they paid attention to *The Death of Wolf*. The postures and positioning of the figures in the frontispiece resemble Trumbull's arrangement more than West's, and the setting in Revolutionary Boston makes it the more likely model for the Boston Massacre engraving. For another reading of the illustration in Nell's *Colored Patriots*, see Fitz, "Commemorating Crispus Attucks," 472–475.

33. My conceptualization here is loosely inspired by "inside" and "outside" politics as discussed in Eddie S. Glaude, Jr., *Exodus!: Religion, Race, and Nation in Early Nineteenth-Century Black America* (Chicago: University of Chicago Press, 2000), 114.

Nell has sometimes been identified as the first African American historian, but many earlier black writers engaged with historical material in some way; see Mia Bay, *The White Image in the Black Mind: African-American Ideas about White People, 1830-1925* (New York: Oxford University Press, 2000), 44-55; John Ernest, *Liberation Historiography: African American Writers and the Challenge of History, 1794-1861* (Chapel Hill: University of North Carolina Press, 2004), 53-113.

34. Michel-Rolph Trouillot, *Silencing the Past: Power and the Production of History* (Boston: Beacon Press, 1995), 2.

35. For Nell's biography, see Robert P. Smith, "William Cooper Nell: Crusading Black Abolitionist," *JNH* 55 (1970): 182-199; Dorothy Porter Wesley and Constance Porter Uzelac, "William Cooper Nell, 1816-1874," introduction to Nell, *Selected Writings*, 5-60.

36. Patrick T. J. Browne, "'To Defend Mr. Garrison': William Cooper Nell and the Personal Politics of Antislavery," *New England Quarterly* 70 (1997): 415-442; Jacobs, "*Liberator* and Boston's Blacks." On Douglass and the *North Star*, see Pease and Pease, *They Who Would Be Free*, 85-90, 116-117; John Stauffer, *The Black Hearts of Men: Radical Abolitionists and the Transformation of Race* (Cambridge, Mass.: Harvard University Press, 2001), 155-168; Kytle, "To Be Free," 113-123.

37. W. A. Hawley, "Response to the Above Petition: House...No. 100," in Nell, *Selected Writings*, 283-285; Nell, *Colored Patriots*, 14; Samuel B. Payne, Jr., "Was Crispus Attucks the First to Die?," *New England Journal of History* 57 (2001): 2-4; Hiller B. Zobel, *The Boston Massacre* (New York: Norton, 1970), 174-179.

38. Nell, *Services of Colored Americans*, 7.

39. Nell, *Colored Patriots*, 91-94, 98-99. Literary scholar Ernest, in *Liberation Historiography*, 132-153, offers the fullest attempt to interpret Nell's historical writing. By contextualizing Nell alongside George Bancroft's synthetic history, as opposed to the work of contemporary local historians and collectors, Ernest overstates the distinctively African American significance of the fragmented quality of *Colored Patriots*.

40. Nell to Phillips, July 8, 1855, Phillips papers.

41. Quotation from a lecture Pennington gave before the Glasgow Young Men's Christian Association and the St. George's Biblical Literary and Scientific Institute of London, in Nell, *Colored Patriots*, 356.

42. Tavia Nyong'o, "'The Black First': Crispus Attucks and William Cooper Nell," *Slavery/Antislavery in New England: Dublin Seminar for New England Folklife Annual Proceedings 2003* (Boston University, 2005), 142. Robert J. Cottrol, "Heroism and the Origins of Afro-American History," *NEQ* 51 (1978): 256-263, also emphasizes this aspect of *Colored Patriots*.

43. George M. Fredrickson, *The Black Image in the White Mind: The Debate on Afro-American Character and Destiny, 1817-1914* (New York: Harper and Row, 1971), chap. 4; Bay, *The White Image in the Black Mind*, 55-74; Paul Teed, "Racial Nationalism and Its Challengers: Theodore Parker, John Rock, and the Antislavery Movement," *Civil War History* 41 (1995): 142-160; Harriet Beecher Stowe, introduction to Nell, *Colored Patriots*, 5-6; Kristin Hoganson, "Garrisonian Abolitionists and the Rhetoric of Gender, 1850-1860," *AQ* 45 (1993): 558-595.

44. Nell, *Colored Patriots*, 11; James Oliver Horton, "Defending the Manhood of the Race: The Crisis of Citizenship in Black Boston at Midcentury," in *Hope and*

Glory: Essays on the Legacy of the Fifty-Fourth Massachusetts Regiment, ed. Martin H. Blatt, Thomas J. Brown, and Donald Yacovone (Amherst: University of Massachusetts Press, 2001), 7–9 (quotation, 8). On calls for black agency in the 1850s, see Kytle, "To Be Free." On manhood and the political theory of American liberalism, see Maggie Montesinos Sale, *The Slumbering Volcano: American Slave Ship Revolts and the Production of Rebellious Masculinity* (Durham: Duke University Press, 1997), 52–56.

45. Mindful of the possible objections of Garrisonians, Nell, *Services of Colored Americans*, 4, felt it necessary to explain "why make a parade of the *military* services of Colored Americans." Coincident with the effort to strike the word "white" from state militia laws, Nell signed on to a petition to remove "male" from the Massachusetts constitution. See *Pennsylvania Freeman*, March 17, 1853, in Nell, *Selected Writings*, 331–332.

46. Cottrol, "Heroism and the Origins of Afro-American History," 256; Nell, *Colored Patriots*, 315. To describe Nell's aim, I use "integration," which implies that all parties were involved in the process as equal players, rather than "accommodation," which suggests that one group merely conformed to the expectations of the other. With Crispus Attucks as the *first* patriot, Nell wasn't saying that people of color merely contributed to an American history made by whites; he was arguing that the American Revolution was fundamentally an integrated event.

47. Nell, *Colored Patriots*, 367–368.

48. Nell, *Colored Patriots*, 368.

49. Though she discusses a different period, my interpretation here is guided by Evelyn Brooks Higginbotham, *Righteous Discontent: The Women's Movement in the Black Baptist Church, 1880-1920* (Cambridge, Mass.: Harvard University Press, 1993), 7–11 (quotations). On the convention movement, see Glaude, *Exodus!*, 112–142; Elizabeth Rauh Bethel, *The Roots of African-American Identity: Memory and History in Free Antebellum Communities* (New York: St. Martin's Press, 1997), 131–139; Patrick Rael, *Black Identity and Black Protest in the Antebellum North* (Chapel Hill: University of North Carolina Press, 2002).

50. See David W. Blight's discussion of the "politics of hope" in *Frederick Douglass' Civil War: Keeping Faith in Jubilee* (Baton Rouge: Louisiana State University Press, 1989), chap. 1.

51. Rael, *Black Identity and Black Protest*, 211–212.

52. Studies situating Delany as a preeminent black nationalist or Pan-Africanist include Victor Ullman, *Martin R. Delany: The Beginnings of Black Nationalism* (Boston: Beacon Press, 1971); Cyril E. Griffith, *The African Dream: Martin R. Delany and the Emergence of Pan-African Thought* (University Park: Pennsylvania State University Press, 1975); Miller, *The Search for a Black Nationality* Robert S. Levine, *Martin Delany, Frederick Douglass and the Politics of Representative Identity* (Chapel Hill: University of North Carolina Press, 1997), complicates the conventional dichotomy between Delany as nationalist and Douglass as integrationist. Tunde Adeleke, *Without Regard to Race: The Other Martin Robison Delany* (Jackson: University Press of Mississippi, 2003), stresses the overlooked integrationist phase of Delany's career. Ernest, *Liberation Historiography*, chap. 2, is perhaps the only scholar to consider Delany and Nell within the same context, though he does not treat their conceptualization of citizenship.

53. Martin Robison Delany, *The Condition, Elevation, Emigration, and Destiny of the Colored People of the United States, Politically Considered* (Philadelphia, 1852), 48–49, 68–69.

54. On the Delany-Douglass collaboration, see Levine, *Martin Delany, Frederick Douglass*, chap. 1.

55. Delany, *Condition... of the Colored People*, 147.

56. Resolutions of Harvard medical students, December 10, 1850, reprinted in Ullman, *Martin R. Delany*, 116; *Liberator*, May 21, 1852, 83. On the Harvard affair, see Ullman, *Martin R. Delany*, 113–119; Philip Cash, "Pride, Prejudice, and Politics," in *Blacks at Harvard: A Documentary History of the African-American Experience at Harvard and Radcliffe*, ed. Werner Sollors, Caldwell Titcomb, and Thomas A. Underwood (New York: New York University Press, 1993), 22–31.

57. Nell, *Colored Patriots*, 118.

58. Note how Nell moved seamlessly from Attucks to Burns in *Colored Patriots*, 18–20.

59. Nell, *Colored Patriots*, 233, 380.

60. Excerpted in *Liberator*, October 26, 1855, 171; January 11, 1856, 8.

61. Nell to Phillips, July 8, 1855, Phillips papers; Watkins, *Our Rights as Men*, 4, 8. On Watkins, see James Oliver Horton and Lois E. Horton, *Black Bostonians: Family Life and Community Struggle in the Antebellum North*, rev. ed. (New York: Holmes and Meier, 1999), 92, 95. Secondary sources on the militia rights crusade include von Frank, *The Trials of Anthony Burns*, 43–49, and Hal Goldman, "Black Citizenship and Military Self-Presentation in Antebellum Massachusetts," *Historical Journal of Massachusetts* 25 (1997): 158–172. For the broader context of black activism in Boston around this moment, see Horton and Horton, *Black Bostonians*, chap. 9.

62. Watkins, *Our Rights as Men*, 9, 6, 13–16; David Walker, *Walker's Appeal, in Four Articles; Together with a Preamble, to the Coloured Citizens of the World, but in Particular, and Very Expressly, to Those of the United States of America* (Boston, 1830), 79.

63. "Speech of Robert Morris Esq. Before the Committee on the Militia, March 3d, 1853," Folder 9, Robert Morris papers, Boston Athenaeum; *An Act More Effectually to Provide for the National Defence, by Establishing an Uniform Militia throughout the United States* (Philadelphia, 1792), 1; "Robert Morris," *American National Biography* online (entry by Robert J. Cottrol).

64. *Liberator*, May 13, 1853, 76; Goldman, "Black Citizenship and Military Self-Presentation," 172–174; *Official Report of the Debates and Proceedings in the State Convention, Assembled May 4th, 1853, to Revise and Amend the Constitution of the Commonwealth of Massachusetts*, vol. 2 (Boston, 1853), 73, 80.

65. Ebenezer W. Stone, *Digest of the Militia Laws of Massachusetts* (Boston, 1851), 24. Robert J. Cottrol and Raymond T. Diamond, "The Second Amendment: Toward an Afro-Americanist Reconsideration," *Georgetown Law Journal* 80 (1991): 332, point out that the 1792 act did not technically exclude blacks from militias; it just did not require them to enroll.

66. Goldman, "Black Citizenship and Military Self-Presentation," 173–176; *Liberator*, August 5, 1853, 122. On the politics of the convention, see Samuel Shapiro, "The Conservative Dilemma: The Massachusetts Constitutional Convention of 1853," *NEQ* 33 (1960): 207–224; Thomas H. O'Connor, "Irish Votes and Yankee Cotton: The Constitution of 1853," *MHSP* 95 (1983): 88–99.

67. On military participation, obligation, and the nature of citizenship, see Linda K. Kerber, *No Constitutional Right to Be Ladies: Women and the Obligations of Citizenship* (New York: Hill and Wang, 1998), 236–243.

68. Jeffrey Kerr-Ritchie, "Rehearsal for War: Black Militias in the Atlantic World," *Slavery and Abolition* 26 (2005): 1–34; Goldman, "Black Citizenship and Military Self-Presentation."

69. Mark R. DePue, "Citizen and Soldier in American History" (Ph.D. diss., University of Iowa, 2004), 139–145; Jerry Cooper, *The Militia and the National Guard in America Since Colonial Times: A Research Guide* (Westport, Conn.: Greenwood Press, 1993), 67–71; Marcus Cunliffe, *Soldiers and Civilians: The Martial Spirit in America, 1775–1865* (1968; reprint, Aldershot, U.K.: Gregg Revivals, 1993), 205–212. Robert F. McGraw, "The Minutemen of '61: The Pre-Civil War Massachusetts Militia," *Civil War History* 15 (1969): 101–108, argues that the volunteer militia was enjoying a renaissance in Massachusetts in the early 1850s. The growing numbers of companies forming and individuals joining in this period might have contributed to black men's interest in forming a militia of their own.

70. Goldman, "Black Citizenship and Military Self-Presentation," 157–166; Susan G. Davis, *Parades and Power: Street Theatre in Nineteenth-Century Philadelphia* (Philadelphia: Temple University Press, 1986), chap. 3; Rael, *Black Identity and Black Protest*, chap. 2. Joanne Pope Melish, *Disowning Slavery: Gradual Emancipation and "Race" in New England, 1780–1860* (Ithaca: Cornell University Press, 1998), 179–182, discusses nineteenth-century broadsides that mocked African American military display. In the midst of the controversy at the Massachusetts constitutional convention, the *Ohio Anti-Slavery Bugle* summed up decades of hostility toward black military parades: "The citizen soldiers don't like the idea of having negroes parading in epauletts, and sporting plumes and red-tailed coats" (*Liberator*, July 15, 1853, 110).

71. The ten petitions (or copies) are in Folder 9, Morris papers, as is all Morris's correspondence relating to these matters. Some of these appear to be incomplete, as they include only a few signatures (several others have over twenty signers). The Boston Athenaeum has tentatively dated all these petitions to 1856, but at least one must be from 1853. See B. Adams to Morris, February 19, 1853.

72. Kerr-Ritchie, "Rehearsal for War," 12; Robert J. Cottrol, *The Afro-Yankees: Providence's Black Community in the Antebellum Era* (Westport, Conn.: Greenwood Press, 1982), 63; Nell, *Colored Patriots*, 11; James Oliver Horton and Lois E. Horton, "The Affirmation of Manhood: Black Garrisonians in Antebellum Boston," in *Courage and Conscience*, ed. Jacobs, 146–150. See also Robert Morris to George H. Devereux, March 14, 1856; George Head to John V. DeGrasse, August 6, 1855; Alexander Ferguson to DeGrasse, August 29, 1855; all in Folder 9, Morris papers. This folder also contains an undated document declaring the reorganization of the Massasoit Guards, containing thirty-eight names of the men considered the new organization's founders; another undated scrap of paper, signed by ten men, reads, "to make our first Annual public parade, in uniform new and complete, on the first day of August next" (regrettably, the paper is torn, with the rest of the text missing). On August First celebrations, see W. Caleb McDaniel, "The Fourth and the First: Abolitionist Holidays, Respectability, and Radical Interracial Reform," *AQ* 57 (2005): 129–151; Mitch Kachun, *Festivals of Freedom: Memory and Meaning in African American Emancipation*

Celebrations, 1808-1915 (Amherst: University of Massachusetts Press, 2003), chap. 2. Kachun notes the existence of several other companies of Attucks Guards (or similar names) in "Forgotten Founder to Indispensible Icon," 275-277.

73. The phrase is Paul Gilroy's, from *The Black Atlantic: Modernity and Double Consciousness* (Cambridge, Mass.: Harvard University Press, 1993); it is useful as an alternative historical conception of "the nation," apart from the territorial and civic limits of "the United States."

74. For examples of the many mid-nineteenth-century depictions of Massasoit, see John Stetson Barry, *The History of Massachusetts: The Colonial Period* (Boston, 1855), 94-103; J. Alden, "The First Fast and the First Thanksgiving in Massachusetts," *New York Evangelist*, 30 March 1848, 52. A slightly later source, Ebenezer W. Peirce, *Indian History, Biography and Genealogy Pertaining to the Good Sachem Massasoit of the Wampanoag Tribe, and His Descendants* (North Abington, Mass., 1878) provides extensive detail. In the preface to this volume, Zerviah G. Mitchell, the book's publisher and Massasoit's direct descendant, calls her ancestor "the great and good Massasoit, whom both the red and white man now venerate and honor" (iii). She could have added "the black man" to that list. Stauffer argues that the "noble savage" appealed to the radical abolitionist men as "the Byronic ideal of a courageous rebel and freedom fighter to an American context" (*The Black Hearts of Men*, 183). Something different must have been at play in the idealization of the diplomatic Massasoit, for to nineteenth-century Americans he signified compromise and conciliation, not armed resistance.

75. Nell, *Colored Patriots*, 11; Bill Belton, "The Indian Heritage of Crispus Attucks," *Negro History Bulletin* 22 (1959): 149-152. J. B. Fisher, "Who Was Crispus Attucks?" *American Historical Record*, 1 (1872): 531-533 is a good source of biographical information as well as an example of certain nineteenth-century whites' insistence that Attucks could not have been black. Nyong'o, "The Black First," 151-152 emphasizes Nell's erasure of Attucks's Native heritage, arguing that "the production of a 'colored patriot' required for its success a symbolic Indian removal alongside the actual one." As I try to argue below, I think the cultural implications of Indian removal for people "of color"—emphasis on the vagaries of that term here—were more complicated. Some people of color found it beneficial to claim an aboriginal past (as, at times, did whites, though the nature and justification of their claims were different).

76. Philip J. Deloria, *Playing Indian* (New Haven, Conn.: Yale University Press, 1998), 5, 21-26; "Speech of Robert Morris." In thinking through the ideas in this section, I have benefited from Judy Kertész's work in progress on the appropriation of the American Indian past in nineteenth-century New England.

77. Horton and Horton, *Black Bostonians*, 60-61; Steven Taylor, "Progressive Nativism: The Know-Nothing Party in Massachusetts," *Historical Journal of Massachusetts* 28 (2000): 167-185; Tyler Anbinder, *Nativism and Slavery: The Northern Know Nothings and the Politics of the 1850s* (New York: Oxford University Press, 1992), 87-94, 159-161, 187-192. The involvement of Irish militiamen in Anthony Burns's rendition to slavery raised tensions between abolitionists and Irish immigrants in 1854. See McGraw, "Minutemen of '61," 109-110.

78. *Official Report*, vol. 2, 80, 72; Cottrol and Diamond, "The Second Amendment," 324-327. On the history of Anglo-American military idealism, see Cunliffe, *Soldiers and Civilians*; DePue, "Citizen and Soldier," 27-37.

79. Benjamin Quarles, *Black Abolitionists* (New York: Oxford University Press, 1969), 150-159; Kathryn Grover, *The Fugitive's Gibraltar: Escaping Slaves and Abolitionism in New Bedford, Massachusetts* (Amherst: University of Massachusetts Press, 2001), chap. 7-8; Gary Collison, *Shadrach Minkins: From Fugitive Slave to Citizen* (Cambridge, Mass.: Harvard University Press, 1997); Kerr-Ritchie, "Rehearsal for War," 8.

80. Kytle, "To Be Free," is particularly good at elaborating the Romantic strand of this discourse.

81. *Liberator*, August 5, 1853, 122; *Official Record*, vol. 3, 647, 724-726. On petitioning as a political strategy, see Ruth Bogin, "Petitioning and the New Moral Economy of Post-Revolutionary America," *WMQ* 45 (1998): 391-425; Linda K. Kerber, *Women of the Republic: Intellect and Ideology in Revolutionary America* (Chapel Hill: University of North Carolina Press, 1980), 85; Susan Zaeske, *Signatures of Citizenship: Petitioning, Antislavery, and Women's Political Identity* (Chapel Hill: University of North Carolina Press, 2003).

82. *Dred Scott v. Sanford*, 60 U.S. 393, 408-414. Taney made reference both to the colonial law of 1705 and to the state law of 1786, both of which outlined punishments for marriages across racial lines. He argued that the 1786 law, which was renewed in 1836, maintained the "mark of degradation" long imposed on blacks, proving that even after emancipation, they were still considered inferior beings. In his dissent, Justice Benjamin Curtis disputed Taney's historical interpretation: "An argument...that they [i.e., people of color] were not, by the Constitution of 1780 of that State [Massachusetts], admitted to the condition of citizens, would be received with surprise by the people of that State, who know their own political history. It is true, beyond all controversy, that persons of color, descended from African slaves, were by that Constitution made citizens of the State; and such of them as have had the necessary qualifications, have held and exercised the elective franchise, as citizens, from that time to the present" (575).

83. Walker, *Appeal*, 25; Glaude, *Exodus!* 5-9.

84. *Scott v. Sanford*, 411. Many sources suggest that the *Dred Scott* decision was issued on March 5, 1857: the coincidence of dates with the Boston Massacre is too good to pass up. However, the opinion of the Court was not read until March 6, and Taney did not issue his majority opinion in print until late May, provoking considerable controversy. See Don E. Fehrenbacher, *The Dred Scott Case: Its Significance in American Law and Politics* (New York: Oxford University Press, 1978), 314-321.

85. William C. Nell, *Boston Massacre, March 5th, 1770: The Day Which History Selects as the Dawn of the American Revolution. Commemorative Festival, at Faneuil Hall, Friday, March 5, 1858* (Boston, 1858).

86. *Liberator*, March 12, 1858, 42. Several scholars have offered insightful readings of the Fifth of March observances: Bethel, *The Roots of African American Identity*, 1-24; Browne, "Remembering Crispus Attucks," 173-175; Ernest, *Liberation Historiography*, 219-221; Teed, "Racial Nationalism and Its Challengers"; Wood, *Blind Memory*, 250-255.

87. *Liberator*, March 12, 1858, 42; August 5, 1859, 124. It is possible that Attucks returned (or was returned) to the Browns after running away in 1750; in that case, it is unclear whether or not he was still a fugitive in 1775. See Nancy Carlisle, *Cherished Possessions: A New England Legacy* (Boston: Society for the Preservation of New

England Antiquities, 2003), 23–25. Accounts of the annual Crispus Attucks celebrations appear in the *Liberator* until 1865; there were also observances in 1869 and 1870 (see Nell, *Selected Writings*, 673, 675).

88. In the final stages of preparing this book, I became aware of two articles by Stephen Kantrowitz that make arguments similar to those advanced in this chapter: "Fighting Like Men: Civil War Dilemmas of Abolitionist Manhood," in *Battle Scars: Gender and Sexuality in the American Civil War* (New York: Oxford University Press, 2006), 19–40, and "A Place for 'Colored Patriots': Crispus Attucks among the Abolitionists, 1842-1863," *Massachusetts Historical Review* 11 (2009): 96-117. Readers interested in the militia movement and Nell's "recovery" of Attucks should consult these pieces, respectively, as well as Kantrowitz's forthcoming book on black activist leaders in Boston, *Colored Citizens: Fighting to Belong in the White Republic* (Penguin).

EPILOGUE

1. Richard Henry Dana, Jr., *The Journal of Richard Henry Dana, Jr.*, vol. I, ed. Robert F. Lucid (Cambridge, Mass.: Harvard University Press, 1968), 166; William Cooper Nell, "Departure of the Mass. Fifty-Fourth Regiment for South Carolina," in *Souvenir of the Massachusetts Fifty-fourth (Colored) Regiment* (1863), 6.

2. Edwin S. Redkey, "Brave Black Volunteers: A Profile of the Fifty-fourth Massachusetts Regiment," in *Hope and Glory: Essays on the Legacy of the Fifty-fourth Massachusetts Regiment*, ed. Martin H. Blatt, Thomas J. Brown, and Donald Yacovone (Amherst: University of Massachusetts Press, 2001), 21.

3. *The Loyalty and Devotion of Colored Americans in the Revolution and War of 1812* (Boston, 1861); George H. Moore, *Historical Notes on the Employment of Negroes in the American Army of the Revolution* (New York, 1862); George Livermore, *An Historical Research Respecting the Opinions of the Founders of the Republic on Negroes as Slaves, as Citizens, and as Soldiers* (Boston, 1863). There is no author identified on the title page of *Loyalty and Devotion*. Most sources attribute it to Garrison, but there are some suggestions that its author was Nell. The pamphlet includes information from *Colored Patriots* and the *Liberator*; Nell and Garrison were, of course, close collaborators.

4. Nell, "Departure," 7–8. On "John Brown's Body" and related songs, see David S. Reynolds, *John Brown, Abolitionist: The Man Who Killed Slavery, Sparked the Civil War, and Seeded Civil Rights* (New York: Knopf, 2005), 465–470.

5. This figure includes seventy-four enlisted men and three officers confirmed dead, though the exact figures are difficult to determine. The popular claim that Shaw lost half his men at Fort Wagner collapses the wounded and the captured together with the dead. Redkey presents a detailed analysis of the casualty figures in "Brave Black Volunteers," 28–32.

6. *Liberator*, December 22, 1865, 202; William Cooper Nell, *The Colored Patriots of the American Revolution* (Boston, 1855), 380.

7. Testimony of John Hill, in appendix to *A Short Narrative of the Horrid Massacre in Boston, Perpetrated in the Evening of the Fifth Day of March*, 1770 (Boston, 1770), 5; *Liberator*, July 15, 1853, 110; "Speech of Robert Morris Esq. Before the Committee on the Militia, March 3d, 1853," Folder 9, Robert Morris papers, Boston Athenaeum.

8. *Boston Evening Transcript*, June 2, 1863; Donald Yacovone, "The Fifty-fourth Massachusetts Regiment, the Pay Crisis, and the 'Lincoln Despotism,'" in *Hope and Glory*, ed. Blatt, Brown, and Yacovone, 35–51.

9. Frederick Douglass, "If There Is No Struggle There Is No Progress," in *Lift Every Voice: African American Oratory, 1787-1900*, ed. Philip S. Foner and Robert James Branham (Tuscaloosa: University of Alabama Press, 1998), 311; David W. Blight, *Frederick Douglass' Civil War: Keeping Faith in Jubilee* (Baton Rouge: Louisiana State University Press, 1989), 156-167. On Madison Washington and the *Creole* (an incident that often gets overshadowed by the *Amistad* case that occurred around the same time), see Maggie Montesinos Sales, *The Slumbering Volcano: American Slave Ship Revolts and the Production of Rebellious Masculinity* (Durham: Duke University Press, 1997), chap. 3. It is worth noting that Martin Delany, often seen as the black nationalist foil to the integrationist Douglass, turned his attention from Africa back to the United States during the Civil War and served as a recruiter for the Massachusetts Fifty-fourth and other regiments; see Tunde Adeleke, *Without Regard to Race: The Other Martin Robison Delany* (Jackson: University Press of Mississippi, 2003), 75-77.

10. William Lloyd Garrison to Samuel May (copy), June 15, 1875, Ms. A.1.1 v. 8, 72, BPL. In the same letter, Garrison apparently made a connection between Revolutionary discourse and women's rights: "It is humiliating to think that, while the old Revolutionary ground of complaint against the mother country was taxation without representation, to this day one half of the inhabitants of the land, though subject to taxation, are deprived of all right of representation either in local or national affairs." On Garrison's politics during the war years, see Henry Mayer, *All on Fire: William Lloyd Garrison and the Abolition of Slavery* (New York: St. Martin's Press, 1998), 518-585.

11. William Lloyd Garrison to Wendell Garrison, June 22, 1875, Ms. A.1.1 v. 8, 73, BPL; Garrison to May, June 15, 1875. On the conflict between "emancipationist" memory and sectional reconciliation, see David W. Blight, *Race and Reunion: The Civil War in American Memory* (Cambridge, Mass.: Harvard University Press, 2001).

12. Robert Lowell, "For the Union Dead," in *The Vintage Book of Contemporary American Poetry*, ed. J. D. McClatchy (New York: Vintage-Random House, 1990), 14.

13. On the controversies surrounding this monument, see Dale H. Freeman, "The Crispus Attucks Monument Dedication," *Historical Journal of Massachusetts* 25 (1997): 125-137; Stephen H. Browne, "Remembering Crispus Attucks: Race, Rhetoric, and the Politics of Commemoration," *Quarterly Journal of Speech* 85 (1999): 178-185. To an outside observer, the monument does not obviously celebrate Crispus Attucks any more than it does any of the other victims of March 5, 1770. However, his name and his race were frequently invoked on both sides of the debate about the value of such a monument. Leading the effort to erect the monument was Lewis Hayden, a fugitive slave turned activist in Boston (William Cooper Nell had died in 1874). For evidence of Attucks's significance at the dedication ceremonies, see *A Memorial of Crispus Attucks, Samuel Maverick, James Caldwell, Samuel Gray, and Patrick Carr* (1889; reprint, Miami: Mnemosyne, 1969). I have quoted from John Boyle O'Reilly's dedicatory poem, "Crispus Attucks," in ibid., 56.

14. Meredith Bergmann, speech at the Boston Women's Memorial Dedication Ceremony, October 24, 2003, http://www.cityofboston.gov/women/MB_speech.asp; "Sculpture by Meredith Bergmann: Public Art," http://www.meredithbergmann.com/pages/publicart.html.

Index

Page numbers in *italics* refer to illustrations.

Printed in the USA/Agawam, MA
October 12, 2011

561841.001